THE ROOTS

OF SOUTHERN

DISTINCTIVENESS

THE ROOTS OF

Southern Distinctiveness

TOBACCO AND SOCIETY

IN DANVILLE, VIRGINIA,

1780–1865

✺ ✺ ✺ ✺

BY FREDERICK F. SIEGEL

THE UNIVERSITY OF NORTH CAROLINA PRESS

CHAPEL HILL AND LONDON

© 1987 The University of North Carolina Press

All rights reserved

Manufactured in the United States of America

Library of Congress Cataloging-in-Publication Data

Siegel, Frederick F.

  The roots of southern distinctiveness.

  Bibliography: p.

  Includes index.

    1. Tobacco industry—Virginia—Danville—History.

  2. Slave trade—Virginia—Danville—History.   3. Danville

  (Va.)—Economic conditions.   4. Danville (Va.)—Social

  conditions.   I. Title.

ゟℸ HD9138.D35S54   1987   338.1′7371′09755666   86-19356

  ISBN 0-8078-1727-9

To my parents,

A L & S E L M A S I E G E L

CONTENTS

❧ ❧ ❧

MAPS AND TABLES

ACKNOWLEDGMENTS

THIS STUDY was made possible by the special setting for the study of social history created at the University of Pittsburgh. Individually, I would like to acknowledge the help I received from the late Carter Goodrich and to thank David Montgomery and Sam Hays for opening up the paths of conceptual history to me. Professor Van Beck Hall generously shared his wealth of knowledge on the eighteenth and nineteenth centuries. I also benefited greatly from the endless hours of debate and encouragement I received from Larry Glasco, Arthur Tuden, John Levine, Bob Doherty, Gabriel Tortella, and Joe White. Larry Glasco, John Levine, and Jane Vadnal gave me invaluable help in organizing and processing the study's quantitative materials. Far and away, however, my greatest intellectual debt is to Julius Rubin, a man whose extraordinary habits of mind can only be palely reflected in this study. Finally, I wish to thank my wife, Jan Rosenberg, whose support and sense of humor helped me to finish this study.

✿ ✿ ✿

THE ROOTS

OF SOUTHERN

DISTINCTIVENESS

🌿 🌿 🌿

INTRODUCTION

F R O M T H E creation of the first permanent New World settlements to the current growth of the Sunbelt, America has been characterized by competing modes of regional development. From the first, historians have been fascinated by the patterns of sectional contrast. Initially, they tried to understand the regions through rough ideal types—Cavalier and Yankee, Planter and Puritan—each defined in terms of the other. Robert King Carter and Ben Franklin were taken to be the representative men. As study moved from hagiography to historicism, American history was placed in the broadening and enlightening context of the rise of capitalism and the creation of an Atlantic economy. Given this context, historians were struck with a great paradox. Marx had argued that capitalism and its revolutionary class, the bourgeoisie, transformed and modernized societies in the process of absorbing them into the world market. But in the South, this process had an ironic twist. The European demand for its agricultural products that drew it into the modernizing market also created seemingly retrograde forms of social and economic organization, slavery and the plantation. The international demand for the Southern staples—rice, tobacco, and cotton—produced growth subject to the cycles of booms and busts, but curiously little in the way of development. The Southern economy, wedded to its regional monocultures, grew not by diversifying but by expanding its geographic domain. By contrast, the North, which was lacking in immediately marketable resources and which grew later and more slowly, developed the mix of agricultural and manufactured goods, market towns, and manufacturing centers that became the model for successful capitalist development.

Recent historians of the antebellum South have dealt with this paradox either by denying it, that is, by arguing that the South as a market economy was far more like the North than has been previously understood, or by heightening it, insisting, in effect, that the South developed a distinctive economy and civilization defined by the master-slave relationship. The former, represented most powerfully by the cliometricians Robert Fogel and Stanley Engerman and more recently by J. Mills Thornton and James Oakes, might be described as "the capitalist school" of pre-

Civil War Southern history.[1] The latter, represented most notably by Eugene Genovese, but which also includes James Roark, Michael Johnson, and Raimondo Luraghi among others, might be characterized as "the paternalist school."[2]

Fogel and Engerman define the paradox away. They consider the plantation to be simply a factory in the field while analyzing slavery as a market relationship. Building on these redefinitions, they argue that the planters' behavior toward their slaves and vice versa can be explained in terms of rational economic choices. The prevalence of such choices indicates to them that, despite some institutional peculiarities, the laws of the market were fully operative in the antebellum South. They then go on to conclude, *ceteris paribus*, that given the free workings of the market there were no major impediments to Southern economic development. Having deduced the success of the Southern economy, they are left to explain away its relative backwardness by evoking the Civil War as the source of the deep-seated economic deficiencies that long antedated the event.[3]

Genovese, by contrast, embraces one part of the Southern paradox virtually to the exclusion of all else. If, as the argument goes, free labor is the sine qua non of capitalism, then even a society heavily oriented toward trade and dominated by merchants could not be considered capitalist if its production was organized with unfree labor. The "paternalist thesis" thus claims that the planters were in the market but not of it. It argues that the singular quality of the master-slave relationship as it developed within the context of semiautonomous plantation squirearchies created an ethos that was at its base hostile to capitalist values. This ethos, which encouraged a disdain for bourgeois rationality, is then used to deduce the South's comparative economic backwardness. Or to put it differently, Genovese asserts, despite an enormous body of contrary evidence, that Southern backwardness was largely willed by the master class.[4]

Whatever their differences, both schools share a methodological essentialism. With the paternalist thesis the master-slave nexus replaces the market as the idée fixe from which all else is deduced. The difference is that with the cliometricians the governing mechanism is an external set of immutable laws that determine the shape of social development, whereas for the paternalists internal questions of personality hegemonically radiate outward and determine external forms through a kind of "mimicry." But in neither case are the contextual factors of soil, climate, or local history allowed to interfere with the logical express train. "The issue here is not the use of ideal types like 'economic man' per se, but rather their limitations. If the keynote of southern history is irony, if indeed the South begins in irony, modern capitalism recreating ancient slavery, will it ever be possible for a single rubric to capture all the subsequent ironies and antimonies?"[5]

Both move from properly seeing slavery as the fulcrum of Southern history to the kind of argument made famous by Thwackum (in *Tom Jones*) whereby when they say the South, they mean slavery; and when they say slavery, they don't mean slavery everywhere but rather slavery where they've studied it. The claims of both Fogel and Engerman and Genovese are based largely on the cotton South. In the case of Fogel and Engerman, evidence from disparate cotton areas is melded into an argument about a singular South, whereas Genovese's evidence for the development of a paternalist ethos is based largely on the oldest areas of Southern settlement, namely the Virginia Tidewater and South Carolina's Sea Islands and coastal regions.[6] In short, both purchase their insights at the price of either avoiding or seriously distorting the evidence that cannot be squared with their deductive assumptions.

The form of the essentialist argument about Southern backwardness follows the schema laid out by Marx in the *Communist Manifesto*, where he describes the extraordinary transformative power of capitalism. The schema takes the following form:

If X (bourgeois values), then Y (dynamic capitalist development) or
    its contrapositive,
If not X, then not Y.

The Roots of Southern Distinctiveness breaks with this logic. It describes a subregion (the hinterlands of Danville, Virginia) that grew but failed to develop despite being blessed by the sort of entrepreneurial spirit the Yankee legend was made of. Its failures were a product not of its values, but of the generative capacity of its economic structure, a structure both created and limited by the changing demands of tobacco production.[7] That is, X (bourgeois values) did not lead to Y (dynamic capitalism). The explanation for this disjuncture is informed by the insights of institutional economists, the so-called "staple theorists," and influenced in part by the *Annales* School's emphasis on the deep structures of historical development.[8] It demonstrates the ways in which the material conditions of production, soil, climate, and the technical peculiarities of the staple being produced shaped the history of a Virginia bright tobacco region in the years between 1780 and 1865.[9]

The narrative history of Danville and its development, politics aside for the moment, is the story on the one hand of its tobacco-generated booms and busts, and on the other of its planters, merchants, and manufacturers, who in response to the cycles of opportunity shaped and reshaped the economic organization of both town and countryside. Underlying the twists and turns of the narrative is the slowly evolving history of tobacco, a crop whose requirements were so demanding, so all encompassing as to have created a "tobacco culture" in both senses of the term.[10] The booms and busts of Danville and the surrounding Pittsylvania County (Virginia's largest) and the strivings of its planters and manufacturers were bound together by that primal source of Southern distinctiveness, the template of soil and climate.

Like the South itself, the history of Danville and its hinterland abounds in irony. The sandy soils that retarded Pittsylvania's early development were the key to its later success as a producer of bright tobacco. And it was the tobacco manufacturing center of Danville, and more particularly the home of its most successful entrepreneur, a home that was harboring a Yankee, that was to gain fame as "the last capitol of the Confederacy." Danville thus came to symbolize "the old South," a South with which it had but a limited resemblance. All this after Danville vainly supported the effort in the Virginia legislature to free the slaves in return for their military service so as to win the fight for Southern independence.

I found the work of an earlier generation of intensely empirical historians and the writings of the "staple theorists" among the economists invaluable for unraveling some of the mysteries of Danville's economic development. I refer primarily to Joseph Robert and Nannie Tilley, but also Lewis Gray, Robert Russel, Avery Craven, and Kathleen Bruce among the historians, and Robert Baldwin, Douglas North, Charles Tiebout, F. Stirnton Weaver, Benjamin Chinitz, and T. W. Schultz among the economists. But far and away my greatest intellectual debt is to Julius Rubin, a rare mix of conceptual historian and empirical economist.

Part One of this volume begins with the settlement of Pittsylvania in the late eighteenth century, moves through to the collapse of the Danville tobacco market in the crash of 1837, and establishes the thoroughly entrepreneurial character of the planters who founded Danville.

Part Two is analytic. It opens by explaining how the soil of Virginia's southern Piedmont precluded the development of any commercially viable alternative to tobacco. The consequences of tobacco production for economic development are amplified by a detailed statistical comparison of Pittsylvania County with the "yeoman's paradise," Augusta, the largest county in the wheat and cattle growing Valley of Virginia. The statistics show that land distribution for whites was roughly similar in both counties, whereas Augusta was burdened with a somewhat larger percentage of propertyless whites.[11] Part Two concludes with a discussion of how bright tobacco promised new hope within the confines of the leafy straightjacket.

Part Three resumes the narrative cut off in 1837 by describing Danville's development as a major tobacco manufacturing center, discusses the politics of social control within Danville, and how the manufacturing center's hopes of becoming a great city colored its response to the North-South conflict. The narrative concludes with a discussion of Danville's pragmatic response to civil war, and the epilogue shows how, despite the economic gains visited on Danville by the war, the city and the region's economic prospects continued to be stunted by their structural dependence on tobacco.

In addition to the standard sources such as diaries, newspapers, and legislative petitions, quantitative sources are used extensively to buttress the argument. The personal and land tax lists were linked with the census to provide a statistically rich account of Danville and Pittsylvania's development. In addition, in some cases it was possible, by linking a particular individual's tax and property lists, to get a nuanced picture of their wealth and property. I emphasize these sources in the hope that their use by other scholars might lead historians away from the broad generalizations of the past fifteen years, and back to a more detailed study of the roots of Southern distinctiveness.

Part One

VALUES, ORIENTATION,

AND FAILURE

I

EARLY PITTSYLVANIA

🖋 🖋 🖋 🖋 🖋 🖋 🖋 🖋

GEOGRAPHIC ANOMALIES dominated the early settlement and development of the southwestern Virginia Piedmont area that became Pittsylvania County. What seemed abundant in waterways and apparent
fertility turned out to be landlocked and agriculturally limited.

Maude Carter Clement, historian of Pittsylvania, describes the region:
"Pittsylvania County is centrally situated in South midland Virginia
touching the NC line. It is the largest county in Virginia with an area of
1,102 square miles. It lies wholly in the piedmont plateau, having a
rolling surface broken by many small mountain ridges. Along the low
ranges and rolling hills are fertile valleys watered by many streams,
Pittsylvania is well drained by three water systems, the Dan in the South,
the Banister in the central areas, and the Staunton which forms the
northern boundary."[1] The area is so thoroughly crisscrossed by waterways that almost every square mile is traversed by a perennial drainage
way or reached by small intermittent branches.[2]

The aesthetic dimensions of the county matched its physical magnitude. Lower Pittsylvania was part of the "Eden" William Byrd described
in his classic *History of the Dividing Line between Virginia and North
Carolina*. Byrd was overwhelmed by the apparent richness of the land he
surveyed. While touring what is now central western Pittsylvania, he
wrote:

All the land . . . is exceedingly rich. . . . Besides whole forests of
canes that adorn the banks of the rivers and the creeks thereabout,
the fertility of the soil throws out such a quantity of winter grass
that horses and cattle might keep themselves in heat all the cold
season without the help of any fodder. . . . In short everything will
grow plentifully here to supply either the want or wantonous of
man.[3]

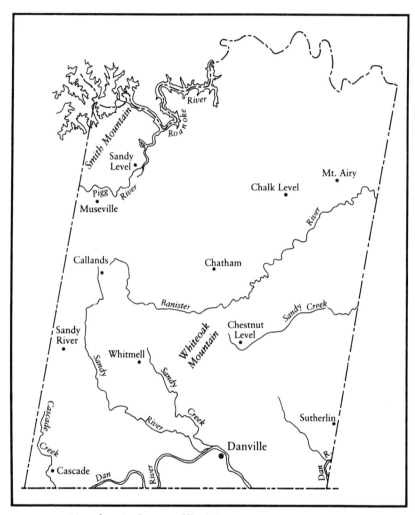

MAP I-I. *Pittsylvania County, Virginia*

Byrd's reaction to the lush and sylvan land of the Dan Valley and its
tributaries was typical of early visitors, none of whom had any sense of
the fragile and vulnerable quality of what they saw. "Happy will be the
people," exclaimed Byrd, "destined for so wholesome a situation, where
they may live to the fulness of days, and which is much better still with
much content and gaiety of heart."[4] Unfortunately, the beauty of the land
was to be only a kind of agricultural fool's gold.

🖋

SETTLEMENT PATTERNS

The first settlers arrived in Pittsylvania County in the mid-seventeenth century, lured by bounty rather than beauty. In response to a purported French threat from across the Alleghenies, the colonial government had offered land to settlers willing to tackle the wilderness. In 1745 Brunswick County, which included much of the Southside (Virginia below the James River), was divided and the western lands became part of Lunenburg County. About the same time, the rate of settlement increased. A major source of this increase was the stream of Scotch-Irish settlers who came from Pennsylvania and New Jersey by way of the great Valley of Virginia. Simultaneously, a smaller group of settlers arrived from the Tidewater of Virginia, particularly from areas between the James and York rivers.

The southwestern Piedmont, unlike the Valley of Virginia, grew slowly, so the government offered further inducements for settlement by granting newcomers a ten-year tax exemption. These inducements were specifically intended to attract the Germans and Scotch-Irish leaving Pennsylvania in search of land. Many of the Scotch-Irish settled in the Valley but many others crossed the Blue Ridge on their way to the Virginia and Carolina Piedmont. Large numbers of Scoth-Irish settlers continued to move into Pittsylvania until the end of the eighteenth century. The settlers from the Tidewater tended to concentrate in eastern Pittsylvania whereas the Scotch-Irish, Germans, and Quakers dominated in the western section of the county.[5]

The population slowly but steadily increased and in 1752 Halifax, including present-day Pittsylvania, and the other counties west of Pittsylvania to the mountains split off from Lunenburg. In 1767 Pittsylvania, which then included Patrick and Henry counties to the west, broke away from Halifax. Finally, in 1777 Pittsylvania was reduced to its present size, though not without protest. The legislature received numerous petitions to further divide what was to be the largest county in Virginia.

Mike Nichols has provided an excellent description of how land was taken up on the Southside. Making extensive use of land patents, the only quantitative sources available, Nichols is able to demonstrate that "the process of taking up the land was marked by a common indifference to the requirements of the land patent laws and widespread squatting."[6] The inability of the provincial government to enforce its land policy encouraged and hastened settlement by those unable or unwilling to pay the necessary fees. Nichols says that suits for the ejection of squatters have not been found. This is so either because squatting was condoned or because the lack of pressure from overpopulation made it relatively unimportant. The farther the land from the courthouse, the more common was squatting. In the area of Lunenburg that became the top half of Franklin and the bottom third of Bedford counties, only 5 of the 107 tithe payers had title to their land or left evidence of ownership by 1750. Nichols describes the consequences of squatting:

> The fact that Royal land policy was unenforceable and ignored all strata of the society allowed one to enjoy the fruits of the land and one's labor until the land could be taken up or left. The widespread participation in the practices indicates a willingness to live outside the law whenever possible and suggests a contemptuous view of non-local society. . . . The elites' lax enforcement, perhaps a partial result of their own participation in illegal land practices, blunted both their potential power and the possible alienation of the lower white classes.[7]

The lack of official ownership and registration was still a problem in Pittsylvania as late as 1811. In a petition to the assembly that year, James Hart, a district commissioner of revenue, complained that 11,640 acres in his district were still unregistered. Hart was concerned because unregistered land posed difficulties for tax assessment. On the same day, another district commissioner claimed—in a virtually identical petition—that 10,191 acres were unregistered in his area.[8]

The population of the western Roanoke Valley (the Dan, Banister, and Staunton rivers are all tributaries of the Roanoke) grew slowly until after the Revolution. In the postrevolutionary years, the areas that are now Pittsylvania, Patrick, Henry, and Franklin counties grew fairly rapidly. The land records of Henry County (Pittsylvania's neighbor to the west) reveal that most of the newcomers acquired their land not by patents but by purchasing small tracts from large landholders who were selling the land as speculators or moving west.[9] There are strong indications that a similar practice was used in Pittsylvania whereby speculators, large landholders, and large farmers sold off considerable portions of their acreage to either newcomers or resident squatters. Between 1780 and 1800 the mean acreage for landholdings in the county dropped 40 percent (from 445 to 252).[10]

It is not clear why the settlers chose Pittsylvania. Rapids made the rivers impassable at a number of points, and even if a cargo could make it east to the main stem of the Roanoke River, until the Dismal Swamp Canal was built in 1817 there was no outlet to the sea. Further, the land was of a poor quality. A petition of 1790 asked for a tax abatement, stating: "Our (Pittsylvania) lands in common are so extremely poor that they cannot be sold for more than ½ or ⅓ of their present estimated value, being taken up merely as range or pasture, having no timber on them, and not with a view of their being tilled or cultivated." The purpose of this petition—tax relief—makes it suspect, and certainly it was wrong in regard to timber (though the indigenous timber was of low quality). But on balance the document is corroborated by an earlier petition of 1776 arguing against the separation of West Pittsylvania (the areas that became Patrick and Henry counties): "considering our inferior situation, together with the great proportion of [Pine] barrens the county contains which lie unfit for cultivation. . . . In a county which contains such bodies of land unfit for tillage, as ours does, where the situation of the inhabitants are so dispersed, the citizens of such a county can never reasonably expect to be as convenient to court as those who inhabit a county more generally fertile."[11]

As late as 1801 petitions called for the separation of the northern and southern halves of the county at the Banister River. The area to the north of the Banister is drained by the Staunton and the area to the south by the Dan. A counterpetition arguing against the division stated: "This county we think, contains more land unfit for cultivation than any other we know of."[12] The petition goes on to point out that the largest percentage of poor land was north of the Banister. (Based on fragmentary clues, it would seem that about two-thirds of Pittsylvania's 11,000 people in 1790 lived in the more fertile Valley of the Dan.)

The relative backwardness of the entire county is also confirmed by the traveler J. F. D. Smyth, who gives the most complete contemporary account of the economy of the Roanoke and Dan valleys:

They also fell great numbers of deer skins and furs; but the principal of the exports are hogs, which they raise in great numbers and drive them in droves of 1,2,3,4, 500 together to the falls of the James River and the Roanoke, and to the more populous parts of the country, as well as the sea ports.

Some few black cattle are also brought from this part of the frontier, but in no considerable numbers. . . .

There is also a considerable quantity of tobacco growing here, which is almost all carried to the James River, and sells there at the rate generally of 16, 18 or 20 shillings per hundred weight.

They make very little wheat, and use still less; . . .

But the great support of the country is indian corn, with which they subsist themselves, their negroes, their horses, and fatten their hogs. . . .

Indian corn is neither sown nor reaped. . . . It is planted and gathered. A bushel of corn will plant nearly 20 acres and on the richest land 20 acres will produce 250 barrels or 1,250 bushels. . . . The (corn) leaves cured are excellent provender for horses; the tops, stalks and husks are exceedingly fine fodder for cattle, and the grain itself supports the inhabitants themselves, both black and white, besides feeding the horses and fattening their hogs.[13]

The impassability of the Roanoke River, with its numerous rapids and obstructions, made transportation from Pittsylvania County rather costly. To compensate, settlers concentrated on producing highly valued items for export, such as tobacco and hogs.

Between 1760 and 1776, when tobacco prices were depressed, hemp production in Virginia assumed a greater importance, with major centers in the Shenandoah and Staunton River valleys. Textiles from hemp and flax became an important source of import substitution, prompting by 1765 a hemp boom further stimulated by bounties offered by the British and Virginia governments. The boom continued, with considerable export production, during the Revolution. Competition from Russia and Kentucky after the war destroyed the Virginia hemp industry.[14]

Fishing was more important to many settlers than flour milling. In 1791, 1799, and again in 1809 petitions complained that the flour mills obstructed fishing on the Banister, Pigg (in the northeastern part of the county), and Staunton rivers: "It was not only those who live immediately on it [the Banister] and who were induced to purchase their lands at a very high price through motives of developing great advantage from the fish, but even the neighborhood for a considerable distance on both sides was plentifully supplied.[15]

Many of the settlers from Pennsylvania expected to establish towns immediately. In 1788, for instance, Harmon Cook petitioned the assembly for a town to be founded on his land at the fork of the roads leading from Houlston to Pittsylvania and Petersburg. The petition stated that many tradesmen were already settled there.[16]

Despite the settlers' intentions, towns failed to develop for two reasons: the generally low level of economic activity in the area and the competition from plantation settlements already providing the kind of marketing and purchasing services typically offered by a town. Plantation settlements along the rivers, particularly at ferrying points, became commercial centers. The most important for early Pittsylvania was that of Sam Pannill, a Scotch-Irishman, who at the end of the eighteenth century, while still a young man, set up a plantation town at Green Hill on the north side of the Staunton River in Campbell. Pannill owned property in Campbell and northern Pittsylvania on both sides of the river. Before he bought the property in 1797 there had been a ferry across the river, but it had been washed away. He revived the ferry service and then, using slave labor, built a covered wooden bridge in the area. The bridge became the main route from Lynchburg to Halifax County. Pannill owned and operated a fleet of flatboats in which he shipped the products of his plantation down the river. His flour was shipped by bateau to Weldon and Gaston, North Carolina, at the falls of the Roanoke. Herman Ginther notes that "the Green Hill plantation with its mills, shops, store, chapel, farm buildings, and other installations, was a completely self-sustaining community."[17]

There were other plantation towns along the Staunton. Patrick Henry owned a large plantation with land on both sides of the Staunton and on the three sides of what is now the town of Brookneal. Henry operated a ferry both for public commerce (at a fee) and to connect the parts of his estate. John Brooke, an enterprising farmer who did much of his business "on the cuff," saw the potential importance of Henry's ferry as a crossing place joining Campbell, Charlotte, and Halifax counties. In 1800 Brooke successfully petitioned for the construction of a tobacco warehouse at that point. In 1803, two years after his warehouse was built, the town of "Brooke Neal" was established by the legislature.[18]

Because the Roanoke River was largely impassable, the tobacco that was grown in Pittsylvania had to be rolled or taken by wagon to the James River, a considerable distance. Given its high value per unit of weight, the tobacco growers were able to absorb the high transportation costs. Despite the difficulties involved, tobacco production increased because, except for the brief boom in hemp, it was the only cash crop.[19]

❧

SLAVERY

With the growth of tobacco production, the use of slave labor increased. In 1767, there were 271 slaves in Pittsylvania County (which included the thinly settled western sections of the county that would split off to form Henry and Patrick counties); by 1800, there were 4,200, representing a sixteenfold increase (see Table 1-1). During the same period, the ratio of slave to adult male population was drastically reversed. In 1767, there were 271 slaves and 801 adult males (tithables), or a ratio of 1 to 3; by 1800, there were twice as many slaves (4,200) as adult males (approximately 2,000).

The distribution of slave ownership changed markedly (see Table 1-2). The dramatic increase in multiple slaveholdings by 1782 came largely from those already resident in 1767 who purchased large numbers of slaves. Of the fifteen residents in 1767 with five or more slaves, the eleven who are listed in 1782 register an enormous increase in slaves. John Wilson, for instance, had eight slaves in 1767 and thirty-two in 1782. At least half of those with twenty or more slaves in 1782 were resident as early as 1767.

There were strong inducements to use slave labor, even for yeomen. In the densely wooded Piedmont, land clearing was extremely difficult, physically exhausting, and time-consuming. It has been estimated that a farm family could clear only five acres a year plus grow its provisions. If a farmer planned to grow tobacco, the area's major cash crop, there would be even less time for clearing. Cleared land was in and of itself a valuable commodity that could be sold to new settlers. Many farmers in the Piedmont, like their Northern counterparts, used slaves to supplement the adult males available for land clearing.[20] Once the land was cleared, tobacco growing demanded an enormous amount of labor. One man could only tend two to three acres; if a farmer wanted to increase the size of his tobacco output, his only alternative (given the lack of mechanical aids for tobacco growing) was to hire slaves.

There was a considerable gap between the rapid growth of slaveholding and the slow growth of the county's largely landlocked economy. Pittsylvania's noncommercial orientation can be demonstrated by comparing the occupations of the members of the Overseers of the Poor in Pittsylvania with those in Accomac and Rockingham counties (see Table 1-3). Accomac was a Tidewater tobacco county that had passed its prime

TABLE I—I

The Number of Slaves in Pittsylvania County between 1767 and 1800

Year	Number of Slaves
1767	271
1782	ca. 2,000
1790	3,100
1800	4,200

Sources: Clement, *History of Pittsylvania*; Pittsylvania (Personal) Property, 1782; First U.S. Census, 1790; Second U.S. Census, 1800.

by the Revolution; its tobacco economy once fully developed had spent itself. Rockingham, settled a few years earlier than Pittsylvania, was located in the heart of the Valley of Virginia. Its economy, which was based on mixed agriculture and some industry, was generally more developed than that of Pittsylvania.

In contrast to the overseers in Accomac and Rockingham, none of the Pittsylvania overseers, with the exception of one contractor, could be described as having primarily commercial occupations. There were for example no merchants, mill owners, or slave traders among them; to the contrary, virtually all of Pittsylvania's overseers were justices of the peace, most of whom were planters.

The composition of the Pittsylvania Board of Overseers was largely unchanged by the Revolution, when the board made a smooth transition from a nominally Anglican body to a secular organization. Pittsylvania had been overwhelmingly pro-Revolutionary. In response to the Continental Congress Resolution of 1774 calling for a boycott of British goods, the county established Committees of Safety to enforce the boycott. The committees appeared to receive wide support but were dominated by the county's leading families, men who sat on the board of overseers, justices of the peace, and representatives to the assembly and state senate. According to Clement, the resolution of the Continental Congress was taken as law: "At the least work or action that could be construed to be unfriendly to the patriot cause, the offending individual was summoned to appear before the committee and if no satisfactory explanation could be given the offender was published in the newspaper as being 'inimical to the cause.'"[21] The drinking of tea was considered

TABLE I–2

The Distribution of Slaves among Slaveholders in
Pittsylvania County, 1767, 1782

	Number of Slaveholders	
Number of Slaves Owned	1767	1782
1	50	60
2–5	43	117
6–9	4	64
10–19	3	48
20+	0	11

Sources: The 1767 figures can be found in Clement's copy of the list of Pittsylvania tithetables and slaves in 1767, *History of Pittsylvania County*; the other figures were found in Pittsylvania (Personal) Property, 1782.

treasonous. Captain John Pigg (the river is named after him), a vestryman and captain of the local militia, was brought before the committee and charged with tea drinking.

After independence Pittsylvania was first anti-Federalist and then anti-Nationalist. J. T. Main identifies Pittsylvania as an ally of the Southside bloc, composed of the less developed debtor counties. That Pittsylvania was only an ally and not a core member is indicative of its future economic and political development, which made it moderately Whig whereas much of the Southside tobacco area was staunchly Democratic. The county was strongly opposed to the Alien and Sedition Acts. And beginning in 1776 a long string of petitions, most with over a hundred signatures, called for increased democracy in state government. A petition of 1796 contains the fullest statement of principles:[22]

That with impatience for some time we have waited expecting to hear the sentiments of the people called for relative to a change in government, as we conceive the present frame to be too complex in its structure and too aristocratic in some of its features to accord well with the simplicity and equality of the democratic principles it was intended for. After the revolution it could be nothing but the force of habit that transcribed those principles from the old, into

TABLE 1–3
Comparison of Overseer Occupations, 1776–1800

Occupation	Pittsylvania	Accomac	Rockingham
Merchant	0	5	0
Mill Owner (Grist or Saw)	0	9	2
Tavern Owner	0	2	1
Warehouse Owner	0	0	1
Peddler	0	0	1
Contractor	1	2	0
Cabinetmaker	0	0	1
Slave Trader	0	1	1
Tanner	0	1	1
Sheriff or Deputy Sheriff	6	2	5
Member, House of Delegates	2	2	0
Constable	0	1	4
Clerk of Court	0	0	1
Justice of the Peace	18	0	7
Member, Committee of Correspondence	4	1	0
Military Officer	9	9	10
Town Trustee	5	1	2
Town Property	0	8	4

Source: Usery, "The Overseers."

the present system, but it appears now to be time to lay aside royal form under Republican name—to act more consistently and to adopt principles more liberal and agreeable to the spirit of liberty— [illegible]—The Spirit of Freedom directs the road to Glory to Honor to the Approbation of Fellow-citizens to be equal by law laid open to all. She knows no distinctions but those which Virtue and ability constitute. When this is the case, what Beast that does not glory to obtain the distinguished Prize. What Bosom that exults not in its country's cause, when public virtue is thus crowned with its own reward. Then may the statesman, the soldier, the citizen catch the Flame of public virtue, and exhibit to the world those shining instances of patriotism and valour which liberty alone can inspire. Men then may be truly sensible that they have exchanged their natural Independence for social liberty alone, their natural strength for Civil Power, which the social union renders invincible—Confidence in each others emulation the love of country, and, above all, Virtue encouraged and rewarded from the very soul of a free and impartial government. The further we are removed from this equable form, the more we must feel the declension, and at length the total abolition of all virtue.[23]

All subsequent petitions of a political-philosophical nature repeated in whole or in part the positions outlined in 1796. Some of the petitions were signed by as many as four hundred people including the area's economic and social elite.

The criticism of an aristocratic and Tidewater-dominated state government, uninterested in providing the internal improvements required to unleash the economic energies of the interior, was fueled by the egalitarian ideology of a revolution made in the name of property rights. Among the most coveted of those rights was the right to hold property in slaves. Antislavery sentiment was equated with Toryism, which in turn was seen as an unnatural check on liberty—liberty here meaning the right of the white population to advance its economic fortunes unhindered by government regulations.[24]

While the gentry of the declining Tidewater and the new wheat-growing areas of northern Virginia were manumitting their slaves in unprecedented numbers, eighty-five of Pittsylvania's leading citizens, many of whom were outspoken foes of "aristocracy," were vehemently reaffirming their support of slavery. They, along with eight other county groups from the developing Southside (the counties in eastern Virginia and south of the James River), sent petitions to the legislature clearly stating their position on the issue.

The wording of the Pittsylvania petition was significant because it was directed both to gentry reformers and to the Methodists and Baptists who were proselytizing among the slaves. Its authors declared that Negro conversion to Christianity would in no way abrogate the owners' property rights in their slaves. They argued: "The freedom which the followers of Jesus were taught to expect was a freedom from the bondage of Sin and Satan and from the dominion of their Lusts and Passions, but as to their OUTWARD CONDITIONS [sic] whatever that was before they embraced Christianity whether BOND or FREE it remained the same afterward." They went on to point out that in verse 20 of Corinthians 7, Paul had instructed: "Let every man abide in the same calling wherein he is called." In verse 21, he had said: "Let every man wherein he is called therein abide with God." The petition warned that emancipation would lead to financial ruin, suffering for black children, and even worse: "the horrors of all the Rapes, Murders, Robberies and Outrages which a vast [illegible] of unprincipaled, unpropertied, vindictive and Remoresefull Bandits are capable of perpetuating."[25]

After this episode, and until 1865 when Pittsylvania was in the forefront of an effort to free the slaves in order to make them soldiers of the Confederacy, there was almost no mention of slavery as an issue within the county. The county's politicians at the state level strongly supported the institution. In the celebrated debate of slavery in 1832 following Nat Turner's Rebellion, for instance, representatives from Pittsylvania endorsed the western and Valley counties' call for internal improvements and political reform but vigorously opposed their antislavery proposals. During the debate Vincent Witcher, Pittsylvania's leading politician, was in the vanguard of the antiabolitionist forces.

ECONOMIC DEVELOPMENT

After 1812 slavery grew rapidly in the county along with agricultural production. Expanded production was evident from the accelerating rate of requests for the granting of town charters and for the opening of state flour and tobacco inspection warehouses that were required for exporting those crops. Between 1790 and 1812 in Pittsylvania and the two counties consecutively to its east along the Roanoke, Halifax and Mecklenburg, there had been only two petitions for flour inspection warehouses, seven petitions for tobacco inspection warehouses, and eight petitions for town charters (Danville's among them). In 1818 and 1819 alone, however, there were six requests for flour inspection warehouses, twenty-one for tobacco inspection warehouses, and five for new town charters.

The labor producing the tobacco was increasingly slave. Whereas the white population increased 48 percent between 1790 and 1820, the slave population increased 300 percent. This great increase in the slave population cannot be attributed to the large Tidewater planters who, fleeing soil exhaustion, moved into the county. Newcomers to Pittsylvania—for instance, those who arrived after 1810—owned fewer slaves than those

who resided there by 1800 or 1810. Only 36 percent of those arriving
between 1811 and 1820 owned slaves and their mean holding was 1.3.
By comparison, of those residing in the county by 1810 or earlier, 60
percent owned slaves and their mean holding was 2.4. A similarity exists
if nonslaveholders are excluded from the calculations. That is, if only
slaveholders are considered, the mean holding for the newcomers who
owned slaves was 3.4 and for the older residents 4.6.[26]

The increase in slave ownership was due primarily to the influx of
small slaveholders from eastern Virginia and to an increase in slave ownership among the older residents of Pittsylvania. The latter group often
acquired more slaves between 1800 and 1820. For example, those owning between 1 and 10 slaves in 1800 had a mean ownership of 2.6 slaves,
whereas in 1820 they had a mean ownership of 4.2 slaves. This was part
of a general increase in economic well-being. Fifty-nine percent of those
residing in the county in 1810 owned considerably more slaves and
horses in 1820.[27]

This gradual tide of prosperity was accompanied by a limited growth
in manufacturing. Although limited, this growth was exceptional because few counties of the southwestern Piedmont were engaged in manufacturing. The low level of manufacturing in the southwestern Piedmont
contrasted markedly with developments just to the northwest in the Valley of Virginia. In the Valley, settled at about the same time, there was
substantial industrial diversification and almost no tobacco production.
Its counties were engaged in extensive flour and saw milling as well as in
the production of boots and shoes, hats, pottery, and liquors.[28]

In 1810, at the time of the first manufacturing census, Pittsylvania was
ranked among Virginia's ten leading counties in the production and value
of distillery products, the production and value of shoes and boots, and
the number of yards of cotton cloth manufactured by its families (see
Table 1-4). It is interesting to note that Augusta and Rockingham counties, in the Shenandoah Valley, ranked one and two in both the number
of footwear items produced and the gallons of liquor distilled.

Between 1810 and 1820 there were important changes in the direction
of Pittsylvania's manufacturing. The most dramatic change was that the
value of the liquors produced dropped drastically, whereas tobacco,
which had not been manufactured to any extent in 1810, was valued at
nearly $15,000 in 1820. Thus began the county's rise to prominence as
the third largest center of tobacco manufacturing in the state. Another
significant change was that the amount of homemade cloth and the number of boots and saddles produced also dropped sharply. It is possible

TABLE 1–4

State Ranking of Goods Produced in Pittsylvania County, 1810

Goods Produced	State Ranking
Gallons of Liquor	8th
Value of Liquor	7th
Pairs of Shoes, Boots, and Slippers	6th
Value of Shoes, Boots, and Slippers	10th
Yards of Homemade Cotton Cloth	2nd

Source: U.S. Census, Manufacturers, 1810.

that Pittsylvania may not have been able to withstand the outside competition for marketing these goods stimulated by the opening of the Dismal Swamp Canal. On balance, then, Pittsylvania's manufacturing picture in 1820 reflected shifts that might be expected of an area competing in a different and wider marketplace. Manufacturing for local markets declined, whereas increased attention was paid to items that could be sold in new and larger markets.[29]

The society being created by this economic growth did not have the accoutrements associated with a cavalier life-style. This can be seen by comparing Pittsylvania with Augusta (of the Shenandoah Valley), which was settled at about the same time and had a similar ethnic composition.[30] In 1815 Augusta, a county of supposedly frugal yeomen, possessed far more luxury items than Pittsylvania (see Table 1-5).[31]

Until the opening of the Dismal Swamp Canal in 1817–19, Pittsylvania was geographically cut off from access to the coast and thus had grown very slowly. Its economy was tobacco-dominated and reliant on a growing slave labor force. It was a county without towns or a commercial center. Plantation villages on the major river thoroughfares were the only centers of trade, until the emergence of Danville.

TABLE 1–5
The Number of Luxury Items Listed for
Pittsylvania and Augusta Counties, 1815

Item	Pittsylvania	Augusta
Houses Whose Value Exceeded $500	73	133
Mahogany Chairs	20	68
Mahogany Chests of Drawers	8	18
Oil Portraits	4	120
Gilt Edged Frames	7	40
Cut Glass Decanters	93	79

Source: Augusta and Pittsylvania (Personal) Property, 1815.
Note: The 1815 tax list, which was used to raise revenue for the War of 1812, was extraordinarily complete, listing many items that had never before been and never again would be taxed.

2

THE PLANTER-
ENTREPRENEURS
AND THE ORIGINS
OF DANVILLE

❧ ❧ ❧ ❧ ❧ ❧

WITH THE assessed land values jumping from $.83 to $5.43 an acre between 1800 and 1820, political economist George Tucker saw a great future for southern Pittsylvania. Tucker is best known as the Virginia Hamiltonian who, while a professor at the University of Virginia, presented the case for protective tariffs, government support of internal improvements, and the expansion of banking.

Tucker argued for a South modeled on the relationship between Philadelphia and its Susquehanna hinterland, envisioning populous cities surrounded by densely settled, fertile districts. He hoped that improvements in the Roanoke River and the eventual opening of the Dismal Swamp Canal would make Norfolk the Philadelphia of the South. With Norfolk as the metropolis, southern Pittsylvania and its fledgling town of Danville would become the commercial center of a thickly settled countryside. He was so taken by the prospects for Pittsylvania that he moved there in 1815 and briefly plunged into politics, winning a seat as the county's representative in the assembly. Tucker moved on to the University of Virginia, but others migrated to Pittsylvania and took up his vision. Among them was planter-entrepreneur B. W. S. Cabell, the scion of a wealthy Episcopalian landowner and a major force in the development of the Dan Valley.[1]

Cabell laid out his case for promoting the commercial interests of Danville in a petition to the Virginia assembly in January 1818:

> There is no point your petitioners believe, which is better situated than Danville for concentrating the trade of this section of the country. The town is at the head of easy and safe navigation. It is low enough on the river to have an extensive back country to support it, and it is high enough not to subject that back country to too great an expense of land carriage. The great road leading from Washington to the Western part of North Carolina, South Carolina and Georgia, passes through it. The only bridge that crosses the Dan is at this place. The river-falls at the town afford excellent sites and an inexhaustible supply of water for mills and machinery.

Cabell pointed out that there was broad local support to make Danville both a trading and a manufacturing center: "Influenced by these obvious and peculiar [geographic] advantages, public opinion seems to have declared decisively in favor of this being the emporium of the upper Roanoke trade; and it is believed that more distant capitalists and adventurers have purchased property in the town and its vicinity than in all the other numerous towns and proposed sites for towns, united."[2]

By 1820 the opening of the Dismal Swamp Canal, linking Pittsylvania to Norfolk, had begun to galvanize the economic energy generated by the rapid expansion of tobacco production. Danville, it was thought, could become the great selling and carrying way station to outside markets. As the mercantile center of southwestern Virginia, an area almost entirely bereft of towns, Danville would stimulate the growth of a bustling and densely populated countryside; the countryside—as in the case of Northern rural areas—would in turn nurture the town.

Despite the persistent efforts of visionaries like B. W. S. Cabell, Danville never became an important commercial center and to this day the piney countryside of Pittsylvania remains thinly settled. The problem from the start was that the county's economy provided an inhospitable terrain for town development.

Pittsylvania's early settlers from Pennsylvania had attempted unsuccessfully to recreate the kind of town life they had known there. The largely subsistence economy of the early years had no need for a town as a place of exchange and transfer. Moreover, in an area of poor soils it would have been disastrous to live in towns for purely social reasons. A farmer had to find the best land available. Later, with the growth of tobacco production, it made sense for the planters to live in the center of their land so they could maintain access to fresh lands when the older ones had been worn out by two or three years' production. When towns did develop, they were centered around and limited by the needs of marketing tobacco. Planter-businessmen established towns as a place to better market their tobacco and as an opportunity for investment.

THE FOUNDING AND
GROWTH OF DANVILLE

Virginia tobacco was generally produced for export. In order to be exported, tobacco had to be inspected by state officials. As of September 1793, there were no inspection warehouses in Pittsylvania County. Planters and farmers of the Dan Valley had to have their tobacco inspected in Lynchburg or Petersburg, a considerable distance away. In October of that year fifteen prominent residents of the Dan Valley petitioned the legislature for the establishment of an inspection warehouse at Wynne's Falls on the Dan River. Just above the falls there was a ford used by mail carriers to connect Washington, D.C., and points south. Maude Carter Clement describes the area: "Low rounding hills by the side of a stately beautiful river form a situation designed by nature for man's abode. The indians were quick to perceive the fitness of the location and established one of their towns there."[3] The petitioners, interested in business rather than beauty, stated that "the situation of the place is suitably calculated for a Town, which will make the convenience of inspection more Serviseable."[4]

In November 1793 the legislature granted the charter for Danville to twelve gentlemen trustees, who were required to lay off the town's land in half-acre lots and establish streets. A subsequent petition led to the construction of a tobacco inspection warehouse on the site, and by 1796 the Danville warehouse was doing a brisk business. Between September 1795 and September 1796, 135 hogsheads or about 135,000 pounds of tobacco had been dispatched and 70 hogsheads were still in the warehouse.[5]

The petitioners, trustees, and early landowners—the sowers of the urban spore—were all tobacco planters. Their leader was John Wilson, the most influential of Danville's founding fathers. He was the son of Peter Wilson, a Scotch-Irish immigrant from Pennsylvania who had settled in Pittsylvania County in 1746.[6] John Wilson was an Overseer of the Poor both before and after the Revolution. He also held a number of other local offices including that of sheriff and justice of the peace. In 1775 he was involved, along with his fellow Virginians George Washington and Thomas Jefferson, in the Virginia Non-Importation Association; later he served as an officer in the Revolutionary army. After the war he represented Pittsylvania in the state assembly and was active in the Methodist church.

Wilson's fortunes rose with those of the county. In 1767 he held land along Sandy Creek a few miles west of Wynne's Falls, and along the Dan River six miles east of Wynne's Falls at a place called Wilson's Ferry. At that time he owned 7 slaves, 2 of whom were employed full time as ferrymen. In 1771, in response to the increased trade in the area, he opened a store at the ferry. Wilson continued to invest in transportation. In 1800 he owned 28 wagons and 20 horses, which were used to transport cargoes around the rapids of the Dan and to take cargoes north to Lynchburg. Wilson's chief interest, however, was in tobacco production. In 1795–96 his 44 hogsheads (about 44,000 pounds of tobacco), shipped out of the newly established Danville inspection warehouse, probably made him the largest planter in the area. Assuming that an acre yielded 750 pounds of tobacco (the average in Virginia for that period), Wilson had about 59 acres in tobacco production. At the time he owned about 48 slaves. If his slaves were as productive as most in Virginia, it took at least 25 of them to produce the crop, including women and children. Some of the others worked as hostlers, draymen, and ferrymen.[7]

Other founding fathers, like John Colquehon and George Adamson, were also large planters. John Dix, another prominent founder, operated the ferry at the ford at Wynne's Falls.

Some information is available for twelve of the sixteen original trustees of the town. Of the twelve, two were younger sons of prominent men. Among the remaining ten, five represented Pittsylvania in the assembly during the 1790s, six were justices of the peace, six were overseers of the poor, two had served as sheriff, and three were members of the influential Masons. Seven of the original trustees lived in the area just west of what became Danville, an area that became the agricultural heartland of the county. Thus, Danville was founded and developed by planter-merchants. This close relationship between the local planters and the development of the town would continue throughout Danville's antebellum history.[8]

Despite the support of local planters and the location of a tobacco inspection warehouse in the town, Danville grew very slowly. When the trustees originally offered the town lots for sale in 1795, the buyers were obligated by the terms of the legislative charter to build within five years "a dwelling house sixteen feet square at least with a brick or stone chimney."[9] As of 1799, none of the seven men who bought lots in 1795 had fulfilled the requirement. So that year the legislature received the first of a number of petitions requesting an extension of time to improve the lots. Four of the seven men who had bought lots had sold them by 1800. There were some newcomers, however, and in 1800 the town had fourteen lot owners, eleven of whom were from Pittsylvania and three from nearby counties in Virginia and North Carolina.[10]

Until 1800, Danville was little more than a transshipment point with a store, tavern, and tobacco inspection warehouse; it had few permanent residents. All of the lot owners from the county owned land outside of the town, and half of them owned land and homes beyond the Wynne's Falls settlement. Some of the owners of town lots were large planters, including John Wilson, Robert and Thomas Barnett, and William Spiller, all of whom held over a thousand acres in the county. Wilson, who owned forty-eight slaves, was the only large slaveholder; no one else owned more than ten. Not surprisingly, transportation—the ownership of horses and carriages—was a common denominator among the owners of town lots. The eleven lot owners residing in the county owned a mean of five (and a median of seven) horses, well above the number held by even large planters, and six owned a total of fifty-six wagons.[11]

In the first decade of the nineteenth century, various improvements in and around Danville began to accelerate the pace of development. To begin with, as a result of legislation passed by the General Assembly in 1796, work was underway to enhance the Roanoke River system, which included the three major rivers in Pittsylvania County (the Dan, the Banister, and the Staunton). In 1800 a post office was established locally, and in 1801 the legislature approved the opening of a flour inspection warehouse in Danville. In the latter year, a group of sixteen local planters asked the assembly for permission to open a school in the vicinity. They said that "being in a remote part of the state we have found it attended with great inconvenience and expense to get our children educated, and have undertaken to build an academy near the said Town, to be known as the Danville Academy."[12] The petitioners also wished to run a lottery to raise money for the school, which was built a few years later. Perhaps the most significant event of 1801 was the legislature's approval of a request for the construction of a toll bridge across the Dan River. The petitioners were John Barnett, one of the planters who held over a thousand acres of land, and Thomas Worsham, who had led the petitioning for the flour inspection warehouse. The bridge, completed a few years later, gave the town a much-needed shot in the arm. By making the crossing so much easier and safer, it attracted travelers and wagons that might otherwise have chosen to cross at one of the nearby fords or by ferry. There is no indication that men like John Wilson, whose ferry was only a few miles up the river, objected to the new bridge, which must have decreased their business in the short run.[13]

In 1809 the legislature chartered a manufacturing company that hoped to take advantage of the town's abundant water power. Although little came of the scheme, it was a precursor of later and ultimately more successful efforts to make Danville a manufacturing center.

In the following years, the would-be metropolis of southwestern Virginia was strongly affected by post-Revolutionary changes in the marketing of tobacco. These changes placed greater emphasis on discerning quality gradations within the tobacco sold. Previously, most tobacco warehousing and sales had been conducted impersonally. A seller brought his tobacco to an inspection point and obtained a receipt from the state inspector. The seller then used this receipt with buyers who preferred to purchase on the basis of the receipt rather than to look personally at the tobacco. But the new emphasis in quality demanded personal attention on the part of the buyers, who were willing to pay a higher price for tobacco they had personally inspected. The sellers in turn would wait at the inspection warehouse to help in the assessment and see how their tobacco fared. As sellers and buyers congregated, a nascent commodities market was created. The sellers and buyers, of course, needed food and drink and perhaps even lodging. And, if they came to a place to sell their tobacco, they might also find it convenient to purchase goods for themselves while they were there. The intense speculation in tobacco after the War of 1812 attracted large numbers of buyers to the most popular inspection points, resulting in the expansion of the more popular market towns and the eclipse of less favored inspection points. Farmers and planters wanted to bring their quality leaf to a place where a host of competing buyers might force up the price.[14]

The changes in marketing practices permitted the producer to bring his crops to market in loose bunches, that is, without being prized. (Prizing is the process of using heavy pressure to compress the loose tobacco into a form more suitable for shipping.) Because of the great labor and effort involved, prizing had usually been done once a year before the tobacco was marketed. With prizing eliminated or reduced, the leaf could be brought into the town warehouse at various times during the year. As a result, Danville experienced a more regular flow of visitors and hence an invigorated life. These changes occurred gradually but they were underway when the town's potential began to crystallize with the opening of the Dismal Swamp Canal.[15]

INTERNAL IMPROVEMENTS AND TOWN RIVALRY

When B. W. S. Cabell arrived in Danville in 1816, the town had just begun to bud. That year he began to organize the building of a canal around Wynne's Falls for the Roanoke Navigation Company. It was to be a rock canal with several locks. When completed, it would make water power available on the south side of the Dan River (where the town was located).[16] The canal project helped set off a great speculative boom in 1818–19 that swept across the entire Roanoke Valley. Eight miles south by southwest of Danville, the town of Milton, North Carolina, was—like Danville—caught up in a frenzy of speculation. The growing rivalry between the two towns is evident from the observations of one speculator, who described the scene in Milton with an eye on the larger Danville:

> As to Milton, speculation has raged there beyond my expectation. Lots on the Main Street have sold for nearly 100 dollars per foot. The Company [probably the Roanoke Navigation Company] have laid out a New Street and sold a few lots. Their Sales have already exceeded $50,000. . . . Lands in the Neighborhood are selling from 20 to $50 per Acre. I understand that more than 500 Hgds of Tobacco have been Received at Danville, and that the property which I sold to Mr. Cabell would now sell for more than $100,000. A great deal of Capital is centering in Milton and Danville.[17]

Thirty miles to the east, the Roanoke Rapids were a major obstacle along the route to the Dismal Swamp Canal and Norfolk. A canal was built around the rapids and a town called Rock Landing established at the upper end of the canal. Walter Coles, of Pittsylvania, a future congressman from the district, explains how the new town developed: "In the spring of 1818, when the whole country was excited by a mania for town speculation, Col. Jones the proprieter, was prevailed on to lay off his lands into lots, a few more were sold at $50.00 and $100.00 each, but the balance soon rose to four or five thousand dollars and in one year the place was sprung up almost to the size of Danville."[18]

In 1818 the legislature was asked to raise the toll on the Danville Bridge, which was nearly one-fifth of a mile long. In justifying the increase, the petitioners pointed out that the bridge was vital to travelers and commerce between the South and Southwest and Richmond and points north. They also noted Danville's historic growth:

> That the bridge was originally built in 1802 at which time the town of Danville was a small village, nor was there then or for many years thereafter any prospect of it becoming a place of commercial importance. . . . [B]ut owing to the great change in the times the progress which has been made and is making in the navigations of the Roanoke River and its branches, the rapid growth of the town of Danville and the consequent demand for building timber of every description the kind of timber which is building the bridge or repairing it has enhanced in price from six to ten fold.[19]

The Danville of 1820 bore no resemblance to the Danville of 1800. In 1800 there had been no buildings; by 1820 the buildings in the town alone were valued at nearly $51,000 (see Table 2-1).

Although Danville had achieved substantial growth through real estate, it still had no security. Moreover, Milton—its nearby rival in North Carolina—was about to gain a bank with state support. This prospect deeply troubled B. W. S. Cabell, who feared that Danville's onrushing growth could be halted if Milton, but not Danville, secured such an advantage. Cabell appealed to the legislature to charter a bank for his town. In the petition, he pointed out that the citizens of Danville had already taken a number of actions on their own behalf:

> . . . the inhabitants of Danville, with the view of availing themselves as soon as possible of the advantages of their situation, have enlarged the limits of their town, have revived an inspection of tobacco, have applied to your honorable body [the General Assembly] for the establishment of lots, actively engaged in preparing to improve the same. That, in consequence of the additional funds acquired to effect these improvements, and the new prospects of trade which are now open to them, they are not provided with a capital which is adequate to the increased and sudden demand. Your petitioners have reason to think that there is a sufficient number of monied men, who, knowing the favorable position of Dan-

TABLE 2–I
Danville Real Estate Development, 1800, 1820

Year	Number of Lot Owners	Number of Lots	Total Value of Lots	Total Value of Buildings
1800	15	21	$ 2,329	—
1820	34	42	$91,270	$50,770

Source: Pittsylvania (Real) Property, 1800.

ville for inland trade, and interested in giving that trade every possible facility, would be ready to furnish the capital of a bank of discount.[20]

Danville finally obtained a branch bank in 1830, largely through the political efforts of a group of about ten planter-entrepreneurs who dominated the town's economy through their ownership of the tobacco warehouses and mercantile firms. The group included Cabell, Sam Pannill, N. H. Claiborne, and Robert and Nathaniel Wilson, sons of the town's planter-patriarch, John Wilson.

Urban lot owners generally fell into one of two categories. The small owners had under $1,000 in town property and a building worth about $500; they owned little or no rural property and at most one or two slaves. The large owners, on the other hand, held on the average $4,000 to $5,000 in town property and $2,000 or so in town buildings. These were the planter-entrepreneurs—all local men, mostly from the Dan Valley—who owned extensive rural property and ten or more slaves. Some of them, like Cabell and the Wilson brothers, maintained town houses in or near Danville in addition to their country estates. The ten largest rural property owners (those in the upper half of the decile ranking among the town lot owners) owned more than 60 percent of the town's property (see Table 2-2).

A PLANTER LIFE-STYLE AND PHILOSOPHY

The planter-entrepreneurs of Danville intermarried with the wealthiest and most respected families in the region. The Wilson family, for in-

TABLE 2–2
Countywide Rankings of Rural Landowners
Who Owned Plots in Danville, 1830

Decile	Total Value of Rural Property	Number of Rural Acres Owned
1	1	1
2	—	2
3	—	1
4	1	—
5	1	1
6	1	—
7	—	2
8	1	1
9	3	—
10	5	7

Source: Pittsylvania (Real) Property, 1830.
Note: This table was created by matching town-lot owners against a decile ranking of rural property owners in terms of the total value and total number of acres owned. In this way, multiple ownership of lots is considered. Deciles are ranked from the bottom to the top.

stance, intermarried with the prestigious Hairstons, known for their large slaveholdings and their political leadership in both the town and the county.[21]

The varied interests and energy of planter-entrepreneur B. W. S. Cabell are particularly noteworthy.[22] According to a prominent Danvillian and fellow Mason, "he [Cabell] was recognized as a gentleman of the Old Virginia Stock."[23] Cabell made his home at Bridgewater, his plantation located a few miles north of Danville, where in 1830 he owned twenty-seven slaves. A few years after his arrival in 1816, he built Danville's first flour, corn, and linseed oil mills. These were the first of many industries to take advantage of the power of the rapidly flowing Dan River. A dozen years later Cabell was heavily involved in the first (but abortive) attempt to bring cotton manufacturing to Danville.

For thirty years Cabell either initiated or participated in every major internal improvement venture in the Dan Basin. In 1824, before the opening of the Erie Canal and a decade before Virginia would slowly begin to aid railroads, he proposed to build a railroad from Norfolk to

Wythe County in the mountains of southwestern Virginia. The railroad would, of course, go by way of Danville. The scheme, which failed, was the precursor of two decades of internal improvements that finally culminated in the chartering of the Richmond and Danville Railroad in 1846.

In the late 1840s Cabell and a partner started the *Danville Reporter and Internal Improvements Gazette*, a weekly newspaper, which Cabell used to trumpet his pleas for state-assisted internal improvements. His articles presented an image of an almost romantic materialism; internal improvements, he argued, would bring incalculable benefits, material prosperity, and a sense of well-being. The paper also supported extending the franchise and opening branch banks. At the same time, Cabell put forth his program for a developing area at odds with the economically backward but politically powerful Tidewater. Cabell shared the states' rights philosophy of the Tidewater leadership. A staunch defender of slavery, he wrote that, to the extent Southerners supported the suppression of South Carolina's rights, "they whet their own swords to cut their own throats."[24] Throughout his life Cabell remained both a militant defender of slavery and a fervid proponent of economic growth and diversification.

This seeming contradiction between what is supposed to be quintessentially Southern—the defense of states' rights—and an entrepreneurial spirit can be seen in other aspects of Cabell's career. He had a penchant for the military as well as the industrial. Educated briefly at Hampden-Sidney College, a Presbyterian institution on the Southside, he left school to become an ensign and later a lieutenant colonel in the War of 1812. Although he left the ranks of the active military after the war, he never completely lost his military bearing, serving in the militia as a major, colonel, major general, and ultimately brigadier general. The last two posts he earned through election by the General Assembly.

The same sort of apparent contradiction in values can be seen in the life of Sam Pannill, paternalist slaveholder and highly successful merchant. The best account of these values is provided in the letters of Samuel Pannill to his son Samuel, Jr., and to his business partner Crispen Dickerson. In the early 1820s, at a time when he was the town's largest property owner, Pannill sent his son to Danville to learn the mercantile business under the tutelage of Dickerson. Pannill wrote frequently to his son and Dickerson and the letters are important for the way they interweave business details and Pannill's philosophy.

It is in his concern for the details of business that we can see the apparent conflict between Pannill's paternalism and his bourgeois spirit dissolve. In February 1830 he wrote to Dickerson and his son: "in a long life I have known few if any to do well of tobacco, indeed, I have known men to get rich on goods and in a few years break on tobacco, there are two late cases in Lynchburg, *we must not attempt to get rich by counting and big notions, solid wealth comes by much time, toil and difficulty and if money comes hard it ought to go hard* [emphasis mine]."[25]

Pannill had specific ideas about what it took to run a good store. At the time of the corn planting he wrote to his store at Green Hill with instructions: "we must . . . be sure to keep up the supply of saleable articles, and to so manage as to have them to hand in full time, it is best never to lack an important article even for one day, it had better be to hand 15 or 20 too soon than to run out, this I have ever considered a very important point."[26] And writing two months later regarding the management of the store, he instructed that "all that we can do or that can be expected of us, is for us to do our best in every respect and never for a moment to be lulled off our guard, but like a cautious warrior on the enemies lines, continually on the alert, this being steadily and uniformly the case all will end well."[27]

In the fall of 1828 Sam, Jr., was, like his father, gravely disappointed at his hero Clay's defeat. In a letter, the senior Pannill admonished his son to keep his mind on what was important, business not politics:

> Let our own whole and vigerous attention be directed to our business and keep our counsuls, we have the world to contend with and as the elections are pretty well over for the present, it will be best to waste no more time in discussing points in relation . . . but go for business . . . we have to work for our living, and pay our debts, there is none that can or will help us. . . .[28]

Again and again in his letters the senior Pannill emphasized the classic bourgeois virtues: steadiness, frugality, and hard work. In the summer of 1829 he was gravely concerned about his son's health. He asked Sam, Jr., if he wanted to go to the springs in the Shenandoah, with a servant to attend to him. Then in a revealing letter to his partner in his Danville store, Crispen Dickerson, he wrote that, if his son were to go to the springs, "[he] will lose only about 4 weeks from business. . . . As health and not pleasure, will be the object of the trip, I hope and I believe there can be no objections."[29]

Samuel Pannill was clearly a man who had internalized a "Poor Richard's" asceticism. His bourgeois morality, however, coexisted with a paternal attitude toward his slaves. Despite the extensive nature of his holdings, he gave considerable personal attention to the slaves who worked on the Green Hill plantation. His letters reveal an intimate personal knowledge of his slaves. In a letter to Dickerson, he identified his slaves by both their first and last names and expressed a knowledge of their marital status. In one instance, he wrote: "I have one of the runaway hands here, there is one in Henry County jail and another is out that has a wife at Major George Wilsons, I hope that some of the neighbors may pick him up shortly, and bring him to me or lodge him in Pittsylvania jail and send me word . . . we commence our inventory and list of balances on Monday next."[30]

The lives of Danville's planter-entrepreneurs clearly extended beyond the traditional definition of what a planter was supposed to have been like. These men engaged in business with relish, not reluctance. If Sam Pannill's attitudes are indicative of the attitudes of the circle he and his family lived and worked within, it would seem difficult to argue that values could have in any sense inhibited the economic development of the Dan basin. Rather than being limited by planter ideology, the town of Danville was built largely by opportunistic planters. They were men who took advantage of the changes in transport and tobacco marketing, which for the first time made town development profitable in their area.

The centrality of the planter-entrepreneurs is related to a number of important threads in the history of Danville and Pittsylvania County. First, there was almost no tension between the interests of the town and the countryside. Their growth was viewed as complementary. This was so, in part, because southern Pittsylvania's largest planters both invested in Danville and sent their sons there to establish businesses. Finally, during the boom periods of 1818–19, the early 1830s, and the late 1840s, the people who took advantage of and helped create the rising tide were almost entirely local—that is, from Pittsylvania and its immediately adjacent neighbors in Virginia and North Carolina.[31]

3

THE POLITICS OF A

DEVELOPING AREA

❧ ❧ ❧ ❧ ❧ ❧ ❧

THERE WAS considerable speculative growth in Danville between 1820 and 1825. But after 1825 growth slackened and Danville's rival, Milton, North Carolina, seemed to be rapidly gaining ground. In an effort to get Danville growing again, the city fathers increasingly turned to politics. They wanted a new injection of state-supported internal improvements. When frustrated by an unresponsive legislature dominated by economically bypassed and fiscally conservative Tidewater planters, Danville's political leaders joined with the insurgent forces of western Virginia in calling for a modification of the state constitution.[1]

Danville's push to reform state government came only after local efforts at self-help failed. A joint stock company was created in 1826 to rebuild the bridge across the Dan River. The new bridge was to be wider and higher to permit heavier freight to pass across it and bigger boats to pass under it. The petition to the legislature asking for the incorporation of the joint stock company to rebuild the bridge was filled with descriptions of Danville successes and roseate projections for the future.[2] The petition began by noting changes that had occurred since the first bridge had been built:

> ... a great change has taken place not only as respects the town of Danville, but as respects the surrounding and adjacent country. This change may be ascribed to various causes but especially to the progress which has been made in rendering the Roanoke River navigable. The town itself has become the depot of an extensive populous and wealthy country. ... The natural resources of the adjacent country are rapidly unfolding and the petitioners think they are not too sanguine when they assess an opinion that the

town of Danville is destined to become at no remote period, one of the most considerable towns in the state of Virginia, above the tidewater.[3]

Given the petitioners' high expectations, the town's economic slow-down in the second half of the decade was all the more disturbing (see Table 3-1). The citizens of Danville and the surrounding area had made heavy personal investments in internal improvement companies: $64,000 was collected in public funds for the improvement of the Dan, and $166,000 had been invested in the Dismal Swamp Canal project. Despite these efforts Danville was not only in a slump; it also appeared that it was about to be eclipsed by Milton, North Carolina, which was located just eighteen miles further down the Dan.[4]

Danville had good reason to fear Milton. Milton, a slightly older town, had grown more rapidly than Danville and was first to establish a newspaper. Moreover, by the mid-1820s Milton was endowed with sev-eral plug chewing tobacco manufactories as well as mills for the process-ing of oil and the manufacturing of woolen and cotton goods. These, to be sure, were on a small scale. But the citizens of Danville were fearful that Danville and Milton were involved in a zero-sum game. They as-sumed, correctly, that there could be only one major town in the Dan Valley.[5]

One response to Milton's competition was the attempt to develop cotton manufacturing in Danville. Almost from the start a keen interest was shown in encouraging mechanics and industry, and as early as 1808 there was a brief attempt to harness the power of Wynne's Falls and establish a manufacturing company.

The importance of and solicitude for the mechanics is revealed in an 1822 petition signed by some of the town's leading businessmen, includ-ing Nathaniel Wilson and transportation mogul Walter Fitzgerald, the owner of more than 150 wagons and carriages. The petition called for the establishment of a polling place in Danville on the grounds that "it is a well known fact that the sedentary life to which mechanics in particular are addicted unfits them in a great degree for exertions on foot—and it is perfectly natural that men thus situated should not only become supine and indifferent toward the general interest."[6]

Six years later Wilson and Fitzgerald, as well as some of the town's leading mechanics like shoemaker John Noble, spearheaded the attempt to establish a cotton mill in Danville. Their petition to the legislature calling for the incorporation of a manufacturing company cited the vast

TABLE 3–1
Danville Real Estate Development, 1820, 1825, 1830

	1820	1825	1830
Number of Owners	34	72	65
Number of Lots	43	132	141
Number of Lots with Buildings	—	50	—
Value of Real Estate	$90,000	$153,000	$135,000
Value of Buildings	$51,000	$ 50,000	$ 52,000

Source: Pittsylvania (Real) Property, 1820, 1825, and 1830.

water power along the bend of the Dan that cradled the town and expressed the hope that "this valuable water capital . . . [be brought into profitable use] . . . by applying machinery adapted to the manufacture of cotton fabrics." With legislative approval, the backers of the plan hoped to also process and manufacture wool, flax, and hemp as well as cotton.[7]

✗

STATE POLITICS

The attempt to initiate manufacturing was only one of the ways Danville's investors tried to meet the challenge from Milton. The central thrust of their efforts was political. It was widely argued that, while Milton benefited from a solicitous state government, Danville was being held back by an unresponsive state legislature. The state assembly had turned down a number of requests for a branch bank to be established in Danville. N. H. Claiborne summarized this argument in a newspaper article:

> The legislature of North Carolina disposed to concentrate the produce of all those counties on their side of the river, have done everything in their power to increase the commercial facilities of Milton, a town 18 miles below Danville. Yes, sir, they have established a bank at Milton. The beneficial effects of this policy are already visible in the increase in population, capital and trade of that place and unless something is done by us—Danville with supe-

rior advantages from healthiness of situation must sink under the unequal contest, and all the sums expended by us and our citizens will serve to advance and augment the interests of our enlightened and liberal spirited neighbors. This has been seen in part already— if I am correctly informed, some of our mercantile men carrying with them their capital, have left us and settled at Milton, and think you others will not follow their example.[8]

Claiborne, who represented Pittsylvania in the state senate, went on to explain why a bank was of crucial importance for Danville: "The great object of a bank should be to enable the merchant to continue his purchases—with the capital of others, while his own was afloat in quest of gain."[9]

Claiborne's remarks helped crystallize the town's antagonism toward the Tidewater-dominated legislature. Claiborne was speaking for the merchants and planters of the Danville Basin, but the resentment in Pittsylvania toward the legislature was long standing and extended well beyond merchant circles. The legislature had long been regarded as an aristocratic and unresponsive body. The state constitution of 1776 had given each county, regardless of size, two delegates to the assembly, the state's preeminent governing body. This system of apportionment allowed the numerous small counties of the Tidewater to dominate the assembly. The constitution of 1776 both sharply restricted white suffrage and placed power in the hands of the conservative Tidewater gentry. In the nearly three-quarters of a century between 1776 and the reform convention of 1850, the developing areas of Virginia—Pittsylvania among them—had fought almost continually against the slowly retreating power of the Tidewater "aristocracy."[10]

The counties of the Dan River Valley and the western Piedmont, in particular, felt cheated by the state's constitutional arrangements. In 1805 and 1806, petitions from Patrick and Henry counties condemned the state's constitution as an affront to the principles of the Republic. In the 1807–1808 session of the assembly, a petition from Patrick, Henry, and Pittsylvania again called for reform. The petition's backers in the assembly gained enough support to pass a bill calling for a constitutional convention, but the bill failed in the senate. The assembly received and ignored numerous other calls for reform. An 1810 Pittsylvania petition called for the establishment of more chancery courts and pointed out that there were only three in the state, and that none of the three was located near the residents of the southwest Piedmont. The petition tied this specific problem to the more general problem of Tidewater domination. It ended by expressing sympathy with the counties west of the Blue Ridge that were calling for a major change in state government.[11]

Between 1810 and 1816 the assembly was flooded with new petitions from the developing areas of the state calling for reform of the courts and the legislature. The consistent refusal of the Tidewater-dominated assembly to respond led to a rump reform convention at Winchester in the Shenandoah Valley in 1816. Representatives from eleven counties attended. The reformers wanted to rewrite the constitution to provide universal suffrage for all white adult males, and they wanted a reapportionment of the state senate on the basis of white population. In the constitution of 1776, the senate had been apportioned on the basis of a formula that considered the size of both the slave and free population. This consideration allowed the heavily slave counties to dominate the senate.

Later in 1816 a larger and more important convention was held in Staunton, also in the Shenandoah Valley. There were sixty-five delegates from thirty-five counties including Pittsylvania. They came from the southwest Piedmont, the Piedmont counties lying along the base of the Blue Ridge, the Potomac area, and the Shenandoah Valley and trans-mountain counties. The reformers, heartened by the support Thomas Jefferson expressed for their efforts, made the standard proposals for reform. The leaders of the Tidewater planters responded with a compromise, hoping to head off further reform. They agreed to apportion the weak upper house, the senate, on the basis of white population in return for changes in the way land values were evaluated for taxes.[12]

The west was far from appeased by the reform of 1817 and in 1825 another reform convention was organized in Staunton. Pittsylvania sent no delegate because the county was divided on the issue. The area of the Staunton River Valley in the north was the center of opposition to the call for further reform, whereas the Banister and Dan Valley areas were strongly in favor.

The split between the upper and lower sections of the county represented a real division of economic interest and constituency. The upper county's chief interest in internal improvements was in clearing the Staunton and opening the Dismal Swamp Canal. This had been accomplished by 1825. In a sense, upper Pittsylvania was like the Tidewater. It stood to gain only minimal benefits from state aid for internal improvements and banks. Forty miles distant from Danville, sections of Pittsylvania along the Staunton were actually closer to Lynchburg.[13]

The picture in Danville was, of course, very different. To begin with, an important section of Danville's citizens, mechanics without twenty-five acres of improved land, were disenfranchised by the constitution of 1776. But more importantly Danville, as Claiborne enunciated, needed state approval for banking facilities and state aid to build roads and turnpikes. The aspirations of the town's entrepreneurs led beyond limited ad hoc support for state measures designed to support Danville, to a political perspective supportive of active governmental aid for the economy.

The concern over governmental support for internal improvements led some of Danville's most prominent citizens to support John Quincy Adams over Andrew Jackson in 1828. Though the county at large went for Jackson, there was strong anti-Jackson and pro-Adams sentiment in the town. A group led by James Lanier and Thomas Wooding accused Jackson of demagoguery, militarism, despotism, and authoritarianism. The pro-Adams group included forty of the leading lights from the Danville area and the county. Among them were transport mogul Walter Fitzgerald, the prominent up-country merchant Philip Grasty, and the early tobacco manufacturer William Linn. Clearly, Danville and its environs as well as the merchants of the county were strongly pro-Adams.[14]

Pittsylvania was politically divided between up-country Democrats and the proto-Whigs behind Adams. Pittsylvania, a divided county, also held an important position in a state increasingly split between the Tidewater planters and their opponents on both sides of the Blue Ridge. The assembly, no doubt mindful of Pittsylvania's position as a potential swing county, voted to authorize the stockholders of the Farmers Bank of Virginia to open a branch in Danville. The authorization came just as pressure was again mounting for a reform convention.[15]

Despite the awarding of a branch bank to Danville, Pittsylvania voted with the Shenandoah Valley, the western Piedmont, the Potomac counties, and the west in calling for a constitutional convention in 1828. This time the reform effort was at least initially successful, and a state constitutional convention was convened. The chief issues revolved around the basis for apportioning representation in the very powerful assembly. The reform elements generally wanted representation to be based solely on the white population. The declining Tidewater aristocrats, ridiculing the Jeffersonian arguments of the reformers, called for a continuation of the existing system based on both the slave and free populations. It was in response to the reformers' attacks that Tidewater leaders like Abel Up-shur increasingly attacked notions supportive of political equality. The second major issue was the basis of suffrage, with the Tidewater refusing to accede to the demands of the reformers for universal suffrage for white male adults.[16]

Pittsylvania's two delegates were both from Danville, but like the county they were split on the issue of reform. The delegates were B. W. S. Cabell, who generally sided with the reformers, and George Townes, who generally sided with the Tidewater. The two men had a great deal in common; both were Episcopalian planters who were actively involved in Danville's development. And Townes, like Cabell, was a promoter of railroad and turnpike schemes designed to expand Danville's hinterland. In the 1840s Townes, along with Whitmell P. Tunstall, was the force behind the ultimately successful Richmond and Danville Railroad. There was little in Townes's public history to suggest that he had any affinities for the regressive economic tendencies of the Tidewater planters.[17]

The key to Townes's support of the Tidewater probably lay in Pittsylvania's role at the convention. Pittsylvania was regarded by both camps as a swing county. Townes's position may have been prearranged with his sometimes collaborator Cabell to maximize Pittsylvania's influence at the convention. It seems more than providential that, within a short time of the convention's adjournment, Danville was given a second branch bank whose first president was to be none other than George Townes.[18]

The convention of 1828 produced only very limited reforms. But the reforms it did achieve split the southwest Piedmont, the western Piedmont, and the Valley away from the transmontane reformers. Pittsylvania was mollified by the reforms because they provided increased representation in the assembly for the Piedmont and an extension of the franchise to leaseholders, which covered Danville's mechanics. More importantly, having established itself as a swing county, Pittsylvania and the town of Danville were ready to reap the rewards of political cooperation with the Tidewater. In the coming decade, the legislature would respond generously to Danville's requests for assistance with internal improvements.[19]

4

DANVILLE, 1829–1837:

A NEW BOOM AND A

NEW BUST

✿ ✿ ✿ ✿ ✿ ✿ ✿ ✿

THE FALLOW YEARS of the 1820s were followed by Danville's second boom tide in the 1830s. For Virginia at large, the 1830s were a period of great decline. Ravaged by soil exhaustion and western competition in tobacco and wheat, the population of the state declined by 26,000 between 1830 and 1840. Danville was decidedly not part of this trend. From 1829 to 1835 the population more than doubled, as the town experienced both economic growth and a rebirth of high aspirations. The flush times initiated a sustained drive for new internal improvements, improvements designed to make Danville the future emporium of southwestern Virginia and bordering North Carolina.

These hopes collapsed, temporarily, with the crash of 1837. Except for a few merchants, only the manufacturers of the town's nascent tobacco industry survived it. What was striking, at decade's end, was not the collapse, which was nationwide, not the process of boom-and-bust per se, but rather how little the boom had wrought even at its high tide. Not only had the boom failed to make Danville a commercial center, but also it had failed to expand the town's economy much beyond the traditional purview of tobacco.

The diary of Thompson Coleman provides a remarkably clear and detailed picture of Danville before the upswing began: "When I went to Danville to reside there in 1829, I approached the place, then a straggling village, by way of the country road. . . . This road was a common country road, unimproved by grading or otherwise." Coleman went on to describe the town's milling and manufacturing area, as tobacco was not yet being manufactured on any scale:

> After crossing the river, the first building to be seen was the flour mill, a frame building three stories high, which stood just below the bridge and between the canal and the river. It was an extensive establishment for those days, running three pairs of stones—two burrs and one common. Just below and connected with the flour mill was a saw mill with an old fashioned sash saw. Just above the bridge, between the canal and the river, was a common "tub" mill, with one pair of stones for grinding corn. Above that was a small building in which were a linseed-oil mill, a cotton gin, and a wool carding machine. These mills were all run by water power from the canal, and were its only improvements.

Coleman detailed each building in the town and its occupants, noting that many of the commercial buildings were only in partial use and the tenements had numerous vacancies. He then gave an overview of the town's economic life:

> The regular business of the town was small. There were only two regular stores, the most extensive of which was kept by Thomas and Samuel D. Rawlins and the other by John Ross and Co (Wilson and Baskerville and Ross, Lansdown and Co having just gone into liquidation).
>
> There was an agency of the farmers bank of Virginia with a very small capital. . . .
>
> There were two tailors shops, one blacksmiths shop and one shoemakers shop (Captain John Nobles). There was one tan yard, (Linn's) operated by Samuel Patton. . . . Hats were manufactured on a small scale by Gilmore and Lyon.
>
> The trade of the place was in general merchandise, . . . and was mostly carried on by barter for country produce, including whiskey and bacon. . . .
>
> The tobacco trade was in its infancy. . . . It amounted to about 350 hogsheads per annum. No leaf tobacco was sold loose, but all was prized in hogsheads, which were inspected by state inspectors and sold at the warehouses; though the greater part of it was purchased from the planters at their barns, then prized and delivered

TABLE 4–1
Rate of Population Growth, 1820–1840

Decade	State	Pittsylvania	Pittsylvania Black	Pittsylvania White	Danville
1820–30	+11%	+22%	+26%	+18%	–
1830–40	–2%	+2%	+7%	–2%	100%

Sources: Clement, *History of Pittsylvania*; Hagan, *Danville*; Hairston, *Danville*.

at the warehouses. There was scarcely any tobacco manufactured here at all, but there was one small establishment.[1]

In 1829 Danville stood a village of less than 500 residents in a county whose growth, like the state's, was coming to a temporary halt. Numerous planters and small farmers were leaving Virginia, taking their slaves with them. The *Norfolk Beacon* later lamented, in an issue devoted to internal improvements, that in 1834 alone over 1,000 Negroes had been taken south from Pittsylvania, and that most of the other counties had been drained in like proportions.[2] As shown in Table 4-1, Pittsylvania did not fare as poorly as the state as a whole, but nonetheless Danville's growth from less than 500 people in 1829 to nearly 1,000 by 1835 was an eddy moving against a wave of decline.

Apparently, Danville was able to buck the tide in part because of George Townes's and B. W. S. Cabell's "bargain" with the representatives of the declining Tidewater aristocracy at the reform convention. It also appears that, in return for Townes's lending Pittsylvania's swing vote to the antireform forces, Danville received one of the major objects of the reform effort, a new and more generously endowed bank. If Thompson Coleman's account is correct, the bank was the catalyst for tapping the dormant potential of Danville's hinterland. The bank's capital spurred the development of the tobacco industry, still in its infancy in most of Virginia, and thus created a local market for tobacco growers.[3] Coleman described the developments in his diary:

> [In 1830] the Bank of Virginia established a branch here, with a liberal capital for the trade of the place. It was managed by a board of directors with Colonel George Townes as president. . . . This made money abundant and gave an impetus to enterprise. The

town commenced to improve in every direction; many new buildings were erected and the population and trade increased. . . .

A tobacco factory was established . . . then other factories were
established and the tobacco trade and other branches of business
rapidly increased and Danville entered upon a period of great
prosperity.[4]

❦

THE FIRST TOBACCO FACTORIES

This success in tobacco manufacturing came on the heels of an attempt
in late 1828 by a group of thirty-one planter-entrepreneurs—including
Robert and Nathaniel Wilson, B. W. S. Cabell, and James Lanier—to
establish a cotton mill.[5] These men had hoped to utilize the abundant
water power of Wynne's Falls, which lay alongside the town, to bring
Danville out of its slump. They failed, and tobacco manufacturing, until
then a largely rural industry carried out by planters as an auxiliary enterprise, became the mainstay of the town's economy.

Unfortunately, little is known about these first tobacco factories,
which were being developed when the industry was in its infancy across
the state. Some indication of the rapid growth in tobacco manufacturing
is provided in Table 4-2, which shows that by 1840 the market value of
tobacco manufactured in lower Pittsylvania alone (that is, Pittsylvania
south of the Staunton River) had increased twentyfold over the countywide total of 1820, totaling more than a quarter of a million dollars.
Although only what were probably the two largest factories in lower
Pittsylvania were located in Danville per se, the rural tobacco manufactories were most thickly concentrated in the Sandy River and Sandy
Creek areas immediately surrounding the town. In any case, it is clear
that this efflorescence of tobacco manufacturing both laid the basis for
the prosperity of the 1830s and paved the way for the great manufacturing expansion of the 1850s. Many of the most prominent manufacturers
of the fifties, including Thomas Neal and William Johns, got their start
in the thirties.

Danville was unusual in that, almost from the start, tobacco manufacturing overshadowed tobacco marketing and shipping. Other towns that
became tobacco manufacturing centers, like Lynchburg and Richmond,

TABLE 4—2
Growth of Tobacco Manufacturing, 1820, 1840

Area	Year	Market Value	Number of Hands	Capital Invested
All of Pittsylvania	1820	$ 14,850	19	$ 6,600
Lower Pittsylvania	1840	$288,000	380	$140,000

Source: U.S. Census, Manufacturers, 1820, 1840.

were first well established as tobacco trading centers. Although there was some tobacco trading and marketing in Danville (two state inspection warehouses and two commission houses were located there by 1836), Danville's growth as a marketing center was constrained by the limitations of its transportation network, and by competition from the established marketing centers of Lynchburg, Petersburg, and Richmond. Generally only the local growers, who wanted to avoid the arduous task of prizing the leaves, brought their tobacco to Danville for manufacturing. The great bulk of the planters continued to ship it either to Lynchburg by wagon if they lived in the northern part of the county or to Norfolk if they lived in the south.

TOWN GOVERNMENT AND INTERNAL IMPROVEMENTS

In an attempt to retain the tobacco marketing trade for Danville, the area's planter-entrepreneurs spearheaded the drive to establish a town government. When the legislature granted a charter providing for a town council and a mayor elected by the council, these same planter-entrepreneurs were chosen, by a vote of all the freeholders and housekeepers within the town, to sit on the first town council. The councilmen, in turn, chose James Lanier to serve as the first mayor.[6]

Lanier's chief objective as mayor was to establish the kind of internal order in Danville that would be conducive to attracting the trade of the countryside. In his first speech to the council, he made it clear that he saw the restraint of rowdyism and the orderly settlement of disputes as

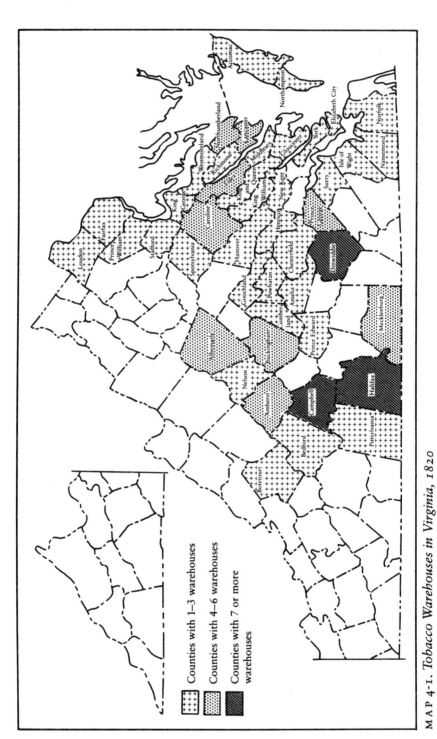

MAP 4-1. *Tobacco Warehouses in Virginia, 1820*

Source: G. Melvin Herndon, "A History of Tobacco in Virginia," M.A. thesis, University of Virginia, 1956.

the first step in making the town a more attractive location for trade. As he explained it, "among the first objects of importance that will present itself to your consideration will be the adoption of such enactments . . . to restrain such exhibitions against common decency and good manners in the public streets as are offensive to the delicacy and feelings of the virtuous and respectable portions of society. . . . To repress all disorder and riots in town." Lanier was directing his remarks at the behavior of the herdsmen and boatsmen, often free blacks, who had a reputation for brawling and rowdyism. But he also may have been referring to the town's growing slave population, because one of the council's first acts was to organize all of the town's white adult males into slave patrols.[7]

Lanier's efforts may have encouraged new money to come into Danville. The initial investments in real estate and businesses came largely from the planters whose lands were in close proximity to the town. Between 1820 and 1840, these planters continued to invest in the town while their initial real estate investments grew rapidly in value. Between 1830 and 1840, the town began drawing investors from the rest of Pittsylvania and from adjacent counties. This new money appears to have been attracted by the promise that Danville might become the commercial and marketing center for the southwest Piedmont. Politically, these new investors became an important source of aid as Danville's leaders mobilized support for the town's road, river, and even railway projects.

In 1833, the same year that the town government was established, B. W. S. Cabell and Joe Megginson, editors of the town's only newspaper, the *Danville Reporter and Roanoke Commercial Gazette*, issued a clarion call for internal improvements. They told their readers: "The Spirit of internal improvements is abroad in our land. . . . No man can forsee the magnitude of benefits which will be enjoyed by the Roanoke Country."[8]

In 1833 Danville's only major connection either to the east or to the west was the Roanoke River. The products from Pittsylvania moved from the Staunton, the Banister, and the Dan rivers down the Roanoke to Gaston. There the boats were unloaded and the goods were transported around the Gaston falls via barge canals to Weldon at the lower end of the rapids and falls. From Weldon the goods went either north by wagon to the Appomattox River and then Petersburg or east, downstream through the Dismal Swamp Canal and on to Norfolk.

The fierce competition between Norfolk and Petersburg for the Roanoke trade was a matter of great concern to Danville, which stood to benefit from it. In his paper, B. W. S. Cabell noted that Petersburg had greatly benefited from improved trade routes and that "we [of Danville] sincerely hope the legislature would afford them [Norfolk] its countenance, in their efforts to enter into fair competition with Petersburg for this trade. The bill which passed the House of Delegates appropriating a sum of money to the Portsmouth and Weldon RR, we see with regret was rejected by the senate by one vote. We hope that body will reconsider its vote."[9]

Danville was very much caught up in the rivalry between the capitalists of Petersburg and Norfolk. The competition intensified in 1829, when Petersburg announced it was building a railroad to Weldon. Norfolk responded by starting a competing line. Danville, still very much in a slump, saw this competition as an antidote for its own sagging fortunes. As a major break in bulk point, Danville was the natural link between the counties to its west—Patrick, Henry, and part of Franklin in the Virginia Piedmont; and Floyd, Carrol, and Grayson in the mountains of the southwest—and the ports of Petersburg and Norfolk.

If Danville was to be the link between east and west, it would have to establish improved connections with the west. In 1831 its only connection west was the forty or so miles of the Dan River above Danville, which was navigable by bateaux and other small boats. The first link proposed was a road to Evansham (or Wythe County Court House) in the mountains of the southwest.[10]

The act incorporating the Danville and Evansham Turnpike Company in 1831 allowed for subscriptions of $100,000 in $50 shares. The directors, most of whom were from the Danville area, attempted to gain subscription support from the counties to the west, which could be expected to benefit from the road, although Danville was expected to provide the bulk of the financing. The Danville directors were drawn from the leading merchants and planter-entrepreneurs of the basin as well as George Townes and Whitmell Tunstall, the men most responsible for establishing the Richmond and Danville Railroad.[11]

Despite this infusion of new investments from Townes and Tunstall, the directors were unable to raise the requisite capital. Too much money may have been required for an area only shortly recovered from the economic doldrums of the late 1820s. Pittsylvania legislators secured a change in the enabling act and in early 1833 the legislature reduced the capital stock requirement to $50,000 and, based on an 1817 law, authorized the Virginia Board of Public Works to subscribe to 40 percent of the $50,000.[12]

Shortly after the new legislation was passed, the proposed dirt pike was waylaid by a grandiose new scheme. Danville entrepreneurs proposed to boldly skip the turnpike stage and link Danville to the west by rail. The hoped for rail line would go through the North Carolina counties to the west along the state border, with a branch to Evansham (B. W. S. Cabell had proposed a railroad to Evansham as early as 1824). If the plan succeeded, Danville would gain a vast market area. It would make itself the indispensible link between the western Roanoke Valley in both Virginia and North Carolina and the coastal ports, and would permanently undercut rivals like Milton.

The North Carolina and Virginia legislatures passed the enabling legislation in March 1833. Under the acts, the line, named the Roanoke, Danville and Junction (R, D & J), was to open subscription books in a dozen North Carolina towns as well as Danville. The proposed road was to connect with the east at Weldon with either the Petersburg or Norfolk trunk lines. There was even a provision for extending beyond the Alleghenies and tying up with the Lynchburg and Tennessee Railroad when it was built.[13]

The plan received widespread support in Danville and the surrounding countryside. Among the directors were George Townes, B. W. S. Cabell, hotel proprietors James and Robert Williams, tobacco manufacturers William Johns and William Linn, merchant John Ross, physician George Craghead, artisan John Price, and one of Sam Pannill's partners John Dickerson. Despite their support the effort folded in short order, even before an engineer's survey could be compiled. The small town's visions far exceeded the capital at its command. The initial failure of the proposed R, D & J, however, did little to cool the town's ardor for a railroad. For the next dozen years, until a charter was obtained for a Richmond to Danville line, the planter-entrepreneurs, businessmen, and politicians of the area were preoccupied with obtaining a new rail connection.

After the initial failure of the R, D & J line, Danville's leaders turned to Norfolk to help revive the plan. The first problems were legal and legislative. The failure to survey had voided the first charter so a new one had to be obtained. In December 1835, North Carolina revived the 1833 legislation. In Virginia, however, attempts to restore the charter were blocked by the internecine warfare over transportation rights and charters between the cities. To marshall support and pressure the legislature, a railroad convention was held in Danville in January 1836. Representatives attended from Pittsylvania and Henry counties in the Virginia Piedmont, Paxson County in the North Carolina border area, and Wythe, Floyd, and Grayson counties in Virginia's mountainous southwest.

The force behind the convention was an alliance of businessmen from Danville and Norfolk. For Norfolk, a city with a small hinterland and powerful enemies in Petersburg and Richmond, the proposed road was a chance to outflank the Kanawha Canal, which linked Richmond to the west. Because Norfolk promised to put up the bulk of the capital, it is not surprising that representatives from Petersburg were ignored at the convention. The convention and lobbying efforts paid off, and in March 1836 the Virginia assembly revived the lapsed charter of 1833.[14]

Once the R, D & J charter was restored, the first order of business was to conduct a preliminary survey. The engineer for the survey demanded full payment in advance. To expedite the work, Danvillians B. W. S. Cabell, George Townes, and William Linn put up $8,000, the cost of the survey, expecting to be repaid at the next stockholders' meeting. When the stockholders met, they voted to fully refund the money.[15]

All of the directors except those from Norfolk, the erstwhile chief backers of the R, D & J line, saw to it that Danville businessmen were repaid. By refusing to compensate the trio, Norfolk in effect withdrew from the project. Norfolk's withdrawal was not merely a matter of caprice. Between the time the enabling legislation was revived and the dispute over the engineer's fee, Norfolk had been badly burned in its railroad rivalry with Petersburg. Norfolk had completed its rail line to Weldon at the lower end of the Roanoke Rapids only to find itself outmaneuvered by Petersburg. Petersburg, which had earlier built a rail connection to Weldon, North Carolina, added an extension to the upper end of the falls, thus intercepting freight before it reached the terminus of Norfolk's railroad at Weldon. Norfolk was then in the position of having expended considerable money on a rail connection to Weldon, with little prospect of a return. It was in this context that Norfolk withdrew from the R, D & J project. With the second collapse of the R, D & J, Richmond became the new focal point for Danville's rail schemes.[16]

The one great success of the period was the building of the Franklin Turnpike from Pittsylvania to Botetourt County. Botetourt was located in the upper Shenandoah, one county due south from Rockbridge and due west of Bedford in the Piedmont. Botetourt, northwest of Danville, was a lesser prize than Evansham, which would have brought in some of the North Carolina and southwestern Virginia trade. Nonetheless, after a string of railroad failures, the prospects seemed alluring, and in 1837

Pittsylvania, Franklin, and Botetourt counties petitioned for a dirt turn-pike to be built from Danville to Fincastle in Botetourt. The petition argued that, in addition to facilitating commerce, the road would aid travelers from the south sojourning to the famed mineral springs of Virginia. This modest project had the additional advantage of improving trade within the county, making it easier to get goods from central Pitt-sylvania to Danville. The project received wide support in Pittsylvania. Among the directors were Robert Wilson and George Townes of Dan-ville, merchant William Rison, William Tunstall (brother of Whitmell, the planter), and Vincent Witcher, one of the county's two representa-tives to the assembly.

The road was quickly surveyed and laid out, and construction pro-ceeded fairly rapidly. The new turnpike was much used, as Maude Carter Clement relates: "Along its dusty way traveled droves of horses, cattle, sheep and hogs; flocks of turkey; wagon loads of chicken, apples and produce of all kinds seeking the market of Danville. It was a rare sight for a country boy who was not so fortunate to live on the turnpike, to be permitted to stand for an hour on the roadside and watch the traffic down this busy highway of trade."[17] Whatever the benefits of the road, however, it was no substitute for a rail connection.

WHITMELL P. TUNSTALL AND THE CAMPAIGN FOR A RAILROAD

The continuing efforts to obtain a rail connection were led by Whitmell P. Tunstall, aided by his brother-in-law, banker George Townes. At first glance, the leader of this drive to transform the economy of Pittsyl-vania and Danville would seem an unlikely figure for such a role. Tun-stall, the master of "Belle Grove," was the scion of one of the wealthi-est, most prominent, and well-respected planter-patriarchs in the county. A wealthy man in his own right, he became politically prominent as one of Pittsylvania's representatives to the powerful lower house of the legis-lature. In the assembly from 1836 to 1841, and then again from 1845 to 1848, he proved himself "forceful in debate and quick with repartee," demonstrating the kind of verve and vision common to the Danville area's leading planter-entrepreneurs.[18]

The opening shot in the campaign unleashed by Townes and Tunstall to bring Danville a railroad connection to Richmond was fired in 1837.

It was a peculiarly long petition to the legislature, which was in effect a manifesto, a proposal, and a plan for Danville's future. The petition opened with a veiled threat, referring obliquely to the sectional disharmony in the state, disharmony that the 1829 convention had far from ended (there would be another reform convention in 1850–51), and it made an invidious comparison between North and South, revealing a respect for the North's achievements:

> It is among the first duties of the legislature to facilitate and improve by means of canals, railroads and other improvements which open communications between different parts of the state. The benign effect . . . has already been produced in strengthening and consolidating the union by means of extensive internal communications. The memorialists believe that these effects will be still more triumphantly displayed if the legislature of Virginia should extend the same fostering and paternal hand to the protection of public works which has been exhibited by some of our sister states. The projects of the great Clinton and his colleagues were pronounced to be visionary when they were first projected but these visionary schemes have proved to be practicable and are daily conferring on the state of New York the most *unspeakable and transcendent benefits* [emphasis mine].

The petition went on to specify the material form of these "unspeakable and transcendent benefits": "It [the railroad] will . . . bring into use the vast and latent mineral wealth of the southwestern part of the state, the iron, salt, lead, gypsum, lime, copper and other valuable materials which are found in Franklin, Patrick, Floyd, Wythe, Washington and Grayson" counties.[19]

Hectoring the assembly, which after a long string of failures refused to supply support for a Richmond to Danville railroad, Tunstall stated that "there is not a town in the United States which is more conveniently situated for the establishment of manufacturing establishments on a large scale." And then playing his trump, Virginia's growing fear of Northern antislavery sentiment, he warned the legislators:

> Should the time in the progress of events arrive when it may be wise and politic to engage more extensively in the manufacture of arms, what other situation in the state unites so many conveniences and facilities as Danville does for operations of this kind, every material which is necessary for the manufacture of guns, swords

and cannons which constitute the munitions of war are afforded in abundance by several of the counties contiguous to this town. . . . And if in the progress of time it may be a consideration of great magnitude that the ancient and renowned commonwealth should possess within herself the means which may enable her to maintain her rights, her dignity, and her peculiar institution, whether they are attacked by an army of invaders or by the more secret and insidious means of those who approach under disguises which conceal from public view their dangerous incendiary and fatal purposes. The memorialists have deemed it most advisable not to encumber this memorial with any hypothetical statement about the probable cost of the intended road.[20]

In some ways, Tunstall's conception was prophetic: twenty-five years later, Danville, then an important tobacco manufacturing center, would in fact become a major economic beneficiary of the Civil War. Tunstall's appeal to sectional pride was to be repeated with good effect two decades later by secession-minded Virginia industrialists, but in the wake of the crash of 1837, it fell on deaf ears. Tunstall persisted in his efforts during a brief stint in the state senate from 1841 to 1842, but the prospects for the state support essential for a Richmond to Danville railroad were foreclosed for a decade by the economic impact of the 1837 depression. It was only when tobacco prices and the Virginia economy rebounded in the late 1840s that hopes for a railroad were revived, this time successfully.

Danville's and Pittsylvania's internal improvements mania was part of an attempt to make the town into an important commercial center for the southwest Piedmont, and although the railroad was not obtained, the town did achieve some notable successes. A first tie to the west, the turnpike to Botetourt, had been built and was thriving; navigation on the Pittsylvania branches of the Roanoke had been improved; the town had attracted a passel of new planter investors; and, what is clearly the bottom line, the growth of business had led in this period to more than a doubling of the town's population from five hundred in 1829 to over one thousand by 1837.

By looking at the structure of the town's economy the profound limitations of the growth that was achieved can be observed. Comparisons of the 1810 manufacturing census, Thompson Coleman's detailed account of 1829, and the precise descriptions of Danville's business given in *Martin's Gazeteer* of 1836 reveal that the town's growth in population was based almost entirely on the expansion of tobacco marketing (and, to a lesser extent, tobacco manufacturing). Other enterprises like tanning and shoemaking, which had long occupied a position of secondary importance in the area's economy, experienced only modest growth during these years. The only new enterprises, other than retail stores, were a plough factory and an iron foundry, both of which operated on a very limited scale. In economic terms, the tobacco-induced prosperity resulted from an expansion of traditional activities rather than an expansion into new areas, that is, there was growth without development.

Despite the energy and verve of its citizens and supporters, Danville's economy had been unable to move much beyond the confines dictated by the requirements of tobacco production. The successful completion of rail ties to the west would have made Danville a way station for transporting that area's mineral resources, but would not have challenged the dominance of tobacco, because the chief product of most of the agricultural hinterland that would have been tapped was also tobacco.

Tobacco was destiny for Danville. When the crash of 1837 occurred, the only enterprises of any size to survive were the tobacco manufactories. In the dark decade of low tobacco prices that followed, Danville failed even to begin to recoup its losses. When recovery did come in the late 1840s, it was based on changes in the culture of tobacco and the consequent expansion of tobacco manufacturing. These two developments are at the heart of Danville's history in the later antebellum period, and Part Two discusses the leafy cage by which Danville was both nurtured and bound.

Part Two

TOBACCO

5

THE CENTRALITY

OF TOBACCO

✐ ✐ ✐ ✐ ✐ ✐

*In Virginia and Maryland Tobacco is our Staple, is our ALL, and
Indeed leaves no room for anything else: It requires the attendance of
all our hands, and Exacts their utmost labor, the whole year round.*
   —Phillips, *Plantation and Frontier*

TOBACCO WAS a culture in more than one sense of the term. Beginning at Jamestown and moving through to the twentieth century, wherever it was the main cash crop it came to dominate the lives of all those associated with it. Ellen Glasgow's novel, *The Deliverance: A Romance of the Tobacco Fields*, set in Virginia during the 1880s, captures this thralldom. In it, a local farmer, Sol Peterkin, speaks to a visiting lawyer who has just arrived on the scene: "Oh you'll find a corn field or two somewhar along . . . but it's a lanky slipshod kind of crop at best, for tobaccy's king down herean' no mistake. We have a saying that a man that ain't partial to the weed can't sleep sound even in the churchyard, an' thar's some as 'll swear to this day that Willie Moreen never rested in his grave because he didn't chaw, an' the soil smelt just like plug. Oh it's a great plant, I tell you suh."[1] Later the lawyer comes upon a planter, who tells him: "Yes I'm a lover of the weed, . . . for my part I believe I took to the weed before I did to my mother's breast. I cut my first tooth on a plug, she used to say."[2]

Tobacco was like a jealous mistress; it was able to absorb ever increasing care, attention, and resources. J. H. Cocke, a prominent Virginia planter, described tobacco as the great monopolist of time and labor: "Whenever anything troubles the tobacco plant directly or indirectly, it never escapes the vigilance of the tobacco maker, and heaven and earth is

moved forthwith, on that plantation . . . till the remedy is supplied cost
what it may in time, in vehicles, in manure-liquid or pulverised."³
John Taylor detailed the impositions:

> It would startle even an old planter, to see an exact amount of
> labor devoured by an acre of tobacco, and the preparation of the
> crop for market. . . . He would be astonished to discover how often
> he had passed over the land, and the tobacco through his hands, in
> fallowing, hilloing, cutting off hills, planting, replantings, toppings,
> suckerings, weedings, cuttings, picking up, removing out of the
> ground by hand, hanging, striking, stripping, stemming, and priz-
> ing, and that the same labor devoted to almost any other employ-
> ment, would have produced a better return by ordinary success,
> than tobacco does.⁴

The duration as well as the intensity of the growing season was a
problem. Tobacco was an eighteen-month crop. Generally eighteen
months elapsed between the preparation of the seedbed and the shipping
of tobacco to market, because the postharvest, premanufacturing process, the curing of the tobacco, was a lengthy operation. What Taylor
referred to as hanging, striking, stripping, stemming, and prizing had to
be carried on while the next crop was in the process of being grown.

Tobacco's insatiable demand for labor and resources had major economic effects. This insatiability made opportunity costs very high. The
cost of spending time and capital on developing other crops or improving the capital plant of a farm might mean a large drop in the value of the
tobacco crop. Edmund Ruffin knew this when he noted: "It is the leisure
time of the farmer judiciously used, that is the most profitable to his land
and ultimately to his income—and of leisure time, a full crop of cotton
permits but little during the year, and one of tobacco none at all."⁵ J. H.
Cocke elaborated on this theme, describing how other needs were sacri-
ficed to those of the infernal weed. Tobacco, he said, was "the idol of the
plantation, before which everything else is thrown down and trodden
under foot: hence every other crop getting only the leavings of this insatiable consumer of manure, labor and time, is starved literally."⁶

As might be expected, it was Thomas Jefferson who most clearly delin-
eated the consequences of Virginia's dependence on tobacco: "It [to-
bacco] is a culture productive of infinite wretchedness. Those employed
in it are in a continual state of exertion beyond the power of nature to
support. Little food of any kind is raised by them: so men and animals

on these farms are ill fed, and the earth is readily impoverished."[7] In Jefferson's eyes tobacco was the historic villain of Virginia's economic difficulties.

THE HISTORIC VILLAIN

All pervasive and ever demanding, the requirements of commercial tobacco production affected almost every aspect of eighteenth- and nineteenth-century lowland Virginia society. The organization of labor and land, the distribution of economic activities and economic transactions were directly and fundamentally influenced by the economic pillar on which Virginia rested: the production of tobacco for extraregional export into at first international and then also national markets. From the beginning, tobacco made Virginia very different from the more northern settlements.

Unlike the Northeast, where economic growth came slowly and only after long years of structural preparation, the Chesapeake area very quickly found what seemed to be the basis for a European standard of wealth, tobacco. In tobacco the settlers of Jamestown had a crop greatly in demand in England, whose high value per unit of weight enabled it to profitably sustain the costs of transatlantic shipment. Under the pressure generated by the possibilities of acquiring great wealth from tobacco, Virginia's first social order—the feudal/military structure of the Virginia Company—collapsed. The social order that replaced it was formed in the boomtown atmosphere of the 1620s, when tobacco was being grown everywhere, including in the streets. The demand was so great and the rewards so high, that men had to be enjoined from producing too much tobacco for fear of not producing enough food.[8]

It was in the years after the Jamestown tobacco boom, long before the development of black slavery, that the distinctive elements of what would come to be seen as Southern backwardness crystallized. The inability to attract a free labor force, the lack of economic diversity, the absence of towns and cities, and the plague of soil exhaustion all antedated the growth of slavery. These problems were directly related to the central fact of Virginia's economic life, the dominance of tobacco. The point here is that the failures of Danville to diversify and achieve substantial growth, described earlier, were not new. Rather, they were a

reenactment of the historic pattern of Virginia's tobacco society. This
was a pattern in which the brief boom tides of tobacco-based prosperity
left in their wake permanent structural inadequacies.

Tobacco and Labor

Tobacco required vast amounts of menial, tedious, and time-consuming
labor. Land was readily available but labor was not, and labor as the
scarce factor of production became the object of enormous pressure.
Edmund Morgan points out that, from the beginning, the members of
the Virginia Company Council had used illegal and violent means to
acquire white laborers. "But whether physically abused or not, Englishmen found servitude in Virginia more degrading than servitude in England. In England the hiring of workers by law and custom gave a servant some control over his life . . . but Virginians dealt in servants the
way Romans dealt in chattels—this at a time when a large scale marketing of men was shocking to Englishmen."[9]

Well before the introduction of African slavery, the exigencies of tobacco production in the New World had led Englishmen to treat men as
property. For the first three-quarters of the seventeenth century most of
the labor force was white, often the English poor or Irishmen who had
been abducted or coerced into service. While crossing the Atlantic, these
individuals were subjected to horrifying shipboard conditions. Once in
America, they were forced to engage in unfamiliar work at a pace and
duration far exceeding anything they had previously known. Their personal mobility was extremely limited, governed by a system of passes and
armed vigilantes. Most importantly, they were treated as a commodity,
whose labor was to be used as quickly and profitably as possible. Because most indentured servants had to serve a tenure of only five to seven
years, it was in the master's interest to get as much work as possible out
of them during that time.[10] Consequently, whereas indenture was originally a contractual relationship and the servant had a legal personality,
this position was eroded. The master class used its inordinate power to
extend terms of servitude, often for trivial and frivolous reasons. Eventually the servant was regarded as chattel, a part of the master's personal
estate, to be treated and disposed of like any other property. In Virginia,
as in Barbados, "the rapid progress was fatally fast: from exploiting the
English laboring poor, to abusing colonial bondservants, to ensnaring
kidnaps and convicts, to enslaving black Africans."[11]

Tobacco and Economic Diversification

Virginia was originally an extension of the economic, social, and demographic processes that were Londonizing the Virginia countryside. Almost from the start, it was a settlement of commercialized Englishmen in pursuit of economic gain. These entrepreneurial settlers were disturbed by the absence in Virginia of the kind of urban existence they had known in England. Cities were seen as essential both for commerce and for social control. James Harrington's argument, in *Oceana*, that the number and size of cities determine the economic health of an entire nation, was common fare in Virginia.[12]

The connection between the absence of cities and the lack of economic diversification was obvious to many in the Virginia leadership, including Governor William Berkeley. To fill this void, Berkeley developed what John Rainbolt has called "The Virginia Vision." This vision, which was shared by most members of the assembly, pictured a multifaceted agriculture of flax, hemp, wheat, silk, and cotton producers. This multifaceted agriculture would, in turn, lead to the development of skilled artisans and thriving cities. In his excellent study, Rainbolt described how, as early as 1620, Governor Edwin Sandys had made extensive efforts to diversify the economy. He instituted numerous disincentives for tobacco production and tried to compel the population to turn its attention to other crops. Sandys failed completely. In the 1660s Governor Berkeley, hoping to have learned from Sandys's mistakes, initiated a better planned and more comprehensive effort to encourage diversification and town development. Supported by a large majority of the assembly, Berkeley proposed a judicious mix of incentives and disincentives to curb tobacco and thus produce other crops. Bounties and tax exemptions were given for growing crops other than tobacco. Berkeley correctly recognized it was unlikely that Virginia would ever urbanize until it reduced its dependency on tobacco.[13]

All in all, a thorough mercantilist program to remake Virginia in the image of the motherland was instituted. But none of the government's efforts to promote diversification or urbanization succeeded. For the overwhelming majority of the planters, large and small, tobacco continued to be the most remunerative crop. Tobacco maintained its grip because it enjoyed an enormous comparative advantage over any other export Virginia could produce. As noted earlier, its high value per unit of weight compensated for the transatlantic shipping costs, and it did not spoil rapidly. It was the one crop whose profits gave the grower the possibility of maintaining his European standard of living in the New World.

Tobacco and Towns

Commentators and early historians of the colony—including Anthony Langston and Henry Hartwell, James Blair, and Edward Chilton—attributed the lack of urbanization to geographic conditions. They argued that Virginia's extensive system of estuaries and rivers gave almost every planter direct access to incoming and outgoing ships. Thus, there were no major break-in-bulk points whose transshipment facilities might serve as the nucleus for a settlement. The riparian system, however, was only one of the factors inhibiting the growth of towns in Virginia's tobacco economy.

Tobacco required little in the way of what Gunnar Myrdal has called backward and forward linkages (backward linkages refer to the tools and other inputs needed to produce a crop; forward linkages refer to the tools needed to process a crop before shipment). The hoe was often the chief tool used in growing tobacco and, well into the nineteenth century, only hand labor was needed for curing tobacco into hogsheads for shipment. By contrast, commercial wheat growing required a small army of middlemen, shippers, and warehousers in addition to millers. Grains required plows and harvesting devices; moreover, "grain has to be marketed, milled and packed or baked into biscuits, then stored, and finally loaded into wagons. . . . All this calls for . . . mills and bakers, storage space, public houses and agencies to establish links between producer and purchaser."[14]

Similarly, the marketing of tobacco required little in the way of support services. In most cases, the individual farmer or planter brought his prized tobacco to a state warehouse where it was inspected and he was given a receipt. He then sold the receipt to a factor, usually the representative of a London or Glasgow firm. The subsequent stages in the marketing of tobacco took place entirely outside of the tobacco colonies. The factor represented, as required by navigation laws, the middle leg of the process whereby the tobacco sold to the continental state monopolies (e.g., the French Farmers General) first had to be brought to London or Glasgow. Because a direct trade between the colonies and their European markets was prohibited, the credit and marketing facilities necessary for tobacco sales helped build cities in the British Isles rather than on the Chesapeake.

Summarizing the first two centuries of urban growth in the South, Carville Earle and Ronald Hoffman concluded that "for the 18th century South . . . tobacco areas rarely generated towns of more than 300 persons. . . . In contrast, the grain regions created towns and cities of varied size, some of which approached 600 by the revolution.[15]

Tobacco and Soil Exhaustion

Virginia was plagued by soil exhaustion and soil erosion before, during, and after black slavery. Tobacco is a voracious consumer of the earth's minerals, a vampire crop that sucks the land dry and constantly demands more virgin lands to be despoiled. As early as 1618 there were complaints that the soil near Jamestown was being exhausted by tobacco. Because land was cheap and labor dear, farmers and planters made no attempt to restore the land; rather, they mined it and then moved on. What evolved was a kind of circulatory agriculture. It was circulatory because the farmer would practice what was in effect a long fallow rotation within the confines of his land; when the soil was exhausted beyond the restorative capacities of fallowing, he would move on. Even when available, manure was rarely used to improve the soil because it imparted a harsh taste to the tender leaf. The premium on potential space meant that, compared to wheat areas, a considerably larger percentage of farm land was kept in an unimproved state as a reserve.[16]

Because of the high percentage of unimproved lands and the tendency to migrate into virgin areas, tobacco regions had a permanently low population density. The recurring impermanence of tobacco production never permitted the countryside to pass out of the frontier stage into a stage of dense settlement and full development. The sparse settlement greatly inhibited the building of roads, which required a heavy expenditure based on expectations of permanence. The very qualities that made tobacco such a good export crop—its high value per unit of volume— also inhibited road development. Paths were sufficient to roll the prized barrels to market. The lack of roads put self-sufficiency at a premium and hindered the division of labor and growth of towns.

Philip A. Bruce has ably summarized the relationship between tobacco and three centuries of Virginia's agricultural history:

> There is serious reason for doubting whether the charge of waste-fullness, not only in the colonial period, but in the period between the revolution and the war between the states, was not to be laid at

the door of the great staple, tobacco, rather than at the door of the institution of slavery itself. . . . The tobacco plant requires for its production loam in the greatest quantity and of the highest quality. There is always a disposition on the part of those engaged in its cultivation to widen the plantation, even now, when artificial manures are so effective in bringing back the fertility which has been lost. The newly cleared field is still the soil most desired. . . . This is not the fault of inherited carelessness in agriculture, but it is a condition which has descended from the 17th century to the present in a form modified only by the growth of population. If the culture of tobacco were very profitable, the tendency to enlarge each estate would be just as strong today in Virginia, with labor emancipated, as it was during the existence of slavery. That institution only promoted the extension of the plantation by cheapening labor. . . . During the first 60 years of the history of the colony, the slave was an insignificant element in the community, and yet during this long period there are to be observed the most marked indications of the tendency to appropriate large tracts. This disposition was manifest from the start, as a result not of the character of the labor system in operation but the nature of tobacco itself.[17]

But if tobacco, and particularly tobacco-created soil exhaustion, was so patently at the center of Virginia's economic problems, why wasn't tobacco either abandoned in favor of other less demanding crops or supplemented by other crops? After all, wheat is also highly soil exhaustive, but Northern farmers eventually came to grips with the problem by incorporating new crops. In other words, why didn't Virginia follow the example of the North and diversify its commercial agricultural production?

SOIL AND CLIMATE:
THE LIMITS OF AGRICULTURAL
DIVERSIFICATION

Tobacco's soil exhaustion was only one of the burdens of the Virginia farmer. He also suffered from soils that were markedly inferior to those of the Northern colonies. There was no way to have known this in

advance. William Byrd, who repeatedly passed through what would become Pittsylvania County while marking the borderline between Virginia
and North Carolina, described the area as Eden-like. He had no hint of
the underlying sandy infertility of its soil. As Arthur Hall explained:
"The first Europeans to view the country could not know the destructive
forces hidden and held in check by the vegetative blanket, nor were they
fully aware of the consequences that would follow its removal or alter-
ation. On the contrary this covering was very attractive, and made the
region appear as a very desirable place indeed."[18]

Driving rains added to the farmers' woes. Indeed, the opening line of
U. B. Philips's *Life and Labor in the Old South* reads: "Let us begin by
discussing the weather, for that has been the chief agency in making the
South distinctive." Philips succinctly described the relationship between
Southern soils and the area's torrential rains:

> Most of the soils are . . . mere sand and clay in varying propor-
> tions, with little or no lime and no humus perhaps on the surface.
> The lack of deep frost in winter and the consequent lack of mel-
> lowing thaw in spring leaves the ground hard packed year round.
> This diminishes the absorbent capacity of the clay, and by the same
> token shortens the beneficial influence of rains and heightens their
> deleterious effects. The Southern rain seldom sifts but commonly
> pelts from a great height.[19]

The consequence was regular and severe erosion, leaving the land de-
nuded of topsoil. A careful student of Southern soil problems has argued
that even if Southern farmers had from the start been careful and enlightened in their farming methods, the probabilities of soil erosion were far
greater in the Southern than in the Northern colonies.[20]

Soil erosion compounded the problem of an already poor soil. Southern soils are in general "low in organic matter and natural fertility, making it difficult to re-establish vegetation once the natural cover has been
stripped off and erosion started."[21] This general problem of Southern
soils directly applies to the Virginia Piedmont. Here the soils were developed under a thick forest cover that blocked the sun and thus limited
other plant development. Basically, then, the soils in the forest were
fertilized only by the falling leaves of the trees. The resulting vegetable
humus was scant. It usually only penetrated the first inch or less of
topsoil, as compared with the grassland soils of much of the Northeast
where the continuous root mass supplied organic matter for a foot or

more in depth. Because of their low organic content, the Piedmont soils were low in the three principal plant foods: nitrogen, phosphorus, and potash.[22]

Virginia's agriculture suffered from a multiplicity of problems, not least of which was its reliance on a single undependable crop, tobacco, for the vast bulk of its export earnings. Beginning in the first quarter of the eighteenth century, there was an attempt to transform Virginia agricultural life by deemphasizing tobacco and moving to a reliance on wheat as the major export staple. This was the start of eighty years of intermittent efforts to create a more diversified and soil-enriching agriculture. For the most part these efforts involved bringing the advances of the English agricultural revolution to Virginia. This new agriculture had a number of phases including an emphasis on animal husbandry to provide manure for fertilizer and dairy products for nutriment and marketing, as well as an increased use of forage crops to provide feed for the cattle and to build the soil. Within the context of these central improvements, mixed farming based on regular crop rotations could be introduced. Where these reforms were successful it was hoped that tobacco could either be put aside or grown as one of a number of crops. In the optimistic crescendo to his masterful study of soil exhaustion in Virginia, Avery Craven assumed that these reforms had taken hold across the state and that all of Virginia was revitalized by the agricultural reform movement.[23]

The reforms Craven described did not spread throughout the state. They were circumscribed by climatic and soil conditions, particularly south of the James River. In an insightful article, E. L. Jones has pointed out that the great practical innovations in agriculture developed in Western Europe were largely inapplicable in tropical and semitropical zones. Virginia below the James had, for practical purposes, many of the characteristics of tropical agriculture. For example, grasses for fodder and soil building were crucial to the introduction of a reformed agriculture. Grass thrives best in a cool, dry climate. But the grasses that did grow in the warm humid South, like the most common grass broom sedge, were of little nutritional value for cattle. The problem was that "in warm, humid areas, many of the forage crops grow rapidly, but this is coincident with the plants maturing rapidly, resulting in a decrease on total digestible nutrients and an increase in fiber content."[24] The hay crops of the North made famous by Hilton R. Helper's jibes—timothy, alfalfa, red clover—could not be grown successfully in the warm, humid climate of Virginia's Southside. The James is also the rough dividing line for a major climatic and soil change within the physiographic region called the Piedmont. North of the James there is a gradual transition from the leached red and yellow lime-deficient soils typical of the quasi-tropical South to the darker colored soils typical of the Northeast. The acid soils of lower Virginia could not, without the aid of twentieth-century science, grow the forage grasses needed for cattle.[25]

"Independently of the effects of poor forage," Julius Rubin tells us, "yields of livestock products must have suffered from the direct effects of climate." Whereas cold weather has almost no effect on a cow's production of milk, that production is severely affected by heat. Modern studies have shown that "dairy animals exposed to a daily mean temperature of 75 degrees or above for a period of 20 days or more will show a significant decline in milk production." Cows need to maintain a constant body temperature in order to maintain their milk production. The Southern sun and the Southern grasses made this difficult. The grasses were also a factor because "the high fiber content of the lower south forage increased the animal's heat levels by raising the metabolic heat digestion and by increasing the intake required to obtain sufficient energy for milk production."[26]

The climate of the lower South, which includes Virginia below the James, also fostered a host of animal parasites unknown to the North. These parasites came largely from worms and larva that were able to survive relatively mild Southern winters. The most common were cattle ticks and kidney worms, which attacked hogs. Parasites had a severe effect on the quality of Southern livestock, but little could be done about them until well into the twentieth century.[27]

In addition to the problems created by the soil and climate, the newest and most important type of tobacco developed in the late antebellum period, the so-called bright leaf, could not be integrated into a system of crop rotation based in part on the use of forage crops. Forage crops like peas and clover created (for bright tobacco) an excess of nitrogen in the soil, lowering the quality of the leaf. Other forage plants harbored parasitic organisms that survived the Southern winter below the thin crust of frozen earth and then attacked succeeding crops of tobacco. "Progressive farmers soon learned that peas or clover preceding the tobacco crop would cause the leaves to spot and become rough."[28] Indeed, improvement-minded farmers in the bright tobacco area found that even the use of cattle manure to improve the soil had deleterious effects on the quality of the tobacco produced. Thus, reforms such as crop rotation, foraging, and fertilizing, which Avery Craven thought would transform Virginia agriculture, had little success in emerging bright tobacco areas of late antebellum Virginia.[29] Rubin has summed up the significant differences that divided Virginia between those areas where Craven's reforms were or were not possible:

> In view of the importance of parasites in preventing a mixed crop and livestock system, the line which bounded the area of infestation by cattle tick before the beginning of the U.S. Department of Agriculture's tick eradication program in 1906 has great significance and can be taken for many purposes as the line that separated the Upper from the Lower South. . . . In the area under this line [Virginia below the James], food crops, forage crops and livestock were lowest in quality and yields. More precisely, it was in this area that the freezing of the ground during the winter was not sufficiently prolonged to destroy the parasites in the soil.[30]

One might well ask, "What about slavery? Wasn't the size of the slave population a major factor in hindering the reform of Virginia agriculture?" Let us consider this by looking at three of the largest and most important counties in the state. Augusta, a mixed agriculture county located in the yeoman's Valley of the Shenandoah, was 23 percent slave; Pittsylvania, of bright tobacco fame in the southern Piedmont along the North Carolina border, was 46 percent slave; and Albemarle, Jefferson's home county located in the foothills of the western Piedmont just east of Augusta, was 55 percent slave in 1850. Based on the size of their slave populations, we would expect Pittsylvania and Albemarle to have more in common with each other than either would have in common with Augusta. But that was not the case.

In terms of rural and urban land values, rural urban building values, and the assessed value of land per capita, Augusta and Albemarle counties closely resembled each other in the years between 1820 and 1850 (see Tables 5-1 and 5-2). This was true despite the fact that Albemarle had twice as many slaves (54 percent to 23 percent).

How did Albemarle, a Piedmont slave county, come to resemble Augusta? As Lewis Gray noted, those western Piedmont counties in the foothills of the Blue Ridge had a higher elevation and thus enjoyed a cooler climate than the counties to the east. In that cooler climate cattle-nourishing grasses could be grown to both replenish the soil and create an improved animal husbandry. Dark tobacco was still grown as a cash crop, but with the reforms it could be integrated with a system of mixed agriculture. Travelers clearly saw the difference between the more ele-

TABLE 5–1

*Land and Building Values in Pittsylvania, Albemarle,
and Augusta Counties, 1820, 1840, 1850*

	1820	1840	1850
Land Values[a]			
Pittsylvania	$ 5.43	$ 4.62	$ 4.62
Albemarle	$ 6.79	$ 8.93	$ 10.46
Augusta	$ 10.39	$ 8.70	$ 13.37
Rural Buildings[b]			
Pittsylvania	$ 18/11	$ 26/14	$ 28/14
Albemarle	$ 54/24	$ 67/32	$ 70/32
Augusta	$ 53/42	$ 55/44	$ 66/57
Urban Buildings[b]			
Pittsylvania	$1.5/.90	$8.70/5	$16/8.50
Albemarle	$ 7/3	$ 18/8	$ 25/11
Augusta	$ 21/17	$ 20/13	$ 20/15
Percent Slave[b]			
Pittsylvania	26%	45%	47%
Albemarle	54%	52%	54%
Augusta	13%	21%	23%

Source: Proceedings of the Virginia Constitutional Convention of 1851.
a. Expressed in the average value per acre for the county as a whole.
b. Expressed in per capita value. Where two figures are given, the first is the per capita
   figure for the white population and the second for the total population.

vated western counties and the rest of the Piedmont. Isaac Weld, traveling through Virginia in the late 1790s, noted:

> [T]he country in the neighborhood of these mountains is far more
> populous than that which lies towards Richmond; and there are
> many persons who consider it to be the garden of the United States.
> All the productions of the lower part of Virginia may be had here,
> at the same time that the heat is never found to be so oppressive;
> for in the hottest months of the year, there is a freshness and elastic-
> ity in the air unknown in the low country.[31]

Almost 150 years later, Clarence Cason noted the continued similarities between the two counties despite the legacy of slavery. He wrote: "If

TABLE 5-2
Land and Building Values, Whites Only, 1850

County	Number of Acres in Farms Per Capita	Per Capita Value of Rural Land, Based on the Rural Population	Per Capita Value of All Land, Based on the Total Population
		(Rounded off to the Nearest $10)	
Pittsylvania	41	$190	$190
Albemarle	39	$410	$440
Augusta	32	$430	$440

Source: *Proceedings of the Virginia Constitutional Convention of 1851.*

all the South were like the Shenandoah Valley, only the promptings of Satan could stir the Southern mind to discontent. Were it possible to regard Albemarle County, Virginia as a microcosm of the South then only an impish perversity could explain a Southerner's dissatisfaction with the bounties of kind providence."[32]

Unfortunately, Albemarle was not a microcosm of the South; it was not even a microcosm of Virginia. For much of Virginia there was no alternative to tobacco production. The distinguished Virginian William C. Bruce wrote of the Southside (Virginia below the James): "It was the most characteristically Virginian of all. The spirit of colonial times lingered there longest after Yorktown; the spirit of Ante-bellum times lingered there longest after Appomattox. As a result, Southside Virginia remained, during both eras, the greatest scene of tobacco culture in the state."[33] Bruce had the causal relationship inverted but he saw something important; there was a sharp difference between the Southside, which was part of Dixie, and upper and mountainous Virginia, which had many of the characteristics of the Middle Atlantic states.

6

PITTSYLVANIA IN

COMPARATIVE PERSPECTIVE

🖋 🖋 🖋 🖋 🖋 🖋 🖋 🖋 🖋 🖋

It is not the tropics with their luxuriant vegetation, but the temperate
zone that is the mother country of capitalism. It is not the mere fertility
of the soil, but the differentiation of the soil, the variety of natural
products, the changes of seasons, which form the physical basis for
the social division of labor, and which by changes in the natural
surroundings, spur man on to the multiplication of his capabilities,
his modes of Labor.
—Marx, *Capital*

IT HAS BEEN argued in the previous chapter that soil and climate, not
slavery, were the crucial factors in determining whether an area could
adopt the innovations of the English agricultural revolution. This can be
demonstrated by comparing the social and economic organization of
Pittsylvania, a county whose soil and climate created a dependency on
tobacco, with that of Augusta, a county in the Valley of Virginia, whose
soil and climate were ideal for mixed agriculture.

In terms of area, Pittsylvania is the largest county and Augusta the
second largest in the state. Both counties were settled in the third quarter
of the eighteenth century largely by Scotch-Irish migrants from Pennsylvania. Both were removed from the culture of Tidewater Virginia, and
neither had easy transport access to fall line ports. Finally, both were
distinctively Whiggish in political outlook, and their representatives often took similar positions on state issues.

Despite these similarities in origin, nineteenth-century travelers and
twentieth-century historians have drawn broad distinctions between the
Valley of Virginia and Augusta County on the one hand and the southern
Piedmont and Pittsylvania County on the other. The storied Valley has

been described in elysian terms. As early as 1790, the traveler Isaac Weld depicted a yeoman's paradise: "The cultivated lands in this country are mostly parcelled out in small portions; there are no persons here, as on the other side of the mountains possessing large farms; nor are there any eminently distinguished by their education and knowledge from the rest of their citizens. Poverty is also as much unknown in this country as great wealth. Each man owns the house he lives in and the land which he cultivates."[1] Its beauty is still the subject of songs, like John Denver's "Country Roads" and plays such as *Shenandoah* that extol the purity and quality of its lands and people. John Schlebecker has described the nineteenth-century Valley as a place where the entire population, black and white, ate well even by modern standards. In his view, the people of the Valley were so prosperous that the "Farmers in the Valley were about twice as well off as the generality of farmers in Virginia."[2]

In contrast to the yeoman's land of the Valley, Pittsylvania and its environs have been described as a typically Southern, planter-dominated, slavery-ridden area. The individual most often associated with the region, Samuel Hairston, was reputed to be the wealthiest man in Virginia and possibly the largest slaveowner in the South. Paul Gates, the distinguished agricultural historian, has argued that "where the soil was peculiarly suited to bright yellow tobacco, ownership of the land was concentrated in the hands of the great planters to a degree that was only exceeded in the rice and sugar counties of the Gulf states."[3]

The data gathered from census and tax lists indicate that the differences between the two counties have been greatly exaggerated. For the white populations, at least, material inequality in Pittsylvania was not measurably greater than in Augusta. In both areas a highly commercial agriculture created severe inequalities within the white population.[4]

The size of landholdings was similar in Augusta and Pittsylvania. Writing about the period of the American Revolution, Freeman Hart emphasized the differences between the areas by pointing out that, in the lower Piedmont counties he had sampled, there were twice as many farms of more than 500 acres as there were in his sample Valley counties. He surmised from this that the Valley was dominated by small farms and the lower Piedmont by large plantations.[5] But if Hart had looked further he would have found that 94 percent of the Valley and 88 percent of the lower Piedmont farms were under 500 acres. Similarly, 74 percent of the Valley and 68 percent of the Piedmont farmers paid taxes on land valued at less than 100 pounds. This pattern, whereby the vast majority of farms were of a similar size, though the Piedmont county had more very large

TABLE 6–I
Farm Size, 1860

Acres	Percent of Farms of Given Size in Pittsylvania	Augusta
0–50	4%	15%
50–100	13%	17%
100–200	31%	28%
200–500	28%	31%
500–1,000	16%	9%
1,000+	6%	4%

Source: U.S. Census, Agriculture Schedule, 1860.

farms, applied to Pittsylvania and Augusta on the eve of the Civil War. As shown in Table 6-1, the vast majority of farms in both counties fell into the common range of between 100 and 500 acres.[6]

This sense of similarity is reinforced by the average size of the plots owned by farmers in Pittsylvania and Augusta (see Table 6-2). The difference was that in Pittsylvania the landowner was more likely to own more than one plot. The tobacco farmer often owned scattered plots, some of which were allowed to lay fallow in order to recover from the ravages of tobacco cultivation. Thus, the average (mean) amount of land owned was somewhat greater in Pittsylvania (see Table 6-3).

The differences in the size of landholding between Pittsylvania and Augusta did and did not follow the pattern of expected contrasts between a plantation and a family farming area. On the one hand, Pittsylvania farms were generally but not dramatically larger; on the other hand, the size of the average plot owned was approximately the same in both counties. The picture becomes even more complex when we realize that, in percentage as opposed to absolute terms, the inequality of holdings was also roughly similar. That is, although Pittsylvania generally had somewhat larger landholdings, the percentage of land held by the largest landowners was approximately the same for both counties. Indeed, in Augusta the top 20 percent of the landowners owned a greater percentage of the land than the comparable Pittsylvania group (see Tables 6-4 and 6-5).[7]

Both the census and the tax lists reveal that in each county most of the land was held by about one-fifth of the landowners. What is striking is

TABLE 6-2
Patterns of Land Ownership, 1820, 1840, 1860

	Average Size of Plots Owned, in Acres			Mean Number of Plots Owned		
County	1820	1840	1860	1820	1840	1860
Augusta	154	190	182	1.4	1.2	1.4
Pittsylvania	199	190	189	1.8	1.9	1.8

Source: Augusta and Pittsylvania (Real) Property, 1820, 1840, 1860.
Note: The average plot size, which can only be derived from the tax lists, should not be confused with the size of the average farm derived from the census, because an individual could own one or more plots without farming all of them. Census reports did not account for multiple ownership.

that landholding was, in some ways, more concentrated in Augusta than in Pittsylvania. In Pittsylvania, in 1860 for instance, the top two deciles owned 62 percent of the land (by the more accurate tax list calculations), while in Augusta the comparable deciles owned 66 percent. Furthermore, in the lower half of the decile range, bottom deciles consistently owned a larger percentage of land in Pittsylvania.

THE BEST LANDS

Even if there was not an inordinate concentration of land ownership in Pittsylvania, the planters may have still dominated agriculture by controlling the best lands. Did the planters monopolize the prime lands? Not surprisingly, there was a strong correlation in Pittsylvania between the total acres a man owned and the total value of his land (see Table 6-6).

The next question concerns the relationship between the size and total value of the property and the per acre value of the land owned. In other words, did the largest landholders, those who owned the most property in land, also own the most highly valued plots and fields, the counties' prime acreage? The answer would have to be a qualified one: only sometimes. As shown in Table 6-7, there was, in the aggregate, only a very slight correlation between the size of Pittsylvania estates and the average

TABLE 6—3
Acres Owned, 1820, 1840, 1860

County	1820 Mean	Median	1840 Mean	Median	1860 Mean	Median
Pittsylvania	348	261	361	277	347	215
Augusta	216	200	228	215	253	178

Source: Augusta and Pittsylvania (Real) Property, 1820, 1840, 1860.

value of the land on those estates. By 1860 the relationship had become mildly negative, that is, the larger the number of acres owned, the less likely the land would have a high per acre value.

It could be argued that the above correlation is deceptive. For instance, isn't it possible that the richest planters owned the best land and the most land, but, because as large landholders they also owned some poor land, their position isn't reflected by looking at value per acre? To answer this question, I looked at all those farmers in the sample who in their respective years owned the most highly valued land: land valued at $6 or more an acre in 1840 and $10 or more an acre in 1860. I then placed these owners in their appropriate decile categories in terms of the total number of acres they owned and the total value of the land they owned. This enabled me to see how many of those who owned the most valuable plots of land were among the largest and (land) wealthiest landholders in the county.

As indicated in Table 6-8, in 1840 only 18 of the 40 individuals (45 percent) who owned the most highly valued land were also ranked in the highest two deciles in terms of the number of acres they owned. By contrast, two-thirds of the 1840 $6 per acre plots were owned by people who were in the top two deciles in terms of the value of their holdings. Between 1840 and 1860 the connection between owning a large number of acres, holding a great deal of wealth in land, and owning the most valuable plots weakened. Thus in 1840 the top two deciles in terms of total acres held owned 45 percent of the most valued plots; by 1860 this same group's holdings declined to 36 percent. Similarly, while the top two deciles in terms of the value of their land held 67 percent of the most valued plots in 1840, by 1860 this had declined to 36 percent. Clearly, then, in the twenty-five years before the Civil War, the best lands in Pittsylvania were not monopolized by the wealthiest planters. If any-

TABLE 6–4
Land Ownership, Ranked by Deciles, 1820, 1840, 1860

| | 1820 | | 1840 | | 1860 | | | |
Decile	Au- gusta	Pitt- sylvania	Au- gusta	Pitt- sylvania	Au- gusta		Pitt- sylvania	
1	.01%	1%	1%	1%	.1%	1%	.3%	2%
2	1%	3%	1%	2%	1%	2%	2%	3%
3	3%	3%	1%	3%	2%	3%	3%	4%
4	5%	4%	2%	5%	4%	4%	3%	4%
5	5%	6%	3%	6%	5%	5%	5%	5%
6	7%	7%	4%	7%	6%	7%	6%	6%
7	8%	9%	5%	9%	8%	8%	8%	8%
8	11%	18%	7%	12%	10%	10%	12%	12%
9	18%	17%	10%	15%	17%	17%	15%	18%
10	44%	40%	67%	41%	43%	43%	48%	36%

Source: Augusta and Pittsylvania (Real) Property, 1820, 1840, 1860.
Note: The figures in each decile, which are ranked from the bottom to the top, represent
the percent of land owned by the members of that decile. In 1860, figures in the right-
hand columns are derived from the U.S. Census, Agriculture Schedule, 1860.

thing, landholding trends were moving in the opposite direction, with
the wealthiest landowners owning a smaller precentage of the prime
plots as the war approached.

THE LANDLESS WHITE POPULATION

It is difficult to determine exactly what percentage of the population in
Pittsylvania and Augusta was landless. Using the tax lists helps because,
unlike the census, the tax list allows one to clearly distinguish between
ownership and tenancy. Using the tax lists, I proceeded as follows: first,
in order to find out the number of household heads in the countryside, I
divided the total non-town population for the sample years by size of the
average household; the average was derived from a one in ten sample of
the census and includes non-family members living with a family. In
Augusta in 1860, for instance, the mean size of a household was 5.6
people. The 5.6 was divided into the total rural population to arrive at

TABLE 6−5
Concentration of Landholding, 1820, 1840, 1860

County	Year	Top 20 Percent Own		Bottom 50 Percent Own	
Augusta	1820	72% of the land		14% of the land	
	1840	78%		7%	
	1860	66%	60%	11%	15%
Pittsylvania	1820	67% of the land		17% of the land	
	1840	66%		18%	
	1860	62%	54%	13%	18%

Source: Augusta and Pittsylvania (Real) Property, 1820, 1840, 1860.
Note: In 1860 the numbers in the right-hand column are derived from U.S. Census, Agriculture Schedule, 1860.

the number of households. The number of households was then divided into the number of landowners to derive a rough percentage of how many households were based on the ownership of land. The findings suggest that in both counties about one-third or more of the white rural households were landless between 1820 and 1860 (see Table 6-9).[8]

Robert Mitchell found that, in the late eighteenth and early nineteenth centuries, landless workers in the Valley of Virginia were in high demand and thus relatively well off. This had clearly changed by 1860, when about 15 percent of Augusta's white male household heads were listed as having neither a skill nor land nor personal property. By contrast, in Pittsylvania, virtually the entire landless labor force of unskilled adult male household heads owned some personal property (see Table 6-10).[9]

The better off of the Pittsylvania landless who owned personal property tended to be men who owned a slave or two and rented land. The remaining, approximately 60 percent of the landless with personal property, tended—like their counterparts in Augusta—to own cattle or horses. Once again, what seems significant is the relative similarity of the two counties. Both were highly commercialized areas with sharply stratified populations, but if anything the landless population seems to have been better off in Pittsylvania (see Table 6-11).

Slaveholding, like other forms of property, was widely distributed in Pittsylvania in 1860. Most studies, Kenneth Stampp's *The Peculiar Insti-*

TABLE 6–6

The Correlation between Total Acreage and the Total Value of Land Owned by Individuals in the Sample, 1820, 1840, 1860

	Pittsylvania		Augusta	
Year	Gamma	Kendall's tau b	Gamma	Kendall's tau b
1820	.9	.7	.6	.5
1840	.9	.8	.8	.6
1860	.9	.8	.7	.6

Source: Augusta and Pittsylvania (Real) Property, 1820, 1840, 1860.

Note: Gamma is a measure of association between ordinal variables. It is used to compare concordant and discordant pairs, and shows the intensity and direction of the relationship between the variables.

Here both gamma and Kendall's tau b are used to measure the association between average value per acre and total number of acres owned. I used tau b as a supplemental measure to insure that values of gamma had not resulted from statistical idiosyncracies of the data. The similar values of gamma and Kendall's tau b lend more confidence to each of the values obtained.

tution being typical, have suggested that about 25 percent of all Southern households owned slaves. In 1860, however, about 40 percent of all households in Pittsylvania owned slaves.[10] Similarly, about 38 percent of all people who owned taxable personal property owned slaves.

If we look at slave ownership in terms of ownership of rural land, that is, if we eliminate the slaveholders residing in Danville, we find that on the eve of the Civil War slightly less than 65 percent of all rural landowners owned slaves.[11] In some areas of the county, the percentage was even higher. In Museville, an area in the west central section with relatively few large landholdings, 77 percent of all landowners and 68 percent of all farm operators (including tenants) were slaveholders.

Slave ownership was far more evenly distributed in Pittsylvania than in the older tobacco counties immediately to the east. In Halifax and Mecklenburg, the counties consecutively to Pittsylvania's east along the North Carolina border, the large slaveholders owned a far greater percentage of the slaves (see Table 6-12). The source of this difference lay in the respective labor demands of the dark tobacco grown in Halifax and Mecklenburg as opposed to the bright tobacco that was increasingly being grown in Pittsylvania.

TABLE 6−7

*The Correlation between the Average Value Per Acre
and the Total Number of Acres Owned, 1820, 1840, 1860*

| | Pittsylvania | | Augusta | |
| | | Kendall's | | Kendall's |
Year	Gamma	tau b	Gamma	tau b
1820	.001	.001	.3	.08
1840	.3	.2	.2	.05
1860	−.1	−.04	−.5	−.2

Source: Augusta and Pittsylvania (Real) Property, 1820, 1840, 1860.
Note: Gamma and Kendall's tau b are explained in Table 6-6.

It is important to note that Pittsylvania had both a larger percentage of small slaveholders and fewer very large slaveholders than did Halifax or Mecklenburg counties. The vast majority of Pittsylvania slaveholders owned fourteen or fewer slaves, and very nearly half owned between one and five slaves. At the other end of the scale, only 6 percent of Pittsylvania's slaveholders owned thirty or more slaves, a figure half the comparable proportion for the other two tobacco-growing counties (see Table 6-13).

MAKING SENSE OF THE DATA

If, as the statistics clearly show, Pittsylvania was not an area of large planters and poor whites, but an area of relative white equality, why were Pittsylvania and Augusta perceived to be so dramatically different? Or to put it another way, given the similarities in the economic status of the white populations, why was Augusta alone seen as a land of opportunity for the white yeoman? The answers to these questions lie in the organization of space and the organization of economic activities within the two counties.

TABLE 6–8
Ownership of the Best Land by Deciles, 1840, 1860

	Total Acres Owned		Total Value of Land Owned	
Deciles:	1840	1860	1840	1860
1	2	9	—	3
2	2	6	—	3
3	—	3	—	2
4	2	2	—	—
5	—	6	4	6
6	3	2	2	4
7	6	3	2	5
8	7	6	5	10
9	2	9	13	9
	45%	36%	67%	43%
10	16	12	14	16
Total	40	58	40	58

Source: Pittsylvania (Real) Property, 1840, 1860.
Note: Deciles are ranked from the bottom to the top. In 1840 individuals with lands valued at $6 per acre are included; in 1860, those with lands of $10 per acre.

The Organization of Space

Although large landholders held a similar proportion of acreage in both counties, there was a marked difference in the location of those large holdings (see Table 6-14). In Pittsylvania, the large landholdings were tobacco plantations, visibly located along the county's main thoroughfares, its rivers. In Augusta, by contrast, the largest holdings consisted mostly of unimproved pasturage situated on the relatively inaccessible slopes of the Blue Ridge. However, below these slopes, in the limestone Valley, there was a dense concentration of intensively cultivated small farms, which, crisscrossed by commercial thoroughfares, gave the area its character.[12]

A second major difference was in the percentage of unimproved land on different sized farms (see Table 6-15). In Pittsylvania, where almost every farm specialized in tobacco production, between 40 and 50 percent

TABLE 6–9
Percent of Landless Households, 1820, 1840, 1860

County	1820	1840	1860
Augusta	37%	32%	38%
Pittsylvania	32%	36%	35%

Sources: Based on Augusta and Pittsylvania (Real) Property, 1820, 1840, 1860. U.S. Census, Population Schedule, 1820, 1840, 1860.

of the land was in improved acreage. In Augusta between 60 and 70 percent of the land was improved in all but the largest landholdings, the mountainside pasturages where the percentage of land improved slipped to 26 percent. This difference in land utilization was a function of the different agricultural systems of the two areas. In Pittsylvania, as was typical of tobacco areas, planters practiced a kind of circulatory agriculture, whereby a large percentage of the land was allowed to lie fallow in order to restore its fertility for future tobacco plantings. In Augusta, a broader range of crops and the integration of animal husbandry made possible a far more intensive use of the soils.

The underlying basis for Augusta's diversification was its soil and climate. Whereas the English agricultural revolution largely bypassed the clay and sandy soils of Pittsylvania, its discoveries had a major effect on the rich limestone—the so-called Haggerstown—soils of the Valley. Soil fertility was maintained in the Valley by a regular rotation of crops, including grasses and hays unable to thrive in the warmer climes of the Piedmont. The grasses and hays left a dense sod that could be plowed under, thus renewing the soil's supply of humus and colloids. Clover in rotation supplied indispensable nitrogen to the soil. In addition to making an excellent arable when preserved, the limestone soils also made for excellent meadows and orchards.[13]

The grains and grasses grown in Augusta provided a variety of opportunities. The grasses, for instance, could be used to feed cattle, which produced manure for the wheat crop; the cattle were then slaughtered and the meat and hides sold in Lynchburg or Richmond. Or the grasses could be used to maintain herds for dairying. Similarly, the grains could be sold directly or they could be used to fatten cattle and swine or converted into liquor. A poem of the period describes one of these interrelationships:

TABLE 6–10
Unskilled Adult White Male Rural Household Heads, 1860

County	Percent Who Own Land	Percent Landless	Percent Landless with Some Personal Property	Percent without Land or Some Personal Property
Augusta	62%	38%	15%	15%
Pittsylvania	65%	35%	28%	2%

Source: Based on a one in ten random sample of the Augusta and Pittsylvania (Personal) Property, 1860.

Without grass you've got no cattle—without cattle 'tis plain,
You'll have no manure and without that no grain.[14]

The Organization of Economic Activity

In Augusta, the diversity of products and the characteristics of the main crop, wheat, entailed the development of a broad range of economic activities. This diversity was clearly reflected in the occupational structure of the countryside. In Augusta, a significantly larger percentage of the population was employed in nonfarming work, primarily as artisans, laborers, or businessmen (see Table 6-16).

Similarly, the demand for a greater range and number of supportive services in Augusta was also reflected both in the number of towns and the size of the town populations (see Table 6-17). What these figures hide is that while Augusta had one large town, Staunton (3,900 in 1860), and one medium sized town, Waynesburg (approx. 650), as well as three other towns with over 200 people, Pittsylvania had, other than Danville, only one other place, Chatham (approx. 350), the county seat, with a population of more than a hundred people. Thus while Danville (3,689) and Staunton (3,900) had a similar population size in 1860, Danville represented nearly 90 percent of Pittsylvania's town population while Staunton was only 60 percent of Augusta's. Obviously, this analysis has left out a number of factors such as the role these two towns played in interregional trade and in manufacturing. The essential point here is that the statistics demonstrate that Augusta's wheat and cattle-based mixed

TABLE 6–11
Value of the Personal Property of Landless Unskilled
Adult White Male Household Heads, 1860

Augusta	Mean	$ 88	Median	$50
Pittsylvania	Mean	$525	Median	$60

Source: Based on a one in ten random sample of the Augusta and Pittsylvania (Personal) Property, 1860.

farming economy generated the kind of pandemic growth of towns crucial to economic development absent in Pittsylvania.[15]

Almost every traveler who passed down the Valley of Virginia remarked on the number and proximity of its towns. It was the visibility of town life which in part explains why, despite the obvious inequalities within the white population, Augusta was seen as a haven for whites. Town life was both the substance and symbol of the broader range of opportunity possible in Augusta. In Pittsylvania, which had few towns, inequality was far more visible among whites; because virtually everyone was engaged in tobacco production, long-term success or failure with that crop could provide a single clear measure of a person's standing. In Augusta, a diverse and protean economy based on mixed farming provided a varied and changing gauge for success.[16]

Finally and most importantly, for a variety of reasons Augusta never experienced the boom-and-bust cycles endemic to an economy based almost entirely on tobacco. Because of the diverse agricultural potential and even-keeled climate of the limestone Valley, Augusta's farmers were able to regularly readjust to the spinning gyroscope of changing regional and national market demand.[17] In the late colonial period hemp was an important Valley crop. With the American Revolution and the end of the British bounty for hemp, as well as increased competition from Kentucky and Russia, the Valley hemp industry suffered a precipitous decline. The Valley farmers responded to the decline of hemp by increasing their production of wheat, in part to meet the demand created by the Napoleonic Wars. Similarly, in the late antebellum period, when faced with increased competition from the new wheat lands opening in the west, Valley farmers began to expand their production of dairy products. After the Civil War this shift away from wheat continued with the expansion of fruit and poultry production (see Table 6-18).[18]

In sum, then, despite the important similarities in their distribution of

TABLE 6–12
Slave Ownership, 1860

County	Total Slaveholders	Total Slaves	Mean Ratio	Percent Slave
Pittsylvania	1,413	14,340	1 to 10	46%
Halifax	1,051	14,897	1 to 14	65%
Mecklenburg	760	12,420	1 to 16	57%

Sources: U.S. Census, Slave Schedule, 1860; Fleetwood, "Southside Virginia."

landholding and landlessness, ethnic composition, and political perspective, Pittsylvania and Augusta were fundamentally separated by the consequences of their respective soil and climatic endowments. In Augusta's case, these endowments permitted the development of an intense and protean agriculture capable of generating a thriving town life and responding to new market conditions. As for Pittsylvania, though its economic prospects were fettered neither by planter domination nor a large population of poor whites, its economy was plagued by its dependence on the booms and busts of tobacco, the only commercially viable crop capable of being produced on the county's clay and sandy soils. Even in good times, the services demanded by a tobacco economy generated only a narrow range of possibilities for development.

Given the constrictive consequences of Pittsylvania's soil and climate, tobacco was almost the sole focus of its entrepreneurial energies. In the 1850s, those energies were channeled into growing a new and more lucrative form of tobacco, bright leaf, which seemed to open up a new range of possibilities for Pittsylvania.

TABLE 6−13
The Distribution of Slave Ownership, 1860

Number of Slaves Owned	Owners					
	Halifax		Mecklenburg		Pittsylvania	
	Number	Percent	Number	Percent	Number	Percent
1−5	401	38%	291	38%	690	49%
6−9	183	17%	124	16%	253	18%
10−14	156	15%	98	13%	153	11%
15−19	76	7%	61	8%	110	8%
20−29	117	11%	80	10%	103	7%
30−69	95	9%	79	10%	78	6%
70−99	15	1%	10	1%	7	—
100+	8	.07%	11	1%	1	—

Sources: Based on U.S. Census, Slave Schedule, 1860; Fleetwood, "Southside Virginia."

TABLE 6−14
The Number of Farms by Location, 1820, 1840, 1860

	River	Road	Town	Unavailable
Pittsylvania				
1820	70	1	6	23
1840	73	1	4	23
1860	68	1	10	22
Augusta				
1820	48	10	11	26
1840	38	14	21	27
1860	35	13	19	33

Source: Based on the description of a farm's location given in Augusta and Pittsylvania (Real) Property, 1820, 1840, 1860.

TABLE 6-15
The Percent of Improved Land on Different Sized Farms, 1860

Acres	Pittsylvania	Augusta
0–50	48%	70%
50–100	37%	68%
100–200	49%	65%
200–500	44%	58%
500–1,000	38%	56%
1,000 +	47%	26%

Source: U.S. Census, Agriculture Schedule, 1860.
Note: Countywide, 40 percent of the land in Pittsylvania is improved; 52 percent in Augusta.

TABLE 6-16
The Percent of White Household Heads in Rural Occupations, 1860

Occupation	Pittsylvania	Augusta
Farmer	70%	43%
Artisan	12%	21%
Laborer	6%	23%
Professional	6%	4%
Businessman	2%	6%
Miscellaneous	2%	—

Source: U.S. Census, Population Schedule, 1860.

TABLE 6–17
Town Population and Number of Towns, 1836, 1860

| | Augusta | | Pittsylvania | |
	1836	1860	1836	1860
Town Population as a Percent of Total Population	16%	27%	5%	13%
Town Population as a Percent of White Population	20%	35%	8%	25%
Number of Towns	7	11	4	5

Sources: The figures for 1836 are derived from *Martin's Gazeteer*; those for 1860, from the U.S. Census, Population Schedule, 1860.

TABLE 6–18
Agricultural Production, 1840, 1850, 1860

	1840	1850	1860
Pittsylvania			
Number of swine	42,513	34,382	22,366
Number of meat cattle	19,451	16,409	15,463
Number of sheep	19,277	14,954	11,611
Value of animals slaughtered	—	$124,610	$223,732
Wheat (bushels)	142,178	—	184,112
Corn (bushels)	679,319	—	519,374
Oats (bushels)	333,763	—	259,053
Tobacco (pounds)	6,438,777	4,700,075	7,053,962
Augusta			
Number of swine	16,424	25,975	31,033
Number of meat cattle	21,479	19,875	20,845
Number of sheep	12,345	16,316	13,013
Value of animals slaughtered	—	$158,501	$254,383
Wheat (bushels)	324,332	419,066	307,402
Corn (bushels)	384,408	505,800	752,530
Oats (bushels)	244,889	278,000	191,379
Dairy (pounds)	—	287,577	466,408

Sources: U.S. Census, Manufacturing Schedule, 1840; U.S. Census, Agriculture Schedule, 1850, 1860.

7

THE ADVENT OF

BRIGHT TOBACCO

🖋 🖋 🖋 🖋 🖋 🖋

PITTSYLVANIA WAS BOTH nourished and constrained by the fortunes of the great leaf. For most of the county's farmers there was no alternative to tobacco as a cash crop. About midway through the antebellum period, however, new possibilities were developed within the realm of tobacco production. The most important development was the increasingly regularized growth of bright leaf tobacco, a lighter, golden, more aromatic leaf than the dark tobacco traditionally grown in Pittsylvania and most of Virginia. The bright leaf was also highly prized as a wrapper for manufactured tobacco. When Pittsylvania began increasingly to grow the bright leaf, tobacco manufacturing became the basis for yet another boom in Danville. To understand how and why bright tobacco became so important to Danville in the decade and a half before the Civil War, the singular qualities of the tobacco plant, qualities that had a significant social meaning, must be considered.

Tobacco was strikingly different from the other major plantation staples—cotton, rice, and sugar—despite their common use of slave labor. Cotton, rice, and sugar could, in the agricultural sense, be mass-produced and mass-handled by gang labor. For instance, little thought was given to making distinctions between different bolls of cotton. But in the case of tobacco, where each leaf could be significantly different from another in terms of its quality and thus market value, mass-handling was something to be avoided. Fernando Ortiz has highlighted these differences by contrasting tobacco and sugar. Despite differences in processing, "in the end there is only one kind of sugar. All sachroses are the same. . . . Uniformity has never been possible, and never will be, where tobacco is concerned. The botanical varieties that contain nicotine are few; but even within each variety, and even in tobacco itself, each crop, each plant and perhaps each leaf has its own unique quality."[1] The sharp differentiation from plant to plant in tobacco occurs because, unlike most other plants, tobacco is true not to its seed but to the soil it is grown in. Seeds taken from the same plant placed in soils that differ only mildly in terms of water or air content can produce leaves with a marked difference in their market worth. A top quality leaf could bring in seven or eight times more than the lowest grade.[2]

In addition to soil, care in handling was one of the keys to growing the most marketable leaves. Tobacco, unlike the other plantation staples, was a delicate crop that required great care and attention at all stages of its growth and curing. The delicacy of the plant was exemplified by its seed: "When St. Matthew mentioned the mustard seed as the least of all seeds he showed an ignorance of the tobacco plant, for ten thousand of its seed will hardly overflow a teaspoon. To strew these in a field is not to be attempted. They must be sown in a seed bed; and even for this they are usually mingled with sifted ashes of other powdery stuff to facilitate an even scattering."[3] The care in seeding was only the beginning of a long process whose every stage demanded that each plant be given nearly individual attention. Whereas an individual slave could usually attend to eight to ten acres of cotton or twenty acres of wheat and corn, he could manage only three or at most four acres of tobacco.[4]

Left unattended, the tobacco stalks would "reach a height of five feet, having clammy hairy stalks and bearing leaves of a yellow-green color of greatest size at the bottom of the stalk."[5] The leaves from such a plant were unmarketable. To be commercially viable, the plants had to be primed and topped when they reached the proper size, which was known only to the experienced eye. Priming was the elimination of the lower four or five leaves. These leaves were often driven into the ground when rain interfered with cultivation, and they had little market value. Topping consisted of cutting off the top of the plant and some of the upper leaves, the number depending on the type of soil and quality of tobacco desired. Topping prevented the plant from going to seed and allowed for richer development of the remaining leaves: the fewer the leaves per plant, the richer the leaf harvested.[6]

Constant vigilance was required to keep the plants free of suckers and worms. It was important to get to the suckers as soon as they appeared to prevent major damage to the plants. Worms presented a similar danger. Produced by a fly whose eggs hatched within twenty-four to thirty-six hours after being deposited, the worms began to feed on the leaf almost immediately after they hatched. Unless destroyed, they grew quickly, posing a threat to the entire crop. Harvesting also had to be conducted carefully on a plant-by-plant basis and increasingly, as the nineteenth century moved on, even on a leaf-by-leaf basis. "Only an experienced planter could tell when tobacco was ripe. There was grave danger from cutting too early or too late. Those who attempted to give written instructions in the art of tobacco culture pushed their powers of description to the utmost."[7]

None of the required tasks—priming, topping, worming, or harvesting—were subject to systematization, let alone mechanization. Skill in topping, for instance, was acquired. J. H. Cocke, the agricultural reformer, described the slaves who were specially chosen for topping: "Tobacco plantation hands who cannot count fifty will acquire a sort of instinct which enables them to top tobacco with invariable accuracy almost as fast as they can walk along the row."[8] A number of "acquired instincts" were required for the later stages of preparing the leaf. According to Nannie M. Tilley, the historian of bright tobacco, "No other agricultural product grown in the U.S. requires as much skill, knowledge, and accuracy in the matter of classing or sorting as tobacco. Proper assortment of bright tobacco is, in fact, an art acquired from close association with soil and plant, often passed on from father to son but seldom attained by those without a tobacco heritage."[9]

Tobacco had an artisanal quality to it. For all the other plantation staples and for wheat, the routinized nature of at least some of the work requirements permitted the use of other gang labor. And while rice, sugar, cotton, and wheat were subject to various degrees of mechanization in the nineteenth century, the mechanical aspects of the industrial revolution barely touched tobacco until well after World War II. No developments in tobacco could compare to steam-powered rice and sugar mills, cotton gins, or mechanical wheat harvesters. There were no factories in the tobacco fields. Indeed, while other crops were being mechanized, tobacco was moving in the opposite direction.[10] Describing the 1890s, Tilley has noted that "throughout this period of change, while other agricultural products were becoming more subject to the use of machinery, tobacco continued to reign in its own peculiar fashion by demanding an even greater degree of meticulous hand labor."[11] Ortiz has summarized the differences between tobacco and its antipode, sugar:

> . . . tobacco requires delicate care, sugar can look after itself: the
> one requires continual attention, the other involves seasonal work;
> the intensive versus extensive cultivation; steady work on the part

of the few, intermittent jobs for the many . . . ; skilled and unskilled labor; hands versus arms; men versus machines. . . .

In the production of tobacco intelligence is the prime factor.[12]

THE TOBACCO PLANTER

What manner of man was created by tobacco planting? The rational capitalist is usually associated with vigorous commercial cities. In the absence of those cities, the lack of a calculating rationality is usually assumed, even where, as in the case of Southern planters, the historical actors involved have been subject to the discipline of national and world markets. The tobacco planter represents a striking counterexample to these assumptions.

In both growing and curing the crop, the tobacco planter was required to make an endless series of rational management decisions. As Cornelius Cathey describes it, "tobacco not only required more after-management [referring to the curing] than any other crop grown . . . but it also, more than any other crop, reflected at all stages of its growth and processing the quality of management it received. Growers who attained a good reputation for the manner in which they handled the crop always received the best prices in the market. Because of this, the acreage per planter per hand was small in comparison with other crops."[13] Joseph Robert, the preeminent historian of tobacco, expressed the same point when he noted that "carelessness in handling was perhaps more costly here than in the case of any other staple; few products showed such a wide price range between mediocre and better grades. To send to market a profitable 'parcel' required a sober crop master who kept a critical eye on the usual labor."[14]

The planter's decision making began with where and when to plant the seedbed. At the tail end of the process, another critical determination was when the crop was ripe for harvest. Soil, weather conditions, and the markets being targeted were all involved in the decision. Once it was made, the leaves were harvested and left in the field until they had wilted from the sun and had become flexible enough to move without breaking. The leaves were then moved into the tobacco barn to be cured.[15]

The curing process was yet another key to a crop's success or failure. There were three major methods of curing: air, fire and flue, along with a number of variations. The planter's choice of a method had a major effect on the marketability of his crop. Smoking is, after all, a matter of personal taste, and the grower had to be extremely sensitive to changes in consumer preference, a problem generally of little concern to the producers of other staples. In the 1820s, when the French showed a preference for fancy colored tobaccos, the planters did their utmost to appeal to that taste. One Nottoway County planter described the competition to produce a colored tobacco: "It was laughable," he said, "to hear the names of the different colors and to see the ambitions of each tobacco-maker to excell his neighbor. There was the 'pie-bald color,' the 'calico,' the 'green streak,' 'straw color,' 'fawn color,' and finally the consummation of all tints, the 'hickory leaf color.'"[16] This planter tended his curing barn like a mother caring for an infant, but curing was a risky business and the returns could be very disappointing. Later, J. R. Gaines, a Charlotte County planter, recounted the demands placed on curing by the craze for fancy colored tobacco:

> The curing process has always been a most difficult and dangerous one, but has been rendered doubly so for the last ten years, by the demand for bright French tobacco. Were a stranger suddenly to open one of our cellared barns, (where the fires had been unremittingly kept up, from Monday morning until Saturday) and see one of the hardy sons of Africa, with his red eyes and sooty locks, he would imagine himself on the borders of the infernal region. But thanks be to the whimsicality of the French, or the avarice of the Scotch, or whatever other cause that has put this kind of tobacco out of fashion.[17]

Given the keen competition to sell quality tobacco, the planter had no choice but to stretch himself to the limit in responding to a coquettish market.

SLAVE LABOR

One of the chief factors in a planter's success or failure was his ability to manage his slaves. It has been estimated that labor represented more than half the costs of producing a crop in the postwar period.[18]

The standard view of slave management in the Virginia tobacco areas is taken from Frederick Law Olmsted, who was convinced that slave labor was inefficient. In the course of his travels, Olmsted came across a "Mr. W.," who told him that "he cultivated only the coarser and lower priced tobacco, because the finer sorts required more pains-taking and discretion than it was possible to make a large gang of negroes use."[19] Nevertheless, while Olmsted was conducting his interview with "Mr. W.," large numbers of Virginia farmers and planters were producing high quality tobacco with slave labor. How did they do it?

First of all, unlike "Mr. W.," most of them did not use gang labor. Typically, the Virginia tobacco plantation involved fewer slaves and fewer acres under cultivation than its sugar or cotton counterparts. The planter often worked in the field himself and, aided by overseers, was able to directly supervise much of the work being done. Second, in at least some of the areas where quality tobacco was being produced, the slaves seemed to understand that the plant required painstaking care.[20] Henrietta Perry, an ex-slave from the Danville area, recalled:

> Marse ain' raise nothin' but terbaccy, ceptin' a little wheat an' corn for eatin', an' us black people had to look after dat 'baccy lak it was gold. Us women had to pin our dresses up roundst our neck fo' we stepped in dat ole 'baccy field,' else we'd git a lashin'. Git a lashin' too effen you cut a leaf fo' its ripe. Marse ain' cared what we do in de wheat an' corn field cause dat warn't nothin' but food for us niggers, but you better not do nothin' to 'baccy leaves.[21]

The importance of care in the "baccy" fields was learned in early childhood. Many ex-slaves stated that as young children their work in the fields began with picking the worms off the tobacco leaves. One slave described her first encounter with worming:

> Guess I was a girl 'bout five or six when I was pit wid de other chillun pickin' de bugs off de terbaccy leaves. . . . Purty soon old Masser come along, dough, an' see dat I done been missin' some of dem terbaccy worms. Picked up a hand full of worms, he did, an' stuffed 'em inter my mouth; Lordy knows how many of dem shiny things I done swallered, but i sho' picked em off carefull arter dat.[22]

Older children were not so lucky. One boy explained how his overseer, a man with hawklike eyes for worms, would give him a choice if he missed some. He could either swallow a bunch or get three lashes. He usually chose to swallow the worms.[23]

The converse of certain punishment in a closely supervised situation was the potential reward for a slave who had mastered the art of tobacco planting. A skilled slave could find himself in a strong bargaining position. One exceptionally skilled laborer ran away after a beating, then gave himself up to a slave trader who, recognizing his worth, was interested in buying him from his master. The runaway's daughter recounted what followed:

> So when de brought father back to his owner and asked to buy him, Mr. Lewis (the owner) said there wasn't a plantation owner with enough money to pay him for Spot (the runaway). . . . Lewis owned a large tobacco plantation and my father was the head man on dat plantation. He cured all de tobacco as it was brought in from the field, made all the twists and plugs of tobacco. . . . Father told his owner after he found out he wouldn't sell him, dat if he whipped him again, he would run away again. . . . So de nigger trader begged my father not to run away from Marse Lewis, because if he did Lewis would be a ruined man, because he did not have another man who could manage the workers as father did. So the owner knew freedom was about to be declared . . . so he sat down and talked with my father about the future and promised my father if he would stay with him and ship his tobacco for him . . . he would give him a nice house and a lot for the family right on the plantation.[24]

The story of Spot and "Marse" Lewis underlines the peculiarities inherent in tobacco. Like the bat that seems to be both bird and mouse, tobacco society is difficult to classify. The economic logic of tobacco production made tobacco society both part of and yet different from the rest of the slave South. The cotton South can be compared to the steel towns of the North in the late nineteenth century. Both the cotton country and the steel towns were organized around large and rigidly hierarchical work units that dominated both the economic and social environment. Both were involved in the regularized production of a primary good aimed at a market of other manufacturers and not subject to the whims of the individual consumer's tastes.

The tobacco farmer, like the family farmer of the North or the owner of a small garment factory, had to work alongside the people whose labor he purchased, though he was clearly separated from his workers by the caste line of racial slavery. Although sharing the racial sensibility of the cotton planter, the tobacco farmer was separated from him by the character of the crop he was growing. The tobacco plantation tended to be far smaller than its counterpart in sugar or cotton, so that the organization of plantation life was less likely to be congruent with the organization of society at large. In short, the tobacco farmer was more likely to be an entrepreneur than a grandee. In terms of his market, the tobacco grower had more in common with the always marginal small garment manufacturer than with the steel baron. He had to market a product with numerous subjective dimensions: taste, texture, and visual appeal, which were not subject to standardized production procedures. The tobacco grower, like the garment manufacturer, was subject to the ever-changing and highly personal taste of the fickle consumer. It was, in part, as a result of the highly competitive effort to improve the taste of tobacco, to please those fickle consumers, that bright tobacco was developed.

THE RISE OF BRIGHT TOBACCO

The rise of bright tobacco in the late antebellum period came, in part, through the intensified emphasis on quality and curing, which had become important in the early nineteenth century. Bright heightened all the peculiarities of the traditional dark or oronoco tobacco. It was hypersensitive to minute variations in the soil and highly dependent on changes in curing techniques. Bright tobacco, that is, tobacco with very light colored leaves which produced a very mild taste, had always been highly valued, but planters had never been able to produce it with any regularity. Nannie M. Tilley explains why:

> It [bright tobacco] is . . . an anachronism in the agricultural system, since the best type of yellow leaf is produced on thin sterile soils unfit for prosperous farming in general. Tobacco possesses a very sensitive nature, adapting itself to a wide range of soils and climates. So great is the influence of the soil on the quality of tobacco that a fine bright plant may grow within a few feet of a course heavy one. . . . It is thus difficult to maintain the characteristics of a distinct variety without exercising extreme care in the choice of soils. . . . In view of the extraordinarily sensitive nature of the tobacco plant and its illogical behavior in the agricultural system, it is not surprising that the bright yellow variety was slow to become a

distinct type, even though the possibilities for such a development had confronted growers since the days of John Rolfe.[25]

Ironically, or perhaps not so ironically, given the cast of tobacco, the exhaustion of some of Virginia's best soils, the rich dark clay soils of the central Piedmont and the alluvial soils of both the central and southern Piedmont, made possible the advancement of bright tobacco. As those relatively rich and heavy soils became exhausted, growers moved southward to the sandy loam soils of Pittsylvania, Halifax, and Henry counties; within the central Piedmont, some of them moved to the gray sandy soil of the interfluvial ridges. The mechanical properties of light, sandy soils are conducive to the growth of bright tobacco, for which a delicate balance of air and moisture in the soil is crucial. Clay soils, which are densely packed, contain an insufficient amount of air and too much water. This is because clay soils are moisture absorbent. They retain a great deal of water, which drowns the plant in fluid, cutting off the oxygen supply. The more porous sandy loams retain some moisture but not so much as to cut off the requisite oxygen.[26]

In Pittsylvania, where most of the soil was a siliceous loam, the early settlers planted only the heavy bottom lands with tobacco; most of the major figures in the county's early history established their estates along the rivers (although their holdings contained a considerable acreage in sandy soils, which would be important later). Indeed, the limited amount of clay loam in the county inhibited its early growth as the relatively barren sandy lands were bypassed by settlers. In the 1820s and 1830s, a few Pittsylvania planters like W. N. Thomas became increasingly aware of the effects of siliceous soils and these farmers developed a reputation for producing quality bright leaf.[27]

At about the same time that the relationship between soil qualities and bright tobacco was being slowly uncovered, major developments were occurring in the curing of tobacco. Until the War of 1812, air or sun curing had been standard. But in the 1820s when the European taste changed, fire curing became necessary to produce the new lighter colored leaf then in demand. As described earlier, an intense competition ensured the creation of the most attractive light color leaves by fire curing. Before the craze for fire curing died out in the thirties, it had produced two major innovations crucial to regularizing the production of bright leaf tobacco—the use of charcoal instead of wood for the fires, and the use of flues instead of open fires. Each of these developments allowed far more control over the curing process. Bright tobacco could be created with consistency only with the use of charcoal and flues in curing.[28]

The early flues were developed in the counties surrounding Danville. One of the earliest was developed by Dr. Davis G. Tuck, of Loves Shop in neighboring Halifax. During the late 1820s, Tuck used pipes, but other successful flues later developed in Henry County, Pittsylvania's neighbor to the west, were made of rock, usually white sandstone. These rock flues were in common use by the 1850s. Whereas the development of flues was the product of calculated experimentation, it appears that the discovery of charcoal's lightening effect was made accidentally in 1839 by Stephen Slade, a slave. For the next decade and a half, Abisha Slade, Stephen Slade's master, and numerous other tobacco planters experimented with the best way of using charcoal to fire the curing. Their efforts, as in the case of attempts to improve the flues, were fired by the premium that Virginia's burgeoning tobacco manufacturing industry placed on bright tobacco. The light golden leaf provided the most attractive and most salable wrapper for the plug and twist tobacco, which was then the mainstay of the industry.[29]

After more than twenty years of gestation, a fairly good knowledge of how to regularly produce bright tobacco emerged in the mid-1850s. The man who was most responsible for spreading that knowledge and the man who emerged as the model planter was Abisha Slade of Caswell County, North Carolina, which lies just south of Danville along the Virginia-North Carolina border. Slade came out of the same mold as the planter-entrepreneurs of Danville. In addition to being a tobacco farmer, he was involved in real estate speculations. He was an early investor in the nearby town of Yanceyville and owned an interest in the town's hotel.[30]

The planters of the Roanoke Valley had been experimenting with ways to regularize the production of bright tobacco for more than twenty years, so it is hardly surprising that Slade's successes aroused a great deal of popular interest. Local newspapers and agricultural societies and state and Southern farm journals gave the developments wide coverage. The implications of the discovery were obvious to all. For the first time the bright leaf, so valued for its superior color and its mechanical properties as a wrapper for manufactured tobacco, could be produced on a regular basis. But even before this discovery, the sandy soils of southern Pittsylvania were producing increasing quantities of bright leaf, albeit on a hit-or-miss basis. The bright leaf, invaluable for tobacco manufacturing, led to Danville's third boom, which began in the late 1840s.

Part Three

DANVILLE, 1840–1866

8

GROWTH AND

TRANSFORMATION,

1847–1860

❦ ❦ ❦ ❦ ❦ ❦ ❦

BETWEEN THE LATE 1840s and the onset of the Civil War, Danville grew from a trading village to the third largest tobacco manufacturing center in Virginia. A few statistics provide a sense of the magnitude of the change. In 1850 Danville's population was about 1,500; by 1860, swelled by the influx of newcomers and slaves, the population had grown to about 3,700 (see Table 8-1). In the same years the value of the town's real estate grew from $331,000 to $767,000. The chief source of this growth was the rapid expansion of tobacco manufacturing.

In 1840, when most tobacco manufacturing was being carried on in the countryside as an adjunct to planting, lower Pittsylvania, including Danville, manufactured tobacco valued at about a third of a million dollars. In 1860, after the advent of bright tobacco, lower Pittsylvania produced tobacco valued at over a million dollars, with Danville proper producing $610,000 of that total. The growth in the value of tobacco produced was reflected in the size of the labor force employed in manufacturing. In 1850, about 425 people in Danville were employed in tobacco manufacturing; in 1860 this number jumped by 150 percent to about 1,050 people. Thus, within a decade the population of Danville grew two and a half times, the value of the town's real estate grew 140 percent, and employment in tobacco manufacturing (including slaves) grew by 150 percent.[1]

The underlying basis for this growth was the revival of tobacco prices, which had collapsed for a decade after the crash of 1837, and the decline of the worn-out central Piedmont tobacco lands, which were following

TABLE 8–1
Population Growth, 1840, 1850, 1860 (to nearest 100)

	1840	1850	1860
Pittsylvania	24,400	28,800	32,100
Danville	1,000	1,500	3,700
Danville as a Percent of the County's Population	4%	5%	12%

Sources: U.S. Census, Population, 1840; U.S. Census, Population Schedule, 1850, 1860.

the Tidewater into the oblivion of soil-exhausted devastation. The value of the later developed and thus fresher soils of Pittsylvania and the south-west of the Southside was enhanced by these changes. In this context, the increasing, though still irregular, growth of bright leaf in Pittsylvania's sandy soils provided a great impetus for the expansion of manufacturing.

The economic potential of these important changes was catalyzed by the continued aggressive efforts of Danville and Pittsylvania's planter-entrepreneurs to improve Danville's transportation connections. The chartering of the Richmond and Danville Railroad in 1847 was the single most important event in revitalizing the town.

TRANSPORTATION

The 1830s had seen literally dozens of internal improvement schemes designed to make Danville a major entrepôt. The two principal types of plans were those which tried to exploit the mountainous hinterlands to the west of Danville and those designed to provide a connection to the coast via Petersburg or Norfolk. All the plans to tie up east and west by rail had failed, and only one of the turnpike schemes had been completed. This was the turnpike that went northwest from Danville through Franklin County and across the mountains into Botetourt County, which was located at the southern end of the upper Valley of Virginia. The more modest efforts at exploiting the areas immediately to the north and south had led to the successful completion of unpaved roads linking the town with upper Pittsylvania and Lynchburg, to the north, and with Yancey-ville and Milton in adjacent Caswell County, North Carolina, to the south. The business brought by road was supplemented by a slim trade from the Dan River. Although navigable forty or fifty miles west of the falls at Danville, treacherous white water stretches severely limited the river's usefulness as a trade route. To the east, Danville was tied to Norfolk and Petersburg by a combined river and rail route.[2]

The leaders in the fight to bring the railroad to Danville were the prominent Pittsylvania planter Whitmell P. Tunstall and his brother-in-law, Danville businessman George Townes. Tunstall had first introduced a bill chartering a railroad from Richmond to Danville in 1838. In the years that followed, the state was devastated by the depression of 1837, and there was little state support for new internal improvements. Tunstall tried again in 1845 but faced strong opposition from Norfolk and Petersburg businessmen who were competing with Richmond for the interior trade. Then, in 1847, after nine years of effort, Tunstall and Townes succeeded in obtaining legislative approval. Unlike earlier charters for a railroad to Danville, none of which had come to fruition, this one provided immunity from taxation and instructed the Board of Public Works to subscribe to a portion of the stock. Tunstall justifiably saw it as the crowning achievement of his life. Shortly after the bill's passage, he wrote to George Townes, "Tis the proudest day of my life and I think I may now say that I have not lived in vain."[3]

The hopes fueled by the promise of a railroad were made clear in the successful 1847 petition to the legislature: "The vast and almost boundless resources of one of the most interesting portions of our country which has hithertofore languished under the repeated efforts of some of her most enterprising citizens to redeem it would immediately assume the garb of promise" if a railroad were built. The petition then went on to recount Danville's long-standing hope of becoming the trading center for southwestern Virginia and bordering North Carolina. The petition proved to be prophetic for, although construction did not begin for another three years and the railroad did not reach Danville until 1854, the very chartering of the road had a catalytic effect on lower Pittsylvania County. The flush prospects engendered a new wave of proposals for internal improvements comparable to the designs of the thirties. The major difference was that the new efforts were far more successful.[4]

The first schemes were aimed at improving the local tributaries of the Dan River so they could serve as feeder routes for the railroad. Of particular interest to the planter-entrepreneurs was the Smith River, one of the Dan's major tributaries. The Smith had its source in the Blue Ridge on the western borders of Patrick County about fifty miles west by north-

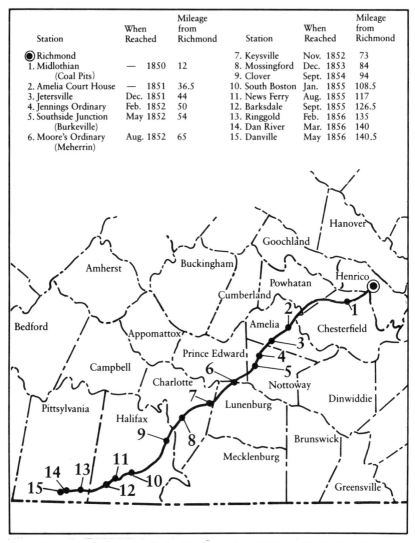

Station	When Reached	Mileage from Richmond	Station	When Reached	Mileage from Richmond
◉ Richmond			7. Keysville	Nov. 1852	73
1. Midlothian	— 1850	12	8. Mossingford	Dec. 1853	84
(Coal Pits)			9. Clover	Sept. 1854	94
2. Amelia Court House	— 1851	36.5	10. South Boston	Jan. 1855	108.5
3. Jetersville	Dec. 1851	44	11. News Ferry	Aug. 1855	117
4. Jennings Ordinary	Feb. 1852	50	12. Barksdale	Sept. 1855	126.5
5. Southside Junction	May 1852	54	13. Ringgold	Feb. 1856	135
(Burkeville)			14. Dan River	Mar. 1856	140
6. Moore's Ordinary	Aug. 1852	65	15. Danville	May 1856	140.5
(Meherrin)					

M A P 8-1. *The Progress of the Richmond and Danville Railroad, 1850–1856*

Source: Malcolm Clark, "The First Quarter Century of the Richmond-Danville Railroad, 1847–71," Ph.D. thesis, George Washington University, 1959.

west from Danville. It descended diagonally through a corner of Franklin County and on through Henry County, passing into eastern Pittsylvania near the hamlet of Cascade until it met the Dan east of Danville at Leaksville in Rockingham County, North Carolina. The *Danville Regis-*

ter was enthusiastic about improving the Smith, contending that it "will render a highly valuable auxilliary to the Richmond and Danville Railroad providing an outlet for tobacco and wheat."[5]

In 1847 George Hairston approached B. W. S. Cabell with a proposal to finance an experimental bateau trip up the Smith River if Cabell would lead it. Thirty years earlier, as a young man, Cabell had made similar explorations down the Dan in preparation for the opening of the Dismal Swamp Canal. Hairston, a member of the area's most prominent planting family, was the owner of an iron forge and foundry in Patrick County near the headwaters of the Smith. According to the *Danville Register*, Hairston's businesses there were "affording a market" that was "the best in the section where it is located, for the surplus products of the neighborhood."[6]

Cabell's expedition began at the Smith's headwaters near Hairston's forge and store. The bateaux, manned by a crew of five, tried to carry six thousand pounds of pig iron from Hairston's Union Iron Works down the Smith to Leaksville, North Carolina, twenty-five miles west of Danville. There the boats had to be moved through a canal built to bypass a rapids before traveling on to Danville. Despite the heavy load and despite having only one experienced crewman, Cabell overcame the Smith's rapids, as well as man-made obstacles like fish traps, to successfully complete the trip.[7]

The expedition had aroused great interest throughout the region. When he arrived in Leaksville, Cabell was greeted by Governor Morehead of North Carolina, who spoke of improving the Leaksville canal to facilitate the passage of heavy loads. The expedition was given banner treatment by the weekly *Danville Register*, which devoted five of its six front-page columns to coverage of the event.[8] Speculations about the possibilities opened up by the trip figured prominently in the paper's accounts. What seemed most tantalizing was the opportunity that Smith River improvements might afford to cut into Lynchburg's share of the Roanoke Valley tobacco trade. The success of the expedition also helped revive interest in one of the failed projects of the 1830s, a plank road to mineral rich Wythe County in the upper Shenandoah.[9]

The proposed Wytheville Pike received support from businessmen along the proposed route in Patrick, Grayson, and Wythe counties. In Pittsylvania, a broad range of interests organized to sell the bonds being floated to pay for the road. The Danville directors of the bond subscription campaign included:

Hobson Johns, tobacco manufacturer
Thomas P. Atkinson, banker and former mayor
Nathaniel Wilson, businessman and member of a prominent planter
    family
Thomas Grasty, merchant
Nathaniel T. Green, physician
George Price, artisan-businessman

Here, as in the case of the Richmond and Danville Railroad, the difference between the outcome of this and earlier efforts was state support. This time the legislature directed the Board of Public Works to subscribe to three-fifths of the company's $30,000 capital stock, once three-quarters of the two-fifths to be bought by private investors (i.e., $8,000) had been secured.

With a railroad to the east and a pike to the west under way, attention after 1851 focused on the building of short feeder roads into the emerging bright belt area immediately surrounding Danville. In 1852 a road was chartered to run from Danville due north to Chatham, the county seat, and then west to the Pigg River, which flowed into western Pittsylvania from adjacent Franklin County. In 1853 the town government acted on its own to build a road south to Yanceyville in neighboring Caswell County, North Carolina. This was the first time that Danville, acting as a corporate entity, had undertaken to spearhead a project. The legislative enabling act authorized the town council to subscribe to up to $20,000 worth of stock, subject to voter approval. The voters assented and within eighteen months four and a half miles of the plank road had been built.[10]

With its own projects secured, Danville had a vested interest to protect, and a new attitude toward internal improvements emerged. Local newspapers, which had fought so long and hard to secure state support for Danville's projects, now began to worry out loud about the state's credit and debt burden. The *Danville Republican* protested that "the building of a railroad without state aid, is an unheard of thing. . . . There are improvements in this section of the state, which many of us would gladly see constructed, but no man who cares anything for the credit of the state, would not prefer to see them fail, for the present, then for the game played by the legislature to be renewed."[11] Further, the paper feared that the many charters granted to private investors in the last session of the legislature would prompt those investors to seek state aid. The problem, the editors asserted, was that many of the newly chartered companies were potential rivals to existing companies. Not coincidentally, the same issue of the paper described a railroad meeting in nearby Leaksville, North Carolina, attended by people from Rockingham County, Virginia, in which there was a call for a railroad to be built from Leaksville to Lynchburg.

POLITICAL SUPPORT FOR INTERNAL
IMPROVEMENTS

Danville and Pittsylvania successfully secured their transportation routes through the work of their representatives in the state legislature. Pittsylvania shared a senatorial seat with the neighboring counties, Franklin and Henry, and the seat seemed to rotate among the counties. But Pittsylvania had two seats in the assembly, and an analysis of the holders of those seats tells us a great deal about the support for internal improvements in the county.

Between 1820 and 1860, twenty men represented Pittsylvania in the assembly.[12] The most influential was probably Vincent Witcher, the "Old Wheel Horse" of the county's Whigs. A self-described Henry Clay Whig, Witcher came out of the classic mold of the Southern politician: he was a skilled parliamentarian, an excellent debater, and the wrong man to have as an opponent. Witcher's parliamentary talents as chairman of the state agricultural society greatly impressed Edmund Ruffin. Ruffin describes how Witcher molded the 1856 meeting of the society. Ruffin's son had nominated the fire-eater Willoughby Newton to replace Unionist J. H. Cocke as the society's president. But then, as Ruffin tells it, Witcher took over:

> . . . it was very doubtful which was the majority. However then the chairman of the meeting Vincent Witcher, with admirable skill and management, declared the majority to be whichever way he (and all reasonable men) thought it to be. And thus by his legislative tactics, he declared the new constitution was adopted, the whole Executive Committee re-elected, and then that the meeting was adjourned sine die, so as to preclude chances for a reconsideration and a reversal.[13]

Although he was a staunch Unionist, Witcher had no doubts about the efficacy of slavery. He first came into statewide prominence during the debate between the *Richmond Whig* and Democratic *Richmond Enquirer* over the role of slavery in the campaign of 1836. When the *Whig* accused the *Enquirer* of soft-pedaling its coverage of Northern "fanatics" for fear of offending Van Buren's supporters, the *Enquirer* retorted that "the Whigs were trying to create an abolition panic in order to defeat Van Buren." Thomas Ritchie, editor of the *Enquirer*, said that Witcher "carried in his pocket the worst pamphlets of the 'fanatics' and the most odious pictures he could obtain from Gerritt Smith, Tappan and Co." He exhibited them to the inhabitants of Pittsylvania County "by way of frightening his people into Whiggery as if they were so many children."[14]

Witcher was an exceptional personality, but he was unexceptional in his strong, almost fervent support for internal improvements and economic growth. As state senator while Whitmell P. Tunstall was in the assembly, Witcher fought long and hard to assist Tunstall in his fight to bring the railroad to Pittsylvania. What seems singularly important about Pittsylvania's elected representatives is that, regardless of their occupation, residence, or political affiliation, they were strong promoters of internal improvements and economic growth.

There were no significant divisions in Pittsylvania between the town merchants and manufacturers and the leading planters. Both groups were committed to what in the twentieth century would be called economic development. It was the planter Tunstall who was central to acquiring a railroad, and he was strongly supported by the town merchants and the tobacco manufacturers. Insofar as one element was dominant, however, it was clearly the town dwellers, as thirteen of the sixteen identifiable representatives came from Danville or Chatham.[15]

As the town had supported the railroad, the railroad buoyed the town. The close ties between the town and countryside and Danville's small size had meant that in general the similarities between life in town and life in the countryside had outweighed the differences. The arrival of the railroad changed this somewhat, as the railroad symbolized the town's growth into a small city. A Danville resident described the town's symbolic response to the railroad:

> When the Richmond and Danville railroad was near Danville, the conductors, engineers and other employees of the road made their headquarters here, and they with some of the young men of Dan-

ville formed what they called a Histrionic Society and gave the first theatrical performance ever witnessed in Danville and vicinity. The Drama was "The Lady of Lyons" and the comedy was "Country Joe, the Country Cousin." The performance was given in the then Masonic Hall. People came in Wagons and buggys for 40 or 50 miles around to see the performance.

Warren Jeter was the country cousin who came to see his city cousin. When Jeter the Country Cousin opened his vest and produced a ginger cake to his city cousin, the audience roared.[16]

As both people from the town and countryside probably realized, the coming of the railroad meant that Danville was becoming a city and its people would have the mores of city folk, so that the people from the countryside would have to watch their etiquette when they came into Danville.

The sense that Danville was becoming different from the countryside can also be seen in letters to the editors of the Danville newspapers. These letters took the form of asking if it were true that such and such an unbelievable idea was circulating in Danville. One good-natured farmer compiled a laundry list of rumors in his letter to the editor. He began:

> It is rumored in the country, that a very unusual occurence has taken place recently in Danville—that a lady preacher has actually held forth to a crowded house in town. Now, Mr. Editor, many strange and unfounded things are told in the country upon you town folks, and lest injustice be done to your town, do let the people of the country know if this woman did in fact come off. Was it a woman or a man in womens attire. . . . Now Mr. Editor, it is currently reported, and many believe, that a woman and not a northern virago, did preach in a church in Danv. . . .

> Some hundreds are right uneasy about their wives. They are afraid that some of them womens rights folks, from the N., are travelling among us, and that some wives are encouraging them. We would rather have an abolitionist among us. . . . One would spoil our negroes, but the other would spoil our wives and sweethearts, and either, would be made a bad piece of property. The accounts given of the performance have produced great alarm, because it looks more like a "womens rights" proceeding. It is even told that good pious wives attended the show, and made their hus-

bands go. . . . It is likely you may see a good many people from the country in Danv., to see the "bloomer" wives and apron string husbands. . . .

It is feared that there will be an insurrection among the women, and that they will begin to chew tobacco and drink whiskey. . . but if worse comes to worse ought there not to be a man's rights convention held? We are sorry for the husbands of Danv.[17]

The husbands of Danville, however, were by and large too busy trying to take advantage of the town's booming economy to worry about the cultural dangers of progress.

※

REAL ESTATE

As the town grew and attracted new businesses and investors, it must have begun to seem strange even to longtime residents. The expectation of growth as well as the growth itself brought both newcomers and a new fluidity to the town's social and economic structure. This is demonstrated by the occupations of its residents. In 1850 Danville had thirteen carpenters, eight of whom had left by 1860. However, between 1850 and 1860 thirty-seven new carpenters moved into the town. Similarly, in the 1850 census only seven people were described as clerks, but by the 1860 census there were thirty-nine. At the same time, other crafts like tailoring declined as the railroad made cheap clothing and other goods from Richmond readily available.[18]

Within this flux there was a core of stability. The town benefited from the continuing support of real estate investors and businessmen, some of whose commitment to the town dated back to the second decade of the century and the opening of the Dismal Swamp Canal. Men like the first mayor, lawyer James Lanier, planter-businessmen Nathaniel and Robert Wilson, and the redoubtable B. W. S. Cabell had owned substantial real property in Danville since at least 1820. Beginning in the 1840s, these longtime investors were joined both by ambitious young men and by some of the county's most prominent planters and tobacco manufacturers.

The town also experienced a continuity in real estate ownership. Of the eighty-five individuals owning property in 1850, forty-two had acquired that property between 1841 and 1850. Of the forty-three individuals who held property as of 1840 or earlier, sixteen owned property continuously from 1820 to 1850; ten, from 1830 to 1850, and seventeen from 1840 to 1850.[19]

The new investors in Danville came overwhelmingly from other parts of Pittsylvania. Between 1850 and 1860 the percentage of property owners in Danville who resided elsewhere in Pittsylvania County almost doubled (see Table 8-2).[20] By 1860 more than half of the people who owned property in Danville lived in rural Pittsylvania. Between 1850 and 1860 the value of Danville land held by rural Pittsylvanians quadrupled, while the value of the buildings they owned increased by a third. By 1860, $247,000 of Danville's land (39 percent of the total) and $62,000 in buildings (20 percent of the town's total) came from this group. Thus, it was rural Pittsylvanians, those most likely to be aware of the emerging developments in Danville, who came forth to seize the investment opportunities, particularly in land.[21]

At least five types of Pittsylvanians began to invest in or move to Danville: young artisans, small tobacco manufacturers, and merchants, all of whom were looking for expanded production opportunities; and speculators and planters, both of whom were primarily interested in buying land. One example of an artisan attracted to Danville was James Voss, a young tailor (he was twenty-four in 1850), who moved to Danville from rural Pittsylvania in the late 1840s. In 1850 he owned only a single slave and his prospects looked bleak, as the local production of garments threatened to be undercut by the goods brought in by the approaching Richmond and Danville Railroad. But Voss stopped making clothes himself and began to merchandise clothes manufactured elsewhere. By 1860 he was calling himself a merchant-tailor, and his holdings in land, buildings, and stock were considerable. He owned $3,000 in real estate and $20,000 in personal property, including a $50 gold watch.[22]

In the late 1840s rural tobacco manufacturers began moving their operations into the town. By 1850 the value of the tobacco manufactured in Danville began to exceed that manufactured in the countryside. This trend continued during the 1850s until most of the large rural manufacturers, including Banister Anderson, who was described as the "Napolean of Tobacco Manufacturers," moved their operations into the town, or in some cases just beyond the town limits. Manufacturing was at the heart of Danville's growth.[23]

While tobacco manufacturers constituted the single largest group of new investors in Danville's real estate during the late 1840s, planters

TABLE 8–2
New Investors in Danville Real Estate, 1850, 1860

Residence	1850	1860
Danville proper	43%	44%
Pittsylvania	28%	52%
Neighboring North Carolina Counties	10%	2%
Elsewhere in Virginia	17%	2%
Other	2%	<1%

Sources: Pittsylvania (Real) Property, 1850, 1860; U.S. Census, Population Schedule, 1850, 1860.

were the second largest group, representing about a quarter of the newcomers. Planter investment continued to grow and between 1850 and 1860, 30 to 40 percent of the new owners of Danville real estate were planters and their sons (see Table 8-3). It was during this period, for instance, that William Tunstall, the county clerk and brother of Whitmell, as well as a prominent planter in his own right, purchased $1,500 in Danville land and $600 in buildings. Other new investors were Jona-

TABLE 8–3
Occupations of Town-Lot Owners, 1850

Year of Acquisition	Artisan/ Entrepreneur	Politician	Minister/ Physician	Lawyer/ Businessman
1820	3	1	—	2
1830	—	—	—	—
1840	—	—	2	—
1850	—	—	2	—
Total	3 (6%)	1	4 (8%)	2

Sources: U.S. Census, Population, 1820, 1830, 1840; U.S. Census, Population Schedule, 1850.
Note: The occupations are given according to the first year the owner acquired a lot in Danville. The occupations are given for 53 of 85 town-lot owners; neither the census nor the other manuscript sources listed the occupations of the remaining 32 owners.

than Beavers, William T. Clark, and John Coleman, all sons of prominent planters.[24]

An interesting case was that of Samuel Hairston, whose brother
George sponsored B. W. S. Cabell's expedition down the Smith River.
Samuel Hairston was often described as the largest slaveholder and
wealthiest planter in the South. A neighboring minister described paradise by saying that it is as beautiful as Mr. Hairston's. When Hairston
chose to invest in Danville, he picked a plot on Wilson Street, which was
named after his close relatives. The Wilsons, as described in earlier chapters, were both one of the county's oldest and most prominent planting
families and a leading force behind the founding and growth of Danville.
Through the Wilsons, Hairston was also related to those two other out-
standing Pittsylvania families, the Tunstalls and the Pannills. What is
significant about all this is that it underlines a point made in earlier
chapters: for Pittsylvania and Danville, at least, it is impossible to make
any real distinction between planting and merchant money. As Karl Polanyi might have it, there were no separate spheres of circulation. The
planters, including the most prominent, were not only drawn into Danville's growth, but were also instrumental in creating it in the first
place.[25]

While Samuel Hairston was only investing money in Danville, other
lesser lights were investing their whole fortune in the town's mercantile
life. Between the mid-1840s and 1854 the number of mercantile estab-

Danville Businessman	Pittsylvania Businessman	Planter	Manufacturer	Teacher
2	1	4	1	—
3	1	—	—	1
5	1	4	1	—
3	3	5	8	—
13 (25%)	6 (11%)	13 (25%)	10 (19%)	1

lishments grew from about six to thirty and included banks, hotels, and the town's first insurance company. One of the new retail shops was a bookstore. In tune with the mood of the town, the bookstore's first advertisement highlighted *Freedley's Practical Treatise on Business.* The book was described as being an "inquiry into the chances of success and causes of failure in business."[26]

Prominent among the new firms was the mercantile house of William Grasty, a man with deep family roots in Pittsylvania. The Grastys were among the oldest and most successful merchant families in upper Pittsylvania. Philip Grasty, the family patriarch, had been a partner of Samuel Pannill. On his own, Philip was the master of what in effect was a proprietary village, Mt. Airy, located in central Pittsylvania along the Staunton River. Philip Grasty owned the Mt. Airy blacksmith shop, tailor shop, tavern, and mercantile store. In addition, he was the justice of the peace and the local postmaster. His main business, however, was in serving as a crop broker, connecting local planters with buyers in Lynchburg and Danville. To service his brokerage work, he ran a simplified banking system, holding money for safe keeping and future payment and advancing loans, all for a fee, of course.[27]

When Philip Grasty died in 1827, his young nephew William Grasty took over the business of the town. William had already proven himself by saving over $700 in three years while clerking in the store of another merchant. William maintained his uncle's business at Mt. Airy until the early 1840s. Then, when faced with the lingering effects of the cyclical downturns that had begun in 1837, he decided to move to Danville. He sold his inheritance through an advertisement in the *Danville Register,* which described the Mt. Airy business as a great catch for an alert capitalist, and then used the proceeds of the sale to establish himself in Danville.[28]

Once in Danville, Grasty both shared in and helped create Danville's success. The move to Danville greatly increased the volume of his mercantile activity. In Mt. Airy, at the end, the volume had not exceeded $100 a month; in Danville, the volume immediately increased to a sum between $800 and $1,000 a month. In addition, as at Mt. Airy, he worked as an agent for the sale of the crops of large planters. A number of his Mt. Airy clients, including the prominent Alexander Bruce of Halifax, transferred their business to Grasty's Danville operation after his move there.[29]

As Grasty prospered, he moved into new and, for Danville, innovative ventures. After a brief fling in smithing and tobacco manufacturing, he became heavily involved in fertilizer importation and cattle breeding. In the late 1850s he bought and sold large quantities of Peruvian guano, and as the Civil War approached he also purchased chemical fertilizers. At about the same time, he began corresponding with Northern experts on ways of introducing Northern cattle to improve the quality of local herds. His correspondence led him to read extensively on ways of introducing Durham-improved short horn cattle into the area. Given the poor grasses and heat of the southern Piedmont, Grasty's cattle studies produced no major benefits for Danville. But while Grasty was pursuing the doomed path of diversification, others were investing in the source of Danville's future, tobacco manufacturing.[30]

9

TOBACCO MANUFACTURING

🖋 🖋 🖋 🖋 🖋 🖋 🖋 🖋 🖋 🖋

"[T]he appropriate American emblem should be not the eagle but the spittoon."
—Heimann, *Tobacco and Americans*

VIRGINIA WAS the largest slaveholding state, and slavery supposedly tainted all that it touched economically. What, after all, could be further from the spirit of innovation and manufacturing than slavery, let alone a society capable of erecting an abstract justification for such a stultifying and wasteful institution?

But deductive reasoning about the inherent nature of slave society cannot explain away the rapid and sustained industrial growth Virginia (and Danville) experienced in the two decades before the Civil War. In the years before secession, at the same time that George Fitzhugh and George Frederick Holmes were trumpeting the cause of atavistic and declining elements in Virginia's social structure, farmers and planters were using their investments to fuel the economic boom that saw Virginia surpass Maryland as the South's leading manufacturing state (see Table 9-1).[1] In 1850 Maryland produced manufactured goods valued at $33 million and Virginia at about $27 million. Over the next decade Maryland's manufacturing grew by a healthy 26 percent, but the value of Virginia's manufacturing almost doubled during the same period. On the eve of the Civil War, Virginia's manufactured goods were worth 21 percent more than those of its Northern neighbor. Within Virginia, the value of manufactured tobacco grew 400 percent between 1840 and 1860, until in 1860 the $16 million product of the tobacco industry accounted for a third of the value of all the state's manufacturing.[2]

Danville's leading citizens were enthusiastic about the growth of industry. In the late 1820s and into the 1830s, there had been attempts to harness the water power of the Dan River for cotton manufacture. These attempts had failed, but a few businesses, notably foundries and flour

TABLE 9–1
Economic Growth, 1840, 1860

	1840	1860	Rate of Growth
Maryland			
Capital Invested in			
Manufacturing in Millions	$14.9	$23.2	56%
Value of Manufactured Products			
in Millions	$33.0	$41.7	26%
Virginia			
Capital Invested in Manufacturing			
in Millions	$18.1	$26.9	48%
Value of Manufactured Products			
in Millions	$26.6	$50.7	90%

Sources: U.S. Census, Manufacturers, 1840; U.S. Census, Manufacturing Schedule, 1860.

mills, had been able to take advantage of the water power. The area's blacksmiths set up shop near the major foundry on the canal, and there, using large forges and tilt hammers driven by water power, they made or maintained ploughs, axes, hoes, mill irons, wrought iron work required for mills, machinery, mechanic's tools, and plantation utensils.

In the late 1840s, as the economy began to open up, Danville's mayor was Ptolemy Watkins, the owner of the largest foundry along the canal. Watkins's main business was in wholesaling ploughs and heavy hardware in the Dan Basin. Seeing the possibilities for growth, he set out to expand the town's hardware production. In this he was strongly supported by the *Danville Register*, which urged the citizenry to:

ENCOURAGE YOUR OWN MECHANICS

Do this, and they can encourage you. . . . No one thing can be more positively injurious to the real interests of any town than to go over the heads of its own mechanics and buy elsewhere. It takes out of the place money which justly belongs at home. It discourages and drives away mechanics. It prevents them from advancing in prosperity, so as to add to the success of their own town.

There are people who think no article can be good for anything, unless it be an imported one. Such persons are enemies to the towns in which they live.[3]

If people who imported were the natural enemies of the town, the people who made it possible to export products were the natural heroes, and the heroes of Danville were its tobacco manufacturers. It was their industry that provided the chief engine of the town's progress.

THE EVOLUTION OF TOBACCO MANUFACTURING

Until the 1830s the bulk of the tobacco grown in Virginia was exported abroad. But in the late 1820s the growth in the size of the domestic market and the development of new styles in tobacco consumption generated the growth of manufacturing in Virginia. Eighteenth- and early nineteenth-century Americans generally took their tobacco in the form of snuff, but in the 1820s there was a dramatic movement away from snuff and toward chewing tobacco. The use of tobacco for chewing was a distinctly American custom. On a cultural level, it was part of the self-conscious attempt to separate America from Europe. It was a rejection of the effete European custom of gently snuffing tobacco for the manly mode of masticating large clumps of the weed. "Chawin tobaccy" belonged to an age when Noah Webster was trying to create a distinctly American language, the Hartford Wits a distinctly American literature, and Benjamin Rush a distinctly American medicine.[4]

Chewing was ideal for the working man; he could carry a twist or plug of tobacco in his back pocket, and when he felt the urge he could bite off a chunk and keep working. It was a natural for a man who did not have the leisure to light up a pipe and who had all of the outdoors as his personal spittoon. A powerful salivant, it kept the mouth moist, and its appetite-suppressing qualities made the long stretches between meals more tolerable. Chaw, popular among both rural and urban people, was a natural symbol of the informality and vigor of the age of Jackson. Visually this produced "the ochre-stained beard, the dark, ground down teeth, and the arching brown trajectory of expectoration leaping through air on its way to a (hopefully) safe home in the dank depths of (indoors) the omnipresent spittoon."[5]

The joys of expectoration became common in part because tobacco manufacturing became widespread. Both grew very quickly in the 1820s and 1830s. Tobacco manufacturing grew quickly not only because of the demand but also because the technical procedures for processing tobacco twists of rectangular plugs were so simple. The skills were fairly easy to acquire and little was needed in the way of capital equipment. In addition, the absence of Northern competition (as in textiles) meant that entry into tobacco manufacturing was very easy, so that about the same time large numbers of planters and urban businessmen began investing in tobacco manufacture. "If Jamestown was the cradle of America's leaf exporting tradition, Danville was the cradle of leaf marketing and manufacturing."[6]

Tobacco manufacturing in Virginia first developed in the centers of the tobacco export trade, Lynchburg, Richmond, and Petersburg. In the late 1820s and 1830s, a considerable business was built up around producing chewing plugs made from the heavy and dark fire cured tobacco grown in the central Piedmont and the Tidewater. Whereas in most areas tobacco manufacturing was concentrated in the cities, in the Dan Basin of Virginia and North Carolina it was centered in the countryside. Joseph Martin (of *Martin's Gazeteer*) described the situation in 1835: "Nearly every planter who raises tobacco to any extent is a manufacturer; but there are some who make a business of it, and purchase the article in leaf from their neighbors, without prizing at a very liberal price." By the 1840s nearly all of the tobacco grown in Henry County, Pittsylvania's neighbor to the west, was bought loose (unprized) by small local manufacturers.[7]

Bright tobacco was the key to the widespread development of manufacturing in the southwestern Piedmont. The bright leaf, grown on a hit-and-miss basis everywhere in Virginia, was grown most frequently in the sandy soils of Pittsylvania and Henry counties. The consumers of chewing tobacco wanted a leaf that not only tasted good but also looked good, and they liked the golden color of the bright leaf best. Manufacturers realized that there was a strong preference for the golden leaf and were willing to pay a premium for it. The bright leaf the manufacturers treasured was more delicate than the standard dark leaf and unable to stand up to the bruising pressure of being compressed and prized for shipment. Because it was difficult to prize raw bright leaf for shipping, and because manufacturing chewing tobacco was a relatively simple process, the planters of the southwestern Piedmont were in a good position to move into tobacco manufacturing.[8]

A writer who studied the manufacturing procedures in Richmond, Lynchburg, and Petersburg in the 1820s was struck by their simplicity. Briefly, this is how tobacco was manufactured in the first third of the century. If the tobacco was dry when it was received, it was watered. When the leaves were sufficiently moist to be easily manipulated, they were detached from the stem or middle rib of the tobacco leaf. Then the leaf was rolled onto a ropelike cylinder and twisted until it gave the appearance of a braided rope. After that the tobacco was prized, that is, placed in wooden containers and then compressed under heavy pressure. With the exception of the prizing, the technique used differed only slightly from those practiced in the seventeenth century. It was only later with the advent of rectangular chaws and flavored plugs that sophistications were added to the process.[9]

In the 1830s most of the Pittsylvania tobacco crop was of the dark and heavy variety. It was generally prized for shipping and then sold either to exporters or Lynchburg or Petersburg manufacturers, who processed it in the manner described above. Probably not even half the crop was shipped by way of Danville. In 1835 there were only two tobacco warehouses there, which were supervised by state inspectors who examined and evaluated the quality of the leaf. A small portion of the quality leaf was acquired by the two small local manufacturers located in Danville. But by the mid-1830s the Danville manufacturers were presented with another way of obtaining their raw leaf. They could buy loose tobacco brought in to them directly from the fields. Loose tobacco was very difficult to transport long distances but it could easily be carried into Danville from the surrounding fields, thus saving the trouble and expense of prizing, a process which could injure the tobacco.[10]

The panic of 1837 was a calamity for most of Danville's tobacco enterprises; the town's two warehouses went under along with a number of the larger mercantile firms. With the merchants ruined they were unable to advance credit to the planters and farmers who had sold through them, so that the local producers had to market their crop elsewhere. The only tobacco enterprises that survived the crash were the manufacturers, who continued to operate on a reduced scale.

The breakdown of the town's established tobacco marketing patterns inadvertently led to a series of marketing innovations, innovations which eventually culminated in the kind of auction marketing system for which tobacco is now famous. The seeds of what became the world-renowned Danville auction were sown when, in the wake of the breakdown of the town's economy, new ways of acquiring tobacco had to be found. Either the manufacturer or his agent rode out to the nearby tobacco curing barns in order to negotiate on the spot for the crop. Alternatively, the manufacturer would buy some of the loose bright leaf which was irregularly brought into the town. "Occasionally a planter would drive into the central part of the town with a load of unprized tobacco. With the assistance of the town crier, nearby tobacco manufacturers were warned by notes from a long tin bugle that tobacco could be purchased from a wagon in the streets. Services of an amateur auctioneer were called into use; manufacturers drew samples from the load and bid according to the merits of the sample. After the conclusion of the sale, the tobacco was carried to the factory of the buyer."[11] The Danville manufacturers already had the advantage of being in the area where bright was most likely to be found, and the auction system gave them another advantage. Their selectivity in purchase allowed them to establish a reputation for producing quality manufactured tobacco.

The local manufacturers played on their advantages, and between 1840 and 1850 the value of the tobacco manufactured in Danville and lower Pittsylvania more than doubled. Although manufacturing thrived, the state warehouse inspections necessary for tobacco exporting were not revived, so that virtually all of Danville's tobacco trade was in tobacco for manufacturing. The surrounding countryside became so focused on producing for the local manufacturers that many of the farmers and planters did not own the tobacco prizing machines used to compress the leaf in preparation for export.[12]

After the collapse of the state inspection warehouse in 1837, there was no state inspection in Danville until the eve of the Civil War. This meant that Danville, despite its rail connection with Richmond and its network of feeder roads and rivers, never became a major tobacco marketing center in the antebellum years. The primary source of Danville's growth was tobacco manufacturing, an almost ubiquitous enterprise in lower Pittsylvania in the quarter of a century before the Union divided. In addition to the relatively large manufactories in Danville proper, there were innumerable small-scale operations run by the tobacco farmers and planters of the surrounding countryside. Indeed, it was not until 1850 that manufacturing production in Danville itself exceeded that of its hinterland.

THE TOBACCO MANUFACTURERS

With a relatively easy entry for producers and a vast number of independent retail sales outlets, tobacco manufacturing and sales was a highly competitive business. The manufacturers faced a rough-and-tumble world. George Kane, a Danville manufacturer, tried to characterize it in a letter to one of his partners, who was a doctor: "Your intercourse in life," he wrote, "has been with gentlemen of the profession—I have known the business world—and you may rely on it, there is very little friendship in the trade."[13] The best known of the Virginia manufacturers, men like John Thomas of Richmond (and later Danville), Maurice Moore of Lynchburg, and William T. Sutherlin of Danville, were famed for their intensity and drive. A eulogizer of Thomas, who was particularly known for his aggressiveness, stated that "in the conflicts of business, he did show a very natural unwillingness to be beaten. He had an imperial nature, perhaps sometimes imperious and the business rival who got in his way might be runover."[14]

Drive and dedication were essential in this classically Smithian industry where the competition was wide open. And, as might be expected, there was a high rate of turnover. Of the forty-three firms operating in the Pittsylvania area in 1850, only twelve remained by 1860.[15]

The intense competition made an intimate knowledge of the crop a prerequisite for success. In his capacity as a buyer, the manufacturer had to choose a leaf wrapper that would appeal to fickle consumers. This required an ability to make small distinctions between the seemingly similar masses of loose tobacco brought before him. It is no wonder that almost all of the tobacco manufacturers in Pittsylvania, whether they were located in the countryside or Danville, were men who had grown up with tobacco.[16]

An intimate knowledge of tobacco was a necessary but not a sufficient condition for success in tobacco manufacturing. Because manufactured tobacco was sold on consignment, the manufacturer had to have considerable credit to maintain his operations until he was paid by the wholesalers and retailers distributing his product. Here the rural manufacturers of central and northern Pittsylvania were at a considerable disadvantage because of their inability to secure credit. Whereas there were five banks in Danville, there was only one in the rest of the county. The legislative petitions of the rural, planter-manufacturers made it clear that their operations were constantly imperiled by a lack of credit.[17]

The most stable and most successful operations were located in Danville where the men who became tobacco manufacturers had already, through their previous occupations, acquired considerable experience in dealing with the problems of credit and marketing. William Ayres, for instance, had run first a confectionary and then a carriage upholstery shop before taking on tobacco. Other Danville manufacturers of the 1860s had been or still were merchants, hotel keepers, machine shop owners, blacksmiths, and foundry owners. Similarly, in the countryside, the most successful manufacturers had been or continued to be tanners, flour mill owners, merchants, and distillers.[18] The movement into tobacco manufacturing did not involve any break with the past; rather, it was a natural extension of the entrepreneurial population's earlier mercantile interests. A brief history of the Williams family will illustrate this point.

The Williams brothers, James and Robert, and their nephew Thomas Neal became tobacco manufacturers in the 1850s, but the family's involvement in Danville began with the patriarch of the clan, Captain Mastin Williams, who was one of the founders of the town. The captain also played a part in the boom years following the opening of the Dismal Swamp Canal. In 1818 he built the Exchange, the town's first hotel. Before his death he also purchased the town grist and saw mills, the first town enterprises to take advantage of the canal B. W. S. Cabell had built along the falls. When the captain died in the late 1820s, his two sons, James Mastin Williams and Robert W. Williams, inherited his enterprises and investments.[19]

Using the Exchange Hotel and tavern as their headquarters, the two brothers diversified their interests during the economic revival of the early 1830s. They built two large brick buildings to house the mercantile and grocery businesses they had started and then established a branch operation in nearby Madison, North Carolina. In 1836 they opened a blacksmith's shop and foundry on land along the canal inherited from their father; here they utilized the water power of the Dan.[20] For the welfare of the town at large, their most significant undertaking was the opening of a bateau line on the Dan River. The bateaux provided a regular connection between Danville and the Petersburg Railroad at Weldon, sixty miles to the east. With some exaggeration, a later observer commented that "this line carried all the freight to and from this whole section of the country."[21] But despite their accomplishments, the Williams brothers were eventually overshadowed by their nephew, Thomas Neal.

Neal got his start when the brothers took him into the family businesses. First he was sent out to learn the milling business and then he
became a salesman and later a partner in the dry goods store. As one
commentator put it, "the junior partner, Mr. Neal was specially noted
for his energy and business push."[22]

In 1835 Neal began to strike out on his own. He became the town's
only regular tobacco auctioneer, serving the three warehouses of Danville's infant tobacco industry. Neal lived the cliché, "he got in on the
ground floor." The warehouses were frequented by the pioneer tobacco
manufacturers of the Dan Basin as well as buyers from Virginia's cities.
When the Danville tobacco market crashed in the depression of 1837,
Neal came out standing on his feet. Although he had no capital to con-
tribute, he was asked, because of his extensive knowledge of tobacco
purchasing, to become a partner in one of the surviving manufacturing
companies.[23]

While his uncles pursued their diversified interests, Neal stuck with his
ailing tobacco manufacturing business through the slack years of the
early 1840s. When the industry began to expand in the late forties, the
Williams brothers took up tobacco manufacturing on a small scale. Neal,
on the other hand, had a thriving business. The 1850s were kind to a
man with Neal's knowledge, drive, and connections. Although a relatively poor man before the boom of the fifties, by 1860 he owned 37
slaves, $22,000 in real estate, and $26,500 in personal estate, far sur-
passing his well-to-do uncles.[24]

THE LABOR FORCE

Just as Thomas Neal came to overshadow his uncles through his success in tobacco manufacturing, so tobacco manufacturing came to overshadow the rest of Danville's economic life. A visitor to Lynchburg, one
of the rival tobacco towns, described the comparable effects of tobacco's
dominance there:

> Tobacco is the idol of the Lynchburgs. In it are their fortunes,
> and in it are beggar's graves. If there are movements in the firma-
> ment, the only concern is to know how they will effect the tobacco
> crops and market. If the earth is shaken by wars and trodden by
> pestilence, they care nothing, should the idolized staple come regu-

larly to their town. They take the planter by the hand, they press him to their bosoms, and inquire, with almost tearfull solicitude, how the crop stands the wet—the drought—the heat—the cold—how it ripens—has he cut yet—has he begun manufacturing or shipping? They talk about the last crop; they grow wise over the prospects of the market; they are full of calculations as to the tobacco still growing in the fields. A merchant may be in the port or whiskey lines, but he knows that he will not sell much of either, if any undue misfortune should befall the tobacco people; another may be in the dry goods way, and yet, if this crop fails, he may hang up his yardstick. Consequently, these interests, and all other interests, are linked with the ups and downs of the weed itself. It is hardly possible to buy a Bible or a tea-kettle, without falling into a discussion of the crop, or at least being affectionately invited to partake of a reviving quid [chew].[25]

If tobacco was dominant in Lynchburg, a larger and more diversified city, what were its effects on Danville? In addition to being a tobacco center, Lynchburg served as the entrepôt for the agricultural products of all of southwestern Virginia (most of which is now West Virginia) and parts of eastern Tennessee. By comparison, Danville serviced a far smaller area composed of the Dan and its tributary river valleys. Moreover, whereas Lynchburg was both a tobacco manufacturing and tobacco marketing center, Danville since the crash of 1837 had focused exclusively on tobacco manufacturing.

In the late 1840s tobacco manufacturing became the linchpin of Danville's economy, employing one-half of the labor force. After a decade of growth and expansion of the hinterland, tobacco manufacturing still employed nearly half the labor force (see Table 9-2). Tobacco manufacturing maintained its centrality for three major reasons. First, Danville was unable to compete with Lynchburg as a center for export sales. Second, tobacco manufacturing itself did little to generate auxiliary industry or business, that is, in the parlance of Myrdal and other economists, it had few spread effects. Finally, although Danville's hinterland had expanded to include some nontobacco areas, most of the area served by the town's transportation network was also caught up in the bright tobacco boom of the 1850s. This was particularly true of the immediately adjacent counties to the west, southwest, and south in both Virginia and North Carolina.

Throughout Virginia, the work force in tobacco manufacturing was

TABLE 9–2
Employment in Danville Tobacco Manufacturing, 1850, 1860

	1850	1860
Tobacco Workers as a Percent of Total Labor Force	51%	46%
Tobacco Workers as a Percent of Total Population	22%	20%

Source: U.S. Census, Manufacturing Schedule, 1850, 1860.

almost entirely black. Unlike industries such as iron manufacturing that used some skilled whites along with semiskilled and unskilled blacks, tobacco manufacturing had no need for specially trained whites. And unlike textiles, which could employ either white or black labor as neither had had any previous experience, tobacco manufacturing needed black laborers because of their extensive experience in the care and handling of tobacco. The initial development of tobacco manufacturing as an auxiliary enterprise on the plantations produced a large pool of trained black labor from which Danville could draw once it had developed its own manufacturing capacity. As a consequence, Danville was the least white of Virginia's small cities. Only 8 percent of Danville's population consisted of white males aged twenty-one or older, compared to 13 percent or 14 percent for similar places like Lynchburg or Staunton (see Table 9-3). Another reason for Danville's small white population was that, although the number of skilled and semiskilled white workers increased almost fourfold between 1850 and 1860, the factory-dominated work force contained a very low percentage of artisans (see Table 9-4).

The unskilled white population increased somewhat between 1850 and 1860, but it was overshadowed—both in absolute and relative terms —by the dramatic increase in black workers, who were largely employed in the tobacco factories and in transportation. During that decade the total black labor force more than doubled, growing from 747 workers in 1850 to 1,668 in 1860 (see Table 9-5).[26]

Although it is difficult to know precisely, it appears that in tobacco manufacturing per se about half of the increase in laborers resulted from the expanded use of hired slaves. It was the tobacco manufacturers, as opposed to the merchants, who made the most use of hired labor. For instance, in 1850 William T. Sutherlin, Danville's largest tobacco manu-

TABLE 9-3
The Racial Composition of the Labor Force, 1860

Town	Percent White Male 21	Percent White	Percent Free	Percent Free Black	Total Population
Danville	8%	46%	51%	5%	3,689
Lynchburg	14%	55%	60%	5%	6,857
Petersburg	13%	52%	72%	20%	18,278
Staunton	13%	74%	77%	3%	3,906
Winchester	14%	68%	84%	15%	4,394

Source: U.S. Census, Population Schedule, 1860.

facturer, owned only five slaves and rented a minimum of nineteen. In 1860, he owned thirty slaves, and (making the unlikely assumption that all of these thirty were used in manufacturing) he rented at least ninety.[27]

Slave hiring gave a manufacturer considerable flexibility in an industry where fixed costs were relatively low and labor costs were one of the two largest (along with the purchase of the leaf) yearly expenditures. The slave hirer did not gain as slaves appreciated in value but the hirer avoided the risk of death or injury to the slave, and, most importantly, the hirer could make seasonal and even intraseasonal adjustments in the size of his labor force.[28]

Slave hiring was traditionally done in late December and early January, with all hires expiring the following December, but if the need arose a manufacturer could hire later in the season if he was willing to pay the price for a full year's hire. There was a wide range of prices for different types of hired slaves. Sutherlin, for instance, paid from between $50 and $145 for an adult male and between $30 and $53 for a boy. At the end of every year the hirer could evaluate the work of the hirees, and thus rid himself of those who had been troublesome or insufficiently productive, while providing bonuses for those he was pleased with and planned to rehire.[29]

Another important way of responding to changed labor needs was joint hiring. It was not uncommon for businessmen to pool their resources to acquire the labor of a group of hires. This was fairly easy to do because in many cases hired slaves in Danville and Pittsylvania circulated within a network of planters, manufacturers, and merchants. After

TABLE 9–4
Artisans as a Percent of the White Labor Force, 1860

City	Percent
Staunton	42%
Lynchburg	33%
Richmond	44%
Danville	18%

Sources: U.S. Census, Population Schedule, 1860; Berlin and Gutman, "Natives and Immigrants."

the harvest, a planter might have an excess labor supply while a merchant might need temporary help in face of the postharvest buying rush, and so on. For instance, Sutherlin rented slaves jointly with a wide range of people including lawyer James Garland, craftsmen George and James Price, planter and transport entrepreneur Walter Fitzgerald (he owned a fleet of wagons), and merchants Levi Holbrook and William Grasty.

Grasty was particularly active in the slave hiring trade. He first became involved in slave hiring in the late 1820s, when he was able to hire out most of the slaves acquired in a fortuitous marriage. When he moved from upper Pittsylvania to Danville in the 1840s, he began to serve as a slave hiring broker for his up-country planter clients interested in renting their slaves out in Danville. The networks created by Grasty helped to integrate rural and urban labor markets, thus vitiating, in part, the rigidities imposed by the slave labor system.[30]

TOBACCO PRODUCTION

The manufacturers' innovative approaches to acquiring a labor force were matched by the increasing sophistication of their product. Tobacco manufacturing was initially a very simple process, requiring little in the way of equipment or machinery. Despite this basic simplicity, new equipment and new techniques were developed in the 1850s as a response to the intense competition between the rival brands of tobacco. As always, taste was the prime mover in the tobacco business, and tobacco chewers increasingly insisted on a sweeter, better-smelling chew. The manufac-

TABLE 9–5
Danville's Population and Labor Force, 1850, 1860

	1850	1860	Percent of Growth
Whites	622 (48%)	1,674 (46%)	132%
Slaves (12 or older, owned by residents)	392 (26%)	805 (22%)	105%
Hired Slaves	286 (12%)	661 (18%)	131%
Free Blacks	69 (5%)	202 (6%)	190%
Number of Workers in Tobacco Factories	327	707	116%

Source: U.S. Census, Population Schedules, 1 (Free Inhabitants), and 2 (Slave Inhabitants), 1850, 1860.
Note: The numbers in parentheses indicate race as a percent of the total population.

turers responded with a wide variety of additives and labeling gimmicks designed to appeal to the buyer's nose, palate, and ego. Time-honored techniques of tobacco production, techniques that had been virtually unchanged for centuries, underwent drastic modification. Joseph Robert succinctly described production under the new techniques. The first stage was unchanged; the tobacco had to be stemmed, but then came a new step, flavoring:

> FLAVORING—dippers soaked the stemmed tobacco in a black, syrupy, compound of licorice and sugar, which had been cooked in massive iron kettles vigorously stirred to prevent scourching. The leaves were then placed in the open air, usually on the factory roof, to dry. To obtain a final bouquet the factory master prepared a fragrant concoction of rum, sweet oil and sundry spices, which some chosen worker sprinkled on the leaves.

> LUMPMAKING—Lumpmakers, seated at benches in a large room somewhat after the manner of school children, took the flavored leaves, molded them into neat rectangular plugs of specified size, and wrapped each in a choice unflavored bright leaf. . . . When the overseer had checked the quality and the amount of the lumpers' work, the lumps were taken to the press room.

PRESSING—In the pressroom, the factory hands fitted the lumps into "shapes," pans subdivided into compartments over which were placed heavy tops, keyed to the rectangular compartments below. The shapes were put in a screw press, which the screwmen operated with a long lever. The first pressing over, the screw was released and the now rather well-formed plugs rearranged in the shapes to attain more perfect alignment of all edges. . . . For the fourth and final prizing the boxes were slipped into billets, or "billies," iron-bound frames, and the screwmen again worked their levers. Workmen fastened the top and branded the box. The plugs were ready for shipment.[31]

The new methods of preparation raised the cost of production substantially. In 1850, when the new techniques were just introduced, in all of Pittsylvania $90,000 was invested in fixed capital to produce $703,000 of finished tobacco products, a ratio of about one to eight. In 1860 the ratio of fixed investment to the value of the product dropped to about one to four, as it took $258,000 in fixed capital to produce $1,104,000 of manufactured tobacco.[32]

The use of water and steam energy to replace the muscle power previously used in pressing increased fixed costs. The tobacco press was similar in form and function to the standard hogshead prize, used to prepare tobacco for shipment, which was common on tobacco plantations throughout the South. Strong male slaves were usually employed to move the presses, even though many of the tobacco factories were located on or near rapid streams. This was because the precise calibration of pressure needed made it difficult to adapt to hydraulic power. This problem was not solved until 1858, when William Cameron of Petersburg developed a sufficiently sensitive mechanism. The hydraulic press was quickly adopted by the larger factories. The 1860 census, while ignoring changes in the Richmond and Petersburg factories, noted that thirteen hydraulic presses were already in use in the rest of Virginia. Three of those thirteen were being used in the Danville firms owned by J. M. Holland, G. T. Pace and Sons, and the jointly owned Sutherlin and Ferrill works.[33]

Steam power was an alternative to the use of water power for pressing. Several Danville companies were in the business of building small steam engines for powering threshing machines, grinders, and circular saw mills. If necessary, they also offered the services of a machinist to install the machine. The local press exulted in these developments. A lead editorial in the Democratic party newspaper announced that "we are pleased to be able to say that for strength, smoothness of operation and workmanship," the steam engine built by the Jonathan Barret Company "surpassed any that came from the shops of the north" and "we understand [it] will sell as low as they can be purchased in northern markets."[34] William T. Sutherlin took advantage of these developments by installing a steam-driven tobacco press in the factory he owned without partners. A pioneer in these efforts, Sutherlin appears to have been the first tobacco manufacturer anywhere in the United States to apply steam power to tobacco manufacturing.[35]

Despite a long tradition of promoting manufactures and a group of enterprising machinists and foundry operators, Danville's economic expansion was based almost entirely on tobacco manufacturing. There was some increase in trade, but no other major sources of income developed either independently of or ancillary to tobacco manufacturing. Tobacco manufacturing, like tobacco planting, generated few backward or forward linkages, that is, supportive services and industries. Similarly, its labor force was either unskilled or so attuned to the peculiarities of tobacco that its skills were not transferrable to other enterprises. Here again, the physical and material limitations of tobacco production are significant, for important segments of Danville's population willingly embraced the ethos of regularity and discipline traditionally associated with the rise of manufacturing in the North.

10

SOCIAL CONTROL

AND SELF-CONTROL

❧ ❧ ❧ ❧ ❧ ❧ ❧

BEFORE THE LATE 1840s and the rapid expansion of the town's manufacturing and transportation capacity, Danville had a small and relatively homogeneous population subject to the kinds of face-to-face controls typical of American village life. Almost all of the slaves lived with their owners or the people they worked for in Danville, most of the laboring whites similarly lived with their employers. There was no way, however, to extend this kind of "supervision" to the new people who streamed into the city in the decade and a half before the Civil War.[1]

The free blacks and slave hires who came to work in the tobacco factories or on roads and rail lines were largely free of the traditional forms of direct personal supervision. At the same time, the railroad, the foundries producing the steam engines for the tobacco manufacturers, and the town's building boom meant that Danville was also faced with assimilating a new and greatly expanded skilled white working class population, a population of strangers who were accustomed to being their own masters. In a town with such a small number of white adult males—they were only 8 percent of the town's population—the skilled workers who represented almost two out of every five white adult males were seen as a potentially disruptive element.[2]

The response to the black influx was straightforward; the city council under Mayor Thomas Grasty instituted regular slave patrols. All white males between eighteen and forty-five were to serve on the patrols. They were to be divided into teams of two and given regular shifts to patrol the town. It was the duty of these two-man patrols to visit the homes of all Negroes, free and slave, "where they had reason to think their services might be required." Furthermore, they had the right to "examine all persons of color, day or night to ascertain their status and their right to be in the town."[3]

The patrol was given the power to "apprehend disorderly white or black." But while force was available, the manufacturers and the merchants tended to think, as in the North, that the gospel was potentially the best policeman of white laborers. In response to the disruptive drinking habits of the white workers, the town's Whig "civic" leaders created a religiously based temperance movement. Temperance speakers and temperance petitions emphasizing self-restraint and discipline became common. Petitions to the legislature requested that all alcohol be banned from Danville, except when used for ceremonial or medicinal purposes. This call for a ban, which was directed at both white and black workers, was led by the largely Methodist merchants and manufacturers. As a stopgap, they took out newspaper ads requesting that their employees (black and white) not be sold liquor.[4]

The temperance campaign produced dividends by 1855, when the Hustings Court refused to issue any liquor licenses for the city, in effect creating a citywide prohibition for those without private means of securing liquor. The court backed up its decision by regularly imposing fines on both those who were caught selling ardent spirits and the buyers. The court followed an evenhanded policy of fining whites and blacks alike for violations.[5]

In response to the initial decision, eleven grateful manufacturers, merchants, and churchmen wrote a revealing epistle of praise to the court. The epistle laid out at length the authors' belief about the connection between personal morality and economic success.

> You have done well to refuse all licenses to a business whose acknowledged influence is not only to destroy both the peace and prosperity but degrade the morals of the community. We know that it is urged by those who oppose your course that it has already greatly impaired and will ultimately destroy the trade of the town. We do not believe that the trade of Danville is based on so slender and insecure a foundation, or that its prosperity is in any degree dependent on the sale of that which ruins not only prosperity and reputation but destroys both body and soul forever. . . .
>
> But if the worst apprehensions of those who favor the license system were well founded, the question would then be, between a

flourishing trade and degraded morals, on the one hand and a crippled traffic with peace quiet and sound morals on the other.

Between the two we do not think you should hesitate for a moment. . . .

If we could but regard the subject impartially, and let reason have fair play we would arrive at the conviction that whatsoever promotes the good order and morality of a place, must increase instead of diminish its trade, unless, it be conceded that depraved appetites rather than enlightened reason rules its inhabitants.

It would be no different matter that most of the liquor which is retailed by those who obtain licenses is by individuals who can ill afford to take from their families. . . .

If the laboring man be bettered the facilities which tempt him to neglect his business and to spend his small earnings in the purchase of that which does not benefit him or his family, but which often reduces them to want, while it destroys himself, he will save the large amounts, thus usually thrown away, and, becoming sober, he will work longer, earn more and *have much more to spend* for the necessaries of life. While he will thus benefit his family in a double ratio, he will not only *spend more with his merchant, but he will now be prompt and certain in his payment.*[6]

While the laboring classes were being exhorted by sermons and policed by patrols, a great number of Pittsylvania's farmers and townspeople were regulating themselves with clocks and watches. Between 1815 and 1860 there was a dramatic increase in the ownership of timepieces. In 1815 there were only 92 clocks in all of Pittsylvania. About one in every twenty-five males aged twenty-one or older owned a clock; in Augusta County the comparable figure was one in sixteen. By 1860 there were 2,000 clocks and watches and more than one adult male in three owned either a clock or watch; in Augusta it was almost one in two. Thus, whereas the county's adult male population increased by about 50 percent, the number of timepieces increased thirteenfold (see Table 10-1).[7]

Along with the locomotive, the clock and the watch symbolized modern economic organization. In 1860, 45 percent of the slaveholders and 63 percent of the adult males in Danville owned either a clock or a watch. Without timepieces work tends to be task-oriented and not sub-

TABLE 10−1

Rural Ownership of Clocks and Watches by White Males over Twenty-one Years of Age, 1850, 1860

	Clocks	Watches
Pittsylvania		
1850	29%	12%
1860	35%	23%
Augusta		
1850	60%	27%
1860	56%	30%

Source: Augusta and Pittsylvania (Personal) Property, 1850, 1860.
Note: These percentages exclude Danville in Pittsylvania and Staunton and Waynesburgh in Augusta.

ject to calibrated controls, but a timepiece allows production to be calculated in measured units of time. As Eugene Genovese puts it: "The advent of clock time represented more than a marking of regular work units—of minutes and hours—and of arbitrary schedules, for it supported the increasing division of labor and transformed that division of labor into a division of time itself. Capitalist production had to be measured in units of labor time, and those units themselves took on the mysterious and apparently self-determining properties of commodities."[8]

The increase in the use of timepieces was part of the growing intensity of economic life in the rural as well as the urban sections of the country. Clocks, which were far more common than watches, may have been of only limited use in gauging field work, but "what made clocks so appealing was their contribution to household efficiency."[9] In affecting the pace of life within the home, where a great deal of productive work still took place, the clock must have also indirectly affected the pace of work in the fields.

Watches were even more significant for field work. Whereas the white population of rural Pittsylvania grew by 12 percent between 1850 and 1860, the number of watches grew by 127 percent, and the percentage of the population owning watches doubled. By 1860 one-quarter of the rural adult males owned a watch. The watch, which could accompany the planter or farmer into the field, allowed for primitive calculations of cost efficiency. And for the slaveholders, more than one-quarter of whom owned watches, they provided a check on the meanderings of an unwilling labor force. "Time was money" even in a Virginia tobacco county.

If a timepiece was useful for a planter or farmer, it was essential for tobacco manufacturers struggling to succeed in a highly competitive industry. A timepiece allowed a manufacturer to gauge the rate of work within each stage of the manufacturing process. But perhaps even more important than the possibility of providing a check on individual and group productivity, it allowed for a precise coordination of the different stages of production, thus eliminating unnecessary waiting time.

In a town blissfully penetrated by the locomotive, the timepiece could only serve as an economic aphrodisiac. By 1860 two-thirds of the white adult males in Danville owned a watch, one-third owned a clock, and one-fifth owned at least one of each. Fully three-quarters of the white adult males owned either a clock or a watch. Many artisans who owned no other taxable item owned a clock. It seems only fitting that the tobacco manufacturers whose industry had transformed the tenor and pace of the town's economic life displayed their leadership and success through the ownership of expensive gold and silver watches.

THE PRODUCER'S IDEOLOGY OF WILLIAM T. SUTHERLIN

William T. Sutherlin, Danville's largest tobacco manufacturer and one of the largest in Virginia, was acclaimed as the town's most prominent and respected citizen. As such his life can be used as a prism through which the history and values of Danville's manufacturers can be viewed.[10]

A classically self-made man, Sutherlin was born in 1822, the son of a yeoman farmer. His father, George Sutherlin, had inherited lands near the confluence of the Dan River and Sandy Creek not far from Danville. William, George's oldest son, was given a formal education despite his father's limited means. William was first sent to a small country school near his home, then to a larger school in Danville, and finally, for a brief period, to a more exclusive boarding academy in neighboring Franklin County. If nothing else, his schooling left him with a taste for literary pretension that later revealed itself in his patronage of Southern Virginia literary societies. He returned to his father's farm and worked there until he was twenty-one, when he went to Danville to try to become a leaf tobacco dealer. Some time after his arrival, he struck a bargain for two wagonloads of manufactured tobacco and headed south to sell it on commission. The trip netted him $700 and provided the capital for further ventures. Little else is known about his early years except that his father, George Sutherlin, was a pious man, deeply opposed to gambling and liquor, who passed this attitude on to William, who refrained from gambling and using alcohol.[11]

Sutherlin gained respect before prosperity. In 1844, at age twenty-two, he was admitted into the Mason's Lodge, a gathering place for the town's leading politicians and businessmen. While Sutherlin was establishing himself in Danville, the town was slowly recovering from the economic doldrums that had plagued it since the depression of 1837. Sutherlin's rise to prominence and the town's revival complemented each other. In 1850 the bridge connecting Danville on the south bank of the Dan with the rest of Virginia washed away. Sutherlin, by then an alderman in the city government, took the lead in organizing a private company to build a new, larger, and sturdier bridge. A year later he became president of the Board of Aldermen, and in 1855, at thirty-three, he was elected to his first mayoral term.[12]

In or out of office Sutherlin was an indefatigable booster. He gave extended and indispensible aid in building the Masonic Temple, a building whose design reflected his outlook. It had three stores on the first floor whose rent paid for the upkeep and mortgage on the building. Sutherlin was also central to building a new and larger Methodist church for the town.[13]

Energetic and well-organized, Sutherlin made time for a wide range of business activities. He was a prominent member of the board of two of the town's banks, a cofounder of the first Danville-based insurance agency, a dabbler in real estate, and one of the founding directors of the Danville Milling and Manufacturing Company, an enterprise aimed at tapping local coal and iron deposits and utilizing the Dan River for textile manufacturing.[14]

His civic and business prominence were born of his success as a manufacturer, a success based in part on his extensive knowledge of all aspects of the tobacco business. He knew the marketing end of the business from his experience in youth as a tobacco peddler, and in 1845 he became what must have been the junior partner in a small tobacco manufacturing operation whose more senior partners were the well-to-do Banister Anderson and A. W. C. Terry. The partnership, begun in 1845, dissolved three years later, and Sutherlin set up his own company, renting a tobacco factory in September 1849. Initially, manufacturing was only a small part of his business. The greater part of his efforts was given over to a standard warehousing operation where he acted as a collector and shipper of other people's tobacco.[15]

It was probably through the contacts he established as a shipper, warehouser, and marketer that Sutherlin learned which farms were the best source of tobacco for manufacturing. During the 1850s, the vast majority of the tobacco produced in the region was the dark, heavy, aromatic tobacco common to the clay lands of most of the Piedmont. In those years Danville and Pittsylvania's growth benefited from the freshness of the soil as compared to the soil-exhausted central Piedmont. But toward the end of the decade bright tobacco became more important. Sutherlin was intensely interested in bright and used his knowledge of the area's farmland to purchase bright whenever he could. At times farmers complained that he was only interested in the bright portion of their crop. He was perhaps the first Danville manufacturer to tap the bright grown on the sandy soils near Yanceyville, North Carolina, twenty-five miles south of Danville, and by the late 1850s he was purchasing the sandy grown tobacco from as far away as Orange County, North Carolina, sixty miles southeast of Danville and thirty miles northwest of Durham.[16]

Sutherlin's success in purchasing bright tobacco was due in part to his detailed knowledge of the region. A similar concern for details was manifest in almost every aspect of his business and private life. He kept at least nine (and probably more) kinds of records. Those that survive include financial records on his investment bonds, savings accounts and loans, records on his tobacco business regarding the purchase of leaf, the sales of manufactured tobacco, the purchase of factory supplies, slave hiring, repair expenditures, and hauling expenditures. There were also more personal records on doctor's expenses for his family and for the slaves, personal expenses for items like cigars and shirts, and records on food purchases. He also kept accounts of his side businesses like home construction and insurance as well as records of his tobacco factories' output.[17]

What these accounts have in common is their chronological and categorical completeness. The records created for Sutherlin a crisscrossed matrix within which he could place his businesses' every motion, including his own actions. The records detailed the exact number of horses' hooves shoed daily; there was almost no item too slight to be recorded, whether it was a small order of nails and tobacco knives or a purchase of cigars for his own pleasure. He knew just how many picks had been

sharpened and how many shoes repaired. Even in the tobacco manufacturing business of which he was sole owner, he listed the money he
personally paid out or received alongside all the other entries in the
ledger.

The vast number of inputs in the way of tobacco, nails, labor costs,
medical costs, and hauling costs led to the production of a great deal of
manufactured tobacco and considerable profit, but very little of that
profit was frivolously expended. His only luxuries appear to have been
cigars and an occasional pair of cuff links.

Sutherlin's frugality was self-conscious. Preaching self-restraint he told
his friend, New England-born Levi Holbrook: "I suppose no one is more
sanguine of the future prospects of Danville than myself and yet I cannot
see any good result from some of the purchases already made in real
estate, for my own part I think I have cause to ask myself, and see that
the prosperity and success which has attended my efforts do not hurry
me into extravagance, all my energy heretofore has been exerted in increasing and improving my business which has uniformly resulted in
profitmaking."[18]

Sutherlin was also a banker and an insurance agent, but his sense of
value was based on production rather than pecuniary gain. Sutherlin
expressed heartfelt attitudes when in a speech before the Danville Mechanics Association he exhorted the men to be thrifty, patient, hard
working, and productive. Extolling the virtues of the producing classes,
he asked the mechanics:

> Why should not a gentleman be a mechanic and a mechanic a
> gentleman? No one can give a reason. Who looks more like a man,
> such as god made in his own likeness—he who stands out in the
> open sunlight, and with healthy ruddy countenance, blended with
> the sweat of toil, and well knit sinewy frame, hurls his good axe
> into the stubborn forest tree, or he who with feeble frame the
> inheritance of a hothouse child, stands in the shade behind the
> merchant's counter, and smilingly measures off, for some fair cus-
> tomer, ten yards of calico, which he positively assures her "Will
> Wash"? Which seems the more elevated position, to hammer the
> red iron on the ringing thundering locomotive, or sit lazily in some
> professional office and talk politics, or study idly at the street cor-
> ner and discuss with learned criticism the dresses of the ladies as
> they pass?[19]

Sutherlin's heroes are producers and men of action, common men with
the mettle to match any aristocrat. At the head of his honor roll was

> Ben Franklin the printer, who was not ashamed, with his own
> hands, to trundle through the streets of Philadelphia the wheelbar-
> row that contained his little lot of paper, all that in his poverty he
> could purchase, and Roger Sherman, the poor Connecticut shoe-
> maker, each by sobriety, industry and intellect, became a member
> of that congress which ushered a nation into being; and both of
> them, as members of the committee that framed the Declaration of
> Independence, stood side by side, acknowledged equals with Jeffer-
> son, Livingstone and Adams, who belonged to the most aristocratic
> classes of society. Sheffey too could rise from his hammer and lap
> stone in the Valley of Virginia, and fearlessly cope with the sarcastic
> wit of the aristocrat Randolph of Roanoke, in the Halls of Con-
> gress; and Andrew Jackson, rising from the humble position of a
> country constable in South Carolina, by dint of energy and intellect
> became the hero of New Orleans, and the idol not merely of a
> powerful party, but of a whole people.[20]

For Sutherlin, the just society was a republican society of self-made men.
He saw classes as inevitable in a commercial and manufacturing society
but he vehemently denied their permanence. Speaking in Jeffersonian
terms, he argued:

> These classes of society remain; they are permanent. But of the
> individuals that comprise them, many are constantly passing from
> one to another as changes occur in their circumstances and for-
> tunes; and to secure such a change and transfer from a lower to a
> higher sphere is one of the great struggles of life. . . . Indeed there
> are but few of our prominent men . . . who if they undertook to
> trace their geneology, would not soon run into the mud; while there
> are many imbeciles now in the mire who can easily trace their
> ancestry back to aristocracy.[21]

For Sutherlin and his ilk, whatever their distaste for abolitionist "fa-
naticism," the notion of the Yankee was not and could not be an ideo-
gram for niggling depravity. Sutherlin's paean to opportunity was born
of his experiences in Danville's expanding and efflorescing economy. He
had no need for the consoling ideology of gentility. At the same time,
however, a prosperity generated by an expansion of traditional forms
simply due to a rising price for dark tobacco would not have created the

sense of fluidity and possibility found in Sutherlin. Rather it was the way that bright tobacco led to the economic reorganization first of the countryside and then the town that provided the basis for Sutherlin's "Northern" perspective. This was the sort of perspective the representatives of Pittsylvania would bring with them into the great secession convention of 1861.

II

A WAR TO

END SLAVERY?

🖋 🖋 🖋 🖋 🖋

A T M I D N I G H T on 2 April 1865, Jefferson Davis fled from the onrushing Union army that was about to seize Richmond. His destination was the burgeoning but relatively obscure southwestern Piedmont town of Danville, a Confederate manufacturing and warehousing center connected to Richmond by rail. In Danville, Davis would use his power—which by then was largely symbolic—in the only way left to him: he would create another symbol. He would make Danville "the last capitol of the Confederacy," so that the town came to exemplify the "lost cause" and the willingness to resist Yankeedom in the face of overwhelming odds.

Both the history of Danville and the history of Davis's brief sojourn there belie all that is resonant in the idea of the lost cause. While in Danville, Davis stayed at the home of William T. Sutherlin, then a major in the Confederate quartermaster corps. Sutherlin's home, Jefferson Davis's final resting place before the collapse of the Confederacy, was the home of a Southern Yankee.

There was another guest in the Sutherlin home when Davis arrived, also a refugee. He was Levi Holbrook, a Yankee both in spirit and birth and a close friend and business associate of Sutherlin. Holbrook's openly Union politics after Sumter had forced him to seek safety within the Sutherlin home. Jeff Davis had fled from one group of Yankees only to land in the bosom of another.[1]

THE RESPONSE TO SECESSION

Danville's path to war was pregnant with possibilities for irony. Danville's response to secession and war were foreshadowed during the statewide tobacco manufacturer's credit crisis of 1857. Credit was the lifeline of the tobacco manufacturer. New banking facilities had been the key to Danville's recovery from the economic slide of the late 1820s. The expansion of credit had played an important role in fueling the town's boom in the late 1840s. And the creditworthiness of the proposed Confederacy was a major concern of Pittsylvania's delegates to the secession convention.[2]

The credit problem which Danville faced in the late 1850s concerned the liquidity of the town's tobacco manufacturers. The *Richmond South* described the situation. An agent for the factors who marketed Virginia's manufactured tobacco in the North

> came to Virginia and offered the usual "liberal" advances on consignments, meaning an acceptance at four months time on from one-half to two-thirds of the value shipped to him. The shipment was made, the tobacco sold, and an account of the sale rendered, with the never failing declaration that the transaction was effected on an EIGHT MONTHS BASIS, when in truth it frequently was for CASH. Even when the product was sold on credit the factor settled balances with the manufacturer only once a year, in the meantime having the use of perhaps a third of the sale price.

Faced with tardy payment on the part of Northern factors, even successful manufacturers were forced to borrow heavily to supply their cash needs. The manufacturers responded to the problem by calling conventions. The first was a regional meeting of the upper Roanoke Valley manufacturers held in Danville in late November 1857. This was followed a week later by a far larger convention in Richmond at which Sutherlin, presumably chosen at the earlier regional meeting, served as the sole representative for all the manufacturers of Danville and Pittsylvania County.[3]

In a time of inflamed sectional tension, the grievances of the Virginia manufacturers could easily have been translated into the political rhetoric of confrontation. Instead, the convention concentrated on a series of concrete proposals designed to tighten credit arrangements between manufacturer and factor by reducing the time between purchase and payment from eight to four months. The convention also called for a reduction in agents' fees and the elimination of a number of minor irritants. It was simply not in the interest of the Virginia manufacturers to exacerbate tensions between themselves and the factors who distributed their goods in the nation's largest markets for manufactured tobacco. Recognizing their mutual self-interest and interdependence with the factors, the manufacturers ended the convention on a conciliatory note:

> We further declare that in exposing what we believe to be the grievances which beset the tobacco trade, nothing has been further from our purpose than to cast imputations of dishonor upon agents; and that such of our strictures as may have a bearing that way, are intended, not for them but for their system of business, which, truth compels us to state, we believe to be radically wrong, and justly liable to all the reforms we have proposed.[4]

The response to the crisis then was a call for reforms, procedural adjustments in the way the trade was to be carried out. Governor Wise responded to the crisis by calling for an expansion of Virginia's banking system. Similarly in Danville the response was to try to secure an increase in the stock and thus the loan potential of the Danville Bank. This required legislative approval and Sutherlin, among others, went to the legislature to solicit their support. The results of his closely watched efforts were widely reported in the press. The *Milton Chronicle* wrote:

> It will hardly be believed that the stock in the Danville Bank, chartered by the legislature of Virginia only a few weeks ago, has all been taken thus soon. Such, however, is the fact. And it is truly astonishing, when we consider the cry of hard times. But what is there in the power of mortal man that William Sutherlin, Esq. of Danville cannot accomplish when he wills the undertaking? To him, we learn, is the institution indebted for almost every dollar's worth of stock obtained. But few, if anyone besides himself, deemed it possible to get half the stock taken, in view of the financial pressure; and we believe that all the other commissioners, despairing of success even before they made a trial, left the whole matter in his hands. To work he went, and almost before the members of the Legislature that chartered the bank returned home and got warm in their seats, Mr. Sutherlin gets $2,000 worth of stock more than is needed. Extraordinary man, truly! The word "fail" is

not in his vocabulary. Ye crackers on whose lips dwell the word "can't" see what energy and perseverance will do! We learn that two thirds of the stock was taken in the county [Pittsylvania].[5]

Already buoyed by the revival of credit, Danville's economy received another boost in 1858, the revival of the nonmanufacturing tobacco market. In the 1830s Danville had been a small center for the ware-housing and sale of state-inspected tobacco. Tobacco, generally destined for foreign markets, was prized by the local farmers and brought into Danville where the inspectors would break open the hogsheads to check them. The panic of 1837 wiped out the Danville warehouse and the state inspections lapsed. Without the state inspection, tobacco could not be sent abroad and since the only buyers to survive the panic were local manufacturers, local farmers who still sold in Danville began bringing loose tobacco into Danville for sale. There was no need to prize to-bacco which was not going to be shipped long distances. The tobacco brought into town was marketed at street auctions attended by the local manufacturers.

Danville's street auction served the manufacturers well. Local farmers who grew quality bright leaf could bring their tobacco into a local com-petitive market without having to trouble themselves and risk damaging their bright by prizing it. But while the manufacturers were well served, a great deal of local dark tobacco was not absorbed by the local manufac-turers and this considerable trade went to Lynchburg or Richmond. In the late 1850s Danville began to recapture this trade lost to Lynchburg. Thomas Neal and his partners spearheaded and waged an aggressive campaign to win over the area's tobacco growers. They personally toured the countryside soliciting new business for the Danville market.[6]

Statewide, the panic of 1857 set off a downward trend in tobacco prices that was still in effect as sectional tensions hardened into civil war. But developments in Pittsylvania and Danville moved counter to this trend; the new infusion of credit, the revival of tobacco marketing and, perhaps most important, the continued high price for the state's pre-mium tobacco, the golden bright leaf, meant that Danville was enjoying a period of prosperity as South Carolina seceded from the Union.

Old Whigs and Democrats alike, Pittsylvania's leaders felt strongly that the South was the aggrieved party in the sectional conflict. Vincent Witcher, the old Whig warhorse, and Democratic spokesman William Tredway made it clear that they saw Northern attacks on slavery as attacks on inalienable property rights the Union created in 1776. But well into the secession crisis, these sentiments were more than counter-balanced by the county's ties to Northern markets and a genuine attach-ment to the Union. In the 1860 election, the county, previously a moder-ately Whig area, gave John Bell a large plurality. In Danville proper, Bell was the overwhelming favorite, collaring 71 percent of the vote, with 15 percent for John C. Breckinridge and 14 percent for Stephen A. Douglas.[7]

As the crisis developed in the months following Lincoln's election, those who spoke out in Danville expressed both a fear of the North and a typically Whiggish fear that secession would unleash social disorder and economic chaos within the South. When a crisis committee formed a home guard of men forty-five and older, it told the guard it was to prepare to defend Danville both from invasion from without and insur-rection from within.[8]

In early January 1861 John Price, the city treasurer, addressed the city council and appealed for his reelection. Price, presumably interested in striking a resonant note, had little good to say about either South Caro-lina or the Northern states. After disparaging both, Price went on to talk about the economic uncertainty that war might engender, stressing the possibility that the war might bring an end to the city's growth.

Similarly, judging by the letters to Sutherlin from his friends and busi-ness associates, the fear of high taxes to pay for a war was as great as the fear of Republican "abolitionism." Virginia businessman Abner Ander-son wrote to Sutherlin that he wanted the state to be the peacemaker, for he saw disunion as bringing only grinding taxes. Henry Muse, patriarch of Museville, an agricultural settlement of about 150 people in central western Pittsylvania, wrote both defending the Union and warning of the economic costs of war: "How can any good man of sense go for the downfall of one of the best governments in the history of the world? Let the wisest man among them tell us what benefit will be derived from such a course of conduct, let them tell us of the cost of arming, and fortifying Virginia, also the supporting and keeping up of armies for all time to come and tell the people where all this expense is to come from, we shall have no federal treasury to call on for aid."[9]

Given the widespread ambivalence if not hostility toward secession, it is not surprising that the two men elected to represent Pittsylvania at the secession convention were both moderate Unionists, William T. Sutherlin and William Tredway, a Douglas Democrat. Tredway, who resided about twenty miles north of Danville near the county seat of Chatham, had been a book and piano salesman in the late 1830s, but by the 1850s he had become a banker. In a speech given at a public meeting in Pitt-sylvania after South Carolina had seceded, he made it clear that while he felt sympathy for the deep South he thought that the Constitution should be preserved. He argued for economic, not political, independence from the North and he condemned both the secession of South Carolina and the Northern abrogation of the fugitive slave laws.[10]

Sutherlin's position as an important public figure placed him under considerable cross pressure. On one hand a business associate from Charleston, South Carolina, wrote to Sutherlin warning of Northern perfidy, stressing that if Virginia joined the secession "the sun would never shine on a more prosperous, happy and contented people, having the only true *Patriarchical* [sic] government."[11] By contrast a business associate from the Mutual Insurance Co. of Greensboro, North Caro-lina, wrote that, "if we were to secede today in less than a year the *middle states* [sic] would have to secede from the *cotton states*. . . . If we cannot live together slavery is gone. . . . I am ready to fight in the union but not out of it. . . . South Carolina rule or ruin democracy has brought us to this."[12]

Sutherlin was subject to cross pressure even from within his family, through his younger brothers. His brother George, an impoverished ne'er-do-well, constantly sought William's succor, in the form of loans, jobs, and introductions. Writing to William, who was then sitting at the secession convention, George complained that, "I am doing nothing and can get nothing to do. Want for some of the necessities of life can't get them." George in his desperate straits may have hoped that secession might bring a new shuffle of the cards: "*I say secede* this week."[13] George went on to warn his brother about black Republican tricks. Days later William received a letter from his brother James, a successful busi-nessman and a partner with William in some Alabama ventures. James assessed the mood in Danville during the convention: "The people here are generally disposed to wait patiently for the results of the peace con-ference at Washington, if that should fail then they will pay more atten-tion to the convention and look for prompt action on their part in some way."[14] This was similar to William's own position; it was only with Sumter that he was willing to vote for secession.[15]

Sutherlin was like other Virginia Whig industrialists in that he was most receptive to the idea of secession when it was couched in terms of the South's industrial growth. One of his business associates, J. B. Sharpe of Memphis, appealed to Sutherlin on just these grounds when he wrote, "You were a Bell man, so were we. We were union so long as any hope remained for its preservation. . . . Would you make Va., Ky., and Tenn., the proudest and wealthiest manufacturing states on the globe, then secede."[16]

The arguments for and against secession centered around its economic consequences. This feeling that Southern independence might be a great boon to Virginia, and for that matter Danville's position as a manufacturing center, was an old and possibly even widely held notion in the town. As early as the 1830s one of the arguments put forth by Pittsylvania legislators for state support for a railroad was that in case of hostility between North and South, Danville would be a natural center for the manufacture of war materials. But while secession held out the possibility of manufacturing prominence for Danville, it also threatened to disrupt the stable conditions under which Danville and Pittsylvania had been prospering for more than a decade. It was the possible disruptive effects of secession that William Tredway, a staunch defender of Southern rights, considered as he spoke at some length before the secession convention.[17]

Tredway called upon the political authority of Edmund Burke and the finanical authority of prominent bankers to buttress his case against secession. He chastised the recklessness of South Carolina, telling his fellow delegates, obviously referring to flush times in Pittsylvania:

> Sir(s), up to the moment of the secession . . . the prosperity of this country was great: all was calm and tranquil; there was no ripple on our political surface; no disturbance of our commercial or social systems; but as soon as secession was resorted to, a panic has spread over this broad land . . . and see the effects . . . not only to the capitalist, with his keen eye, who looks to political causes where he undertakes to invest his money; not only to the workshop, where the operations have been stopped; not only has enterprise everywhere been thwarted and brought to a stand, but panic has gone into the very dwelling of our citizens. . . . Until secession occurred, there was no such evil known in this land.

Because of these consequences Tredway thought South Carolina's secession wrong and unjustifiable. He argued further that the Confederacy which Virginia was being asked to join would, according to respected English bankers, have serious financial problems. Finally, dealing with a subject central to Pittsylvania's burgeoning tobacco economy, he warned that Virginia secession would adversely effect its credit standing: "The credit of the union, . . . has stood high . . . but this shock which has been brought on our commerce, has affected government securities, and no capitalist from Europe or elsewhere will invest his funds in a Southern Confederacy, or the government in Washington as readily as before." Finally, he argued, quoting from Burke, "They [referring to South Carolina] commit the whole to the mercy of untried speculation; they abandon the dearest interests of the public to those loose theories to which none of them would choose to trust the slightest of his private concerns."[18]

Tredway's fears were unfounded as far as Danville was concerned. Although rural Pittsylvania suffered from severe food shortages, Danville became a major economic beneficiary of the war. Securely behind the battle lines, Danville became a haven for Richmond and Petersburg and Lynchburg tobacco manufacturers and warehousemen. Early in the war a large number of these men, including James Thomas, Richmond's largest manufacturer, transferred their operations to Danville. Thomas established a factory in Danville and lived there during the war, but others merely moved their stocks and equipment there. This was a great boon to Danville merchants like Thomas Grasty and William Rison, who rented space to commission merchants from all over Virginia seeking a safe place for their stocks.[19]

Danville's position as a rail center was similarly improved. Danville was never invaded and throughout the war maintained her rail ties to Richmond via the Richmond and Danville Railroad. In 1862 the Confederate government gave top priority to extending Danville's rail connection south to Greensboro, North Carolina, both to provide for increased troop maneuverability and to tap a broader area of supply for the Confederate capital. The net effect was to dramatically increase the level of traffic on the Richmond and Danville line while making Danville a major Confederate supply base and warehousing center. The commander of this supply operation was William T. Sutherlin. Also Danville became an important Confederate ordinance center as some of the tobacco factories in the town and nearby countryside were converted to arms production. In assessing Confederate wartime growth, Mary E. Massey has noted that Danville and Lynchburg came to be symbols of wartime economic growth.[20]

Sutherlin played a central role in organizing this economic change. For example, he was involved in supplying wool, shoes, fertilizer, grain, and coal to the Confederacy. In order to do this he had to organize the expansion of already-existing local production, as in the case of shoes, or create new industries in the case of fertilizer and coal. Existing manufacturing companies like the Danville Manufacturing Co., of which Sutherlin was a director, were expanded and moved into new areas like the production of harvesting tools. Perhaps the most important development for the city was the building by the Confederate government of the Piedmont Railroad connecting Danville to Greensboro. Danville investors, with Sutherlin as their chairman, played a major role in financing the road, but its construction was made possible only because the Confederate government gave the project a top priority. The War Department, insisting on the logistic importance of the line, hired thousands of slaves to build the road. The difficulty Sutherlin had in acquiring slaves for grain harvesting provides an interesting insight into Confederate supply problems. He found the local slave population, which was weaned on tobacco, insufficiently skilled in grain harvesting and so he had to make extensive though unsuccessful efforts to acquire northern Virginia slaves with grain experience.[21]

Sutherlin's efforts on behalf of his government and his city still left him time for purely personal economic ventures. He continued to operate at least part of his tobacco manufacturing and supply operation in Danville, and he maintained his Southern network of salesmen and agents for his products. At one point in the face of the war-induced labor shortage he considered plant modernization through the purchase of another hydraulic tobacco press (used for packing the tobacco). In March 1864, while the Confederate position was deteriorating, he was scheming with R. O. Davidson of Richmond to gather a group of investors for a new venture. He considered some new land speculations in Virginia, but his most extensive new business interests involved buying a large plantation in Alabama with his brother James who had moved there. James and William kept up an extensive correspondence, only part of which has survived. James's letters to William dealt almost entirely with detailed descriptions of crop, slave, and land prices in Alabama. In these long letters there is only one reference to the Yankees and that is oblique. The only references to the war are concerned with the war's inflationary effects. James took no part in the war, ostensibly because of his asthma. But in 1863, faced with dim business prospects and a rampant inflation, he decided to join the war effort by getting a job with the Confederate government.[22]

James Sutherlin was by no means alone in avoiding active participation in the war. Antiwar sentiment was widespread in the southwest Piedmont of Virginia during the last years of the war. "As a result of the seeming hopelessness of the southern cause, many of the best people in parts of Bedford, Botetourt, Montgomery, Giles, Floyd, Franklin, Patrick, Henry and Pittsylvania were said to be completely demoralized."[23] Colonel Robert Withers, a friend of William T. Sutherlin and commandant of one of the prison camps located at Danville, described a category of people he called Danville's "Before breakfast Secessionists." These were men of prominence who, having supported secession, would only enter the military when compelled. Withers included in this category a majority of those who had supported secession. Those who opposed disunion were presumably even less supportive of the Confederacy. As an example of a "Breakfast Secessionist" he cited a young and wealthy Danville man who, rather than joining the army, prepared instead to raise an artillery company. When this scheme fizzled, he prevailed on his grandmother, a wealthy plantation owner, to name him manager of her estate, thus providing for an exemption. When this loophole was closed, he availed himself of another and bought a newspaper in North Carolina and made himself editor-in-chief, editors being exempt from military service. The young man avoided the army for the duration. Sutherlin had considerable personal experience in this regard. In the early spring of 1864, he received a flow of inquiries from friends asking how their children could avoid military service. The tone of their letters indicated that, despite Sutherlin's position as commandant and chief quartermaster, they expected him to be sympathetic. Within Sutherlin's inner circle of friends, his tobacco manufacturing partner B. Ferrel obtained, perhaps with Sutherlin's help, a questionable medical discharge for his son.[24]

Planters, similarly, gave less than their all to the war effort. Pittsylvania regularly failed to meet the quota for slaves requisitioned for military construction work by Governor William Smith. The planters were even reluctant to have their slaves used in less dangerous work as hospital orderlies in Danville. Large numbers of orderlies were needed, and the hospital administration was authorized to hire slaves at a fee of twenty dollars per month. The fee plus patriotic pleas failed to secure anywhere near the number of orderlies needed and a message was sent to the surgeon general:

Having failed after dilligent efforts to procure colored men and women in sufficient numbers to meet the demands of the hospital, I respectfully suggest the expediency of authorizing the Quartermaster of this post to impress the hands of the planters engaged in cultivating tobacco. It would I presume be inexpedient to cripple the agricultural force of the farmers who are raising breadstuffs and other subsistence supplies, but who have turned a deaf ear to every appeal of patriotism and have appropriated their best hands to the production of tobacco during the current season.[25]

Sacrificing the growth of bright tobacco for the Confederacy was sacrificing the future, no matter who won the war. During the war the bright tobacco which had always been prized as wrapper for high-grade manufactured plug was put to new uses as smoking tobacco. Smoking tobacco had been little used before the war. But the war brought about a change in both taste and production which created a great demand for bright smoking tobacco. Danville and Durham to the south were initially the chief beneficiaries.[26]

Before Lee surrendered to Grant, the Confederate army had surrendered to the pleasures of tobacco. Smoking, as opposed to chewing tobacco, was made far easier by the development late in the antebellum period of the friction match, but the great appeal of smoking may have been psychological. Tobacco stimulation is received far more quickly by smoking rather than chewing tobacco, and thus smoking may have had a great appeal to a soldier in need of a quick lift.

Initially at least, smoking tobacco was forced on the Confederate soldiers by the condition of the available chewing tobacco. Chewing tobacco (plug) spoiled, and some of the plug manufactured before the war began to spoil. "The dealer or the manufacturer merely followed the example of pipe smokers who had long obtained their tobacco by slicing off flakes of plug." As the war progressed and the flavoring materials needed to sweeten the chews were increasingly hard to come by, manufacturers began to intentionally produce smoking tobacco. They had a great captive audience for the efforts, the huge number of Confederate soldiers who moved in and out of Danville along the Richmond and Danville Railroad. The soldiers came to enjoy smoking their tobacco, and Danville tobacco manufacturers had every reason to expect a postwar boom based on the mild and light bright leaf.[27]

Paradox flows freely through Southern history; the growth of Danville's wartime industry and the rise of bright tobacco led in part to one of the small paradoxes alluded to in the introduction. This same area, which only halfheartedly supported entering the war, was willing to transform the labor system to maintain Southern independence. Important factions in Danville wanted to augment the Confederate army with slaves, who in return for fighting would be given their freedom after the war. The *Danville Appeal*, which before the war led the fight for secession by attacking both black Republicanism and Sutherlin, gave considerable favorable attention to arming the slaves in return for their freedom. The newspaper presented its own views on this revolutionary proposition when it quoted the *Richmond Enquirer* to the effect that "If this war was being waged on our part for rights in the territories, this proposition to arm the negroes and liberate negro soldiers would be suicidal. But as it is it is the white man's liberty and not the negroes for which these people are really fighting."[28]

In March 1865, as part of a larger Confederate debate on arming the slaves, two bills were introduced into the Virginia House calling for the use of slave soldiers in return for the slaves' freedom. The first bill, representing the majority report of the committee investigating the issue, recommended that the consent of the owner be required and that the owner receive compensation. This, a relatively mild bill given the perilous state of the Confederacy, received major opposition. The Virginia legislature never formally approved the freeing of slaves who might serve in combat. Representative A. S. Buford of Danville, "tall and slender, the handsome Buford epitomized the Virginia gentleman," presented the second bill, the minority report, and recommended to the legislature that any slave who volunteered be given his freedom and admitted into the army whether the master consented or not.[29]

Buford, who was by both marriage and business closely connected with the county's leading planters and entrepreneurs, used his ownership of the Whig *Danville Register*, the town's oldest and most prestigious paper, to advance his position. He was supported in his efforts by his erstwhile opponents at the Democratic *Danville Appeal*. Further support came from Democrat William Tredway, who ran for the House of Delegates on only one issue, the need to arm the slaves. Tredway also promised that if he were elected, he would try to transform the state legislature into a combat unit.

Elsewhere Whigs, fearing the total breakdown of the social order if the war continued, had been anxious to bring the war to a speedy and orderly end. Similarly, some of the large planters of Louisiana were more than willing to come to terms with the Union if in doing so they could maintain their slave property. Why was Danville different? Perhaps it was not so different. Just as their economic self-interest propelled some large planters into a willingness to accept the Union again, Danville's economic self-interest led it to support the last-ditch efforts for an independent South.

There was support for arming the slaves in Danville because a substan-

tial section of the business and manufacturing class had come to believe
that the city's economic interests would be best served in an independent
South, even if that independence meant the elimination or modification
of slavery. The war had made Danville an important commercial, manufacturing, and rail center, and the growth of the smoking tobacco industry promised to make it the tobacco capital of Virginia. If the war were
lost, however, and older commercial and rail patterns were reestablished,
Danville might sink back into regional obscurity.[30]

Slavery, on the other hand, had already been greatly transformed as a
labor system and as a means of racial control. For nearly a decade and a
half before the war, the city's manufacturers had had extensive experience with a labor force of free negroes and almost free hires. During the
war, Danville swelled with large numbers of hired slaves employed by the
Confederate government. Those black men had worked hard for the
Confederacy during the war when they had every opportunity to be
provocative; why should they be a problem afterward? Slavery had not
been presented as a positive good before the war, but rather as something
that could be dispensed with. For Danville, at least, it seems that the
questions of slavery and racial control were no longer linked. The advo-
cates of arming the slaves for the Confederacy may have come to understand what G. W. Cable meant when he said that "the ex-slave was not a
free man, he was a free negro."[31]

Before the slaves could be used, however, the Confederacy collapsed.
Danville's support for freeing the slaves so that they might fight for
Southern independence could be seen as a manifestation of the kind of
flamboyant Southern nationalism that might be associated with a city
known as the "last capital of the Confederacy." But the response to the
Yankee victory and occupation makes clear the foolishness of such a
proposition. Just as the call for arming the slaves had been designed to
serve the city's best economic interests, the response to the defeat was
similarly pragmatic.[32]

The most heated resistance was not to the invading Federal troops but
to the attempt by the departing Confederate army to blow up the railroad bridge across the Dan. On the morning of 10 April, Jefferson Davis
fled Danville; that afternoon General Lomax's Confederate cavalry entered the town with orders to destroy the span across the Dan and burn
the remaining military warehouses. Lomax was aggressively repulsed by
local elements led by Sutherlin's friend, Colonel Robert Withers. Withers
asked Lomax to desist, but Lomax insisted he had to carry out his orders, whereupon Withers dispatched men to guard the bridge and resist,

by force if necessary, any attempt to destroy it. The matter was not finally resolved until four days later when, at the request of Mayor James Walker, supported by Sutherlin and top manufacturer T. D. Neal, Lomax finally agreed to end his efforts.[33]

Between 13 April and the arrival of Federal troops on 27 April, the town was in chaos. Thousands of Confederate troops were stranded in Danville due to a breakdown of railroad service, and the town was rocked by rioting and looting and by rumors that there were still large food supplies left in the city. Colonel Withers, the men still under his command, Mayor Walker, and his augmented police force had to contain a number of violent mobs. Given the situation in Danville, it is not surprising that the arrival of the Federal troops was greeted with a minimum of hostility. When General Wright, the Union military commander, arrived in Danville, he pitched his tent opposite the Sutherlin mansion, and "he [Major Sutherlin] lost no opportunity to cultivate kindly relations with northerners of influence and to inaugurate a reign of goodwill generally." Sutherlin was not alone in his affability. Other leading citizens like Mayor Walker and top manufacturers W. T. Clark and C. W. Watkins and G. W. Dame, Episcopal priest and leading Mason, dealt peacefully, efficiently, and even sociably with the Union occupation and leadership.

Colonel Withers symbolized the situation. A Colonel Fletcher of Maine was stationed with Withers and asked permission to eat with the Withers family. "Mrs. Withers agreed to the proposition, and he proved a most agreeable and pleasant intimate of the family. The day before he made the arrangement to eat at our table, I had noticed in front of Sutlers door, who had established himself on Main St., a large dried Codfish, and had told my wife that as we all had to turn Yankee now, we had better begin the transformation by learning to eat Yankee food, and advised her to send and purchase a codfish." Withers was not the only one to make personal accommodations. Two days after the arrival of the Union troops, the Union army newspaper personals column was filled with propositions for liaisons made by Danville women to Union soldiers; it was hardly a frosty welcome.[34]

Sutherlin saw the war's conclusion, unfavorable as it was, as a release from the dampers of the "Old Virginia." He mourned neither the passing of slavery nor the passing of the "old Tidewater aristocracy"; he told the Border State Agricultural Society in 1866:

Let us abandon the unprofitable and corrupting study of politics, and devote our leisure hours to the reading of agricultural journals. . . . We should remember . . . that no laws or forms of government can relieve us from the necessity of labor. Our future success will depend on our individual effort. Those who make nothing, will have nothing; whilst each citizen will be allowed the proceeds of his own labor, no one being allowed to claim the proceeds of another's earnings without just compensation. . . . We would demonstrate to the world that if we cannot *command* we can do more, we *can deserve success.*[35]

Rather than being seen as a denouement, the war's end was seen as a release, as the Episcopal priest, G. W. Dame, wrote shortly after the war: "The energy of the people of Danville is such that it cannot be kept down a moment longer than the iron rod binds. The town is destined to be one of the important inland towns of Virginia." Dame envisioned Danville using its water power to become a major textile manufacturing center, but while it would be fifteen years before textile manufacturing would be important, the promise of tobacco blossomed at the war's end. New manufacturers and new money were attracted to the golden lure of the bright leaf, and tobacco manufacturing quickly reestablished itself.[36]

Duval Porter, the "poet laureate" of Danville, described the excitement and energy of postwar Danville:

[W]hen the conflict was over a marvelous change came over Danville. The war prices paid for tobacco soon drew to it a crowd of tobacco speculators from both Virginia and North Carolina. There was a rush and roar on all sides. . . . Fortunes were made in a single year. Men who came there on foot a few years before, rode back to see poor relations in phaetons. The whole town seemed to revolutionize, and the most extravagant dreams of its future greatness began to be indulged in.

Porter, a self-ordained spokesman for the old gentility, went on to describe these developments in the manner of a Roman who was witnessing the breach of the city walls by the onrushing barbarian hordes:

[W]hen the speculation craze struck the town, there poured in from the counties adjacent to Danville, a crowd of adventurous spirits who did not know "B from a bulls foot," so far as books were concerned who could hardly, in some instances, sign their names, and in others not at all. But they were sharp businessmen for all that. Most of them had spent their lives from boyhood to manhood in the tobacco fields of Virginia and North Carolina, and they were the best judges of tobacco under the sun . . . their ambition knew no bounds.

He went on to bemoan that these aggressive yokels "pushed the enlightened . . . citizens" of Old Virginia "quite into the rear." Before the war, he argued, Danville's "leading citizens were men of culture and refinement"; they had "a grace and dignity born of the Old Virginia gentlemen."[37]

So it was that through Porter, the litterateur, Danville acquired what was denied it by experience, a cavalier history. But the barbarians had entered the gates long before the end of the Civil War. In fact, they had always been there.

✖ ✖ ✖

CONCLUSION

In those areas where tobacco is grown almost exclusively there is the most apparent poverty—not a poverty of money alone, but a poverty of culture, a poverty of soil, a poverty of good homes and social environment, and a poverty of health and everything else that goes to make an ideal mode of living.
  —Griffin, Young, and Chatham, *Anglo-America*

B Y 1 8 6 7, Danville was being swept away in yet another boom, a boom propelled by the skyrocketing demand for the golden leaf and by "men whose ambition knew no bounds." Danville's promise was such that again "dreams of its future greatness began to be indulged in."[1] Danville did, indeed, go on to become the center of bright leaf tobacco marketing from the postwar years until the end of World War I when the city was overtaken by North Carolina rivals. In the 1880s, the profits from tobacco marketing and manufacturing went into the development of the massive textile mills that utilized the water power of the Dan River. If this were the whole story, the history of Danville and Pittsylvania could be seen in terms of an economist's saga, whereby entrepreneurship and the free play of market forces had triumphed over adversity in the form of a narrow resource endowment to create a dynamic regional economy.

The view from the countryside, however, was far less sanguine. The transition from slave to nominally free labor was far more difficult on the farms than in Danville, which had already experienced a partially free black labor force. In Pittsylvania, as elsewhere in the staple South, the farms were smaller and tenantry was more widespread than before the Civil War. But tenancy had been growing in the late antebellum period and bright tobacco demanded even more intensive labor than the dark leaf tobacco, so there had also been a trend toward smaller units of production before the war. Moreover, the postwar transition was cushioned by high tobacco prices. "Northern and Western manufacturers scarcely waited for the victory of the federal army before entering the Virginia-Carolina area to purchase tobacco for blending with their heavier leaf." High prices stimulated production and to encourage quality, sets of silver spoons were offered as prizes by a Danville firm for the farmers who grew the best tobacco. A trade journal in Liverpool reported on developments in the emerging bright belt by telling its readers of tobacco farming, "NOT A BAD BUSINESS. A gentleman in Halifax County, Virginia [the county directly to the east of Pittsylvania], CULTIVATED 130,000 hills of tobacco with 5 hands. He will make over a $1,000 for each hand."²

Not a bad business, not at least for the time being, but the flush of high postwar prices obscured the fundamental continuities in the countryside. While tobacco manufacture would be repeatedly transformed by changing consumer tastes (the rise of the cigarette being most important) and by the mechanization of production, tobacco growing was being carried on in its almost immemorial manner. If anything, the postwar years saw an intensification of the use of meticulous hand labor.³

Continuity, not transformation, is at the core of a tobacco-based economy. In the 1790s, after describing the beauty of the Valley of Virginia, the traveler Isaac Weld rode through the mountains east onto the southern Piedmont where he saw a "country [which] is flat and sandy, wearing a most dreary aspect. Nothing is to be seen for miles together, but extensive plains that have been grown worn out by the culture of tobacco, overgrown with yellow sedge and interspersed with groves of pine and cedar trees. . . . In the midst of these plains are the remains of several good homes which show that the country was once different."⁴ But it would never be different again. The culture of tobacco exacted a lasting price from the land and its people. Almost ninety years after Weld, Ora Langhorne, a reformer and reporter for the *Southern Workman* and *Hampton School Record*, echoed Weld as she reported this scene while traveling through Pittsylvania:

> Having spent my early life in the beautiful Shenandoah Valley with its flocks and herds, its fine crops of wheat and corn, its large population of thrifty Germans, and its comparatively small African element, I met many contrasts and novel scenes in this part of the state. The country and the people are as new to me as if I were not a Virginian. . . . The principal crop of Pittsylvania County is tobacco which forms the principal interest of the district. . . . There are great forests stretching as far as the eye can see. Often one sees no human habitation except for a log cabin in a little clearing, *as*

if the sturdy pioneers had just reached a new country [emphasis mine].[5]

In the forty years between the time when Langhorne wrote and the mid-1920s, there were numerous efforts to reform the Southside by introducing grasses and using fertilizers to improve the quality of the soil. The attempts at introducing the grasses failed and the chemical fertilizers served only to shore up the old patterns by permitting the continued profitable growth of tobacco on lands which in the past would have had to lie fallow. Tobacco culture was impermeable to the advances of early twentieth-century science.

The rural population of the Southside tobacco areas was poorer than their compatriots in the mixed farming areas of the Valley and the northern Piedmont. They were served by fewer roads, had fewer newspapers, magazines, and radios, and suffered from less in the way of health and medical care. This continued backwardness was almost overwhelming to Halifax's William Cabell Bruce, the literary light of the Southside's most prominent family. Speaking in the voice of a fictional Northern roommate from Harvard, he echoed the words of earlier writers when he noted that the Southside

> compared but poorly with the beautiful Valley of Virginia . . . or even the piedmont territory of northern Virginia. . . . Not that it lacked natural beauty far from it. . . . When I spoke of the impression of inferiority left upon my mind by my first glimpse of the Southside . . . I was referring to industrial rather than natural shortcomings . . . the countryside . . . after we left behind us the fertile meadows of the Staunton River (in the Valley) . . . was a singularly backward one; so backward, indeed that when the superior character of the English and Scotch-Irish stock was taken into account, it was impossible (even after all allowances had been duly made for the calamitous effect of the Civil War) to avoid the conclusion that its economic developments had been stunted by the influence upon human energy and enterprise of a great mass of squalid servile negroes, now happily free.[6]

Bruce's racism had led him astray; the freeman and the white farmers were victimized by the very soil and climate which at the same time provided tobacco to sustain them but prohibited any other form of market sustenance. If, as Wilbur Thompson has argued, "the essence of long run growth is the transition of the local economy from one export base to another,"[7] then the Virginia tobacco country lacked that essence. The power of what, in an earlier context at least, were nature's ineluctable constraints is suggested by an agricultural poem of the 1880s:

Our Agriculturalists Experience in Chemical Manures
In a Nutshell

He put his foot in America
    a hundred years ago,
Tramped to Old Virginia
    Where he fixed his "habito"
He smote the great big oaks;
    Forest-pines and ash,
Cedars, gums and jacks,
    All went down in the crash
He sopped up the virgin soil
    Then sniffed about for Guano
Tried this, tried that, tried all
    And made some chaffy 'bacco
He plowed and dragged this stubble,
    Then sowed it down in wheat,
Yet got for all his trouble
    Little but straw and cheat,
Now Reader, ask him, make him say it;
    "Farmer, has fertilizer made ye
Rich? What and where's your money?"
    "Is it stocks, bonds of money?"
Answer comes triumphantly,
    Mid-smile, squint and wink:
"I've got" (besides bankruptcy)
    "TEN ACRES IMPROVED, I think" (!)[8]

The farmer in the poem, like many farmers in Pittsylvania, looked for an alternative to tobacco but found none. The growing season in Pittsylvania and most of the Southside was too short for cotton, and the temperature was too warm for dairying, while the sandy and clay soils were not capable of producing exportable wheat. Thus Pittsylvania stood and fell with tobacco.

In the 1950s, Douglas North took the lead in arguing that the development of a successful export sector was the sine qua non of economic development in a newly settled region. Subsequently North's argument was modified by critics like Charles Tiebout, who argued that a successful export sector was a necessary but not a sufficient condition for successful long-term growth. Tiebout placed an emphasis on the diversity and flexibility of a local economy. His strictures apply well to Danville, for finally, what was crucial is that even when tobacco prices were high, there was only a limited range of intercourse between town and countryside. Tobacco short-circuited the kind of symbiotic relationship between town and countryside enjoyed in Augusta and which was typical of Northern development.[9]

In the case of Danville and surrounding Pittsylvania, the town was unable to supply the tools and knowledge needed for the improvement of agriculture, first because tobacco required so little in the way of tools and second because the technical knowledge needed was simply beyond the reach of nineteenth-century science. On the other hand, the countryside, because of limitations of soil and temperature, was unable to fully supply to Danville basic foodstuffs like milk, cheese, and even, to some extent, grain. What this suggests is that what was peculiar about Pittsylvania was not just the peculiar institution of slavery or the values that that institution spawned, but rather the limitations on economic development imposed by the fortunes of nature.

✒ ✒ ✒

NOTES

INTRODUCTION

1. Fogel and Engerman, *Time on the Cross*; Thornton, *Politics and Power*; Oakes, *The Ruling Race*. Thornton and Oakes assimilate the South in the broader trends of Jacksonian and Republican ideology. Oakes says (p. 227) that "except for its defense of bondage, the slaveholders' ideology was strikingly similar to the Republican party ideology of the 1850's."

2. Genovese's seminal work was *The Political Economy of Slavery*; Roark, *Masters*; Johnson, *Patriarchal Republic*; and Luraghi, *Rise and Fall*. Other works influenced by Genovese include Davis, *The Problem of Slavery*; Shalhope, "Race, Class and Slavery"; and Greenberg, "William Byrd II and the World of the Market." Discussing this either/or tendency in "The Virginia Ideology," I wrote: "Confronted with the spectacle of free market chivalry an historian is tempted to throw up his hands and cry fraud. What is he to make of a man like Beverley Tucker (1784–1851) who is at the one moment attending a jousting tourney and at the next delivering speeches on the importance of free trade and the cultivation of the commercial arts. Usually after some preliminary remarks about the Janus-faced character of the South, the historian grabs on to one of the bulls horns and tries unsuccessfully to wrestle it to the ground" (p. 344).
For a discussion of the Genovese thesis, which places its appeal in the context of the 1960s, see the opening pages of Siegel, "The Paternalist Thesis."

3. The arguments in *Time on the Cross* tend to be circular in that their explanations are derived from the very free market assumptions they set out to prove. For an account of some of the methodological problems in *Time on the Cross*, see Siegel, "Time on the Cross." Fogel and Engerman's misuse of economic theory is discussed in David and Temin's "Capitalist Masters, Bourgeois Slaves."

4. Rather than being a product of the master-slave relationship, paternalism as a conscious ideology in Virginia was a response on the part of economically bypassed Tidewater plantation owners to a political challenge from the still developing areas of Virginia. On this see Siegel, "The Paternalist Thesis" and "The Virginia Ideology."

5. Siegel, "Parameters for Paternalism?" p. 66. Genovese has acknowledged the importance of the methodological assumptions he shares with his erstwhile rivals. In "The Debate over *Time on the Cross*, a Critique of Bourgeois Criticism," a chapter in *Fruits of Merchant Capital*, Genovese defends Fogel and Engerman. He contends that whatever their substantive failings, the holistic logic of their approach should be applauded.

6. For a discussion of Genovese's insensitivity to intraregional variations, see Siegel, "Parameters for Paternalism?" pp. 60–67, and Genovese's response, "A

Reply to Criticism," p. 94. For a similar criticism of what is described as Genovese's "monolithic" perspective, see Oakes, *The Ruling Race*, pp. xi–xii.

7. For a similar concern with problems of a "generative structure" in the current debates over America's transition from industrialism to "post-industrialism," see Reich, *The Next American Frontier*.

8. On the *Annales* School see Willis, "The Contribution of the *Annales*," and Forster, "Achievements of the *Annales*."

9. See Cowdrey, *This Land, This South*.

10. In *Tobacco Culture*, T. H. Breen argues that, broadly speaking, it was the mentality created by the exigencies of tobacco production that led the colonists to revolution.

11. On the broad consequences of an area—climate permitting—being able to shift from tobacco to wheat, see Shifflett, *Patronage and Poverty*, and Fields's carefully nuanced study, *On the Middle Ground*.

CHAPTER I

1. Clement, *History of Pittsylvania*, p. 22.

2. U.S. Department of Agriculture, *Soil Survey of Pittsylvania County*, p. 44.

3. Quoted in Clement, *History of Pittsylvania*, pp. 22–24.

4. Ibid., p. 138.

5. Quoted in Ginther, *Captain Staunton's River*, pp. 3–4.

6. Nichols, "Origins of the Virginia Southside," p. ix.

7. Ibid., pp. 169–70.

8. Pittsylvania Petition, 10 December 1811, from District Commissioner of Revenue James Hart. James Williams, another district commissioner from Pittsylvania, sent a virtually identical petition the same day.

9. Mitchell, "Henry County," p. 14. Patrick Henry owned 8,000 acres of land in the county that had been named after him. Richard Beeman, *Patrick Henry* (New York, 1974).

10. These figures are derived from Pittsylvania (Personal and Real) Property, 1780 and 1800.

11. Pittsylvania Petitions, 1776–1801. The 1776 petition calling for a division of the county insisted on the need to maintain a large undivided county because of the area's inability to support a dense population. It was followed by four similar petitions between 1776 and 1801 (on 13 November 1794, 10 November 1796, 6 December 1798, and 10 December 1801) which used the same argument to draw the opposite conclusions.

12. Petition to the legislature, 10 November 1796.

13. Smyth, *A Tour*, pp. 190–93. This progression from cattle rearing to cash crops was typical of large sections of the South. For a recent interpretation of this transformation, though it does not seem to apply to Pittsylvania, see McWhiney, "Alabama Agriculture," pp. 3–32.

14. Herndon, "A War Inspired Industry," pp. 301–11.

15. Pittsylvania Petition, 21 October 1791.

16. Ibid., 28 October 1788.

17. Ginther, *Captain Staunton's River*, pp. 18–19.

18. Ibid., pp. 10, 13.

19. Clement, *History of Pittsylvania*, p. 112.

20. Primack, "Land Clearing," pp. 448–71. The recognized value of slaves for land clearing in both North and South is discussed in McColley, *Slavery and Jeffersonian Virginia*, pp. 175–81, and Freehling, "The Founding Fathers," pp. 81–93; Ginther notes that in some cases the "yeomen may have brought their slaves with them from Pennsylvania" (*Captain Staunton's River*, p. 5).

21. Clement, *History of Pittsylvania*, p. 141.

22. Main, "The One Hundred," pp. 354–84. Main's contention is supported by Risjord ("The Virginia Federalists," p. 493) and Clement (*History of Pittsylvania*, p. 198).

23. Pittsylvania Petition, 17 October 1796. See also the petitions of 12 December 1806 and 24, 30 December 1807.

24. Pittsylvania Petition, 10 November 1785, with fifty-four signatures. This petition from Pittsylvania was one of a number of petitions sent to the legislature by economically expanding counties where there was vociferous support for slavery. These petitions are discussed as a group in Schmidt and Wilhelm, "Proslavery Petitions," pp. 133–46.

25. Pittsylvania Petition, 10 November 1785.

26. These figures are based on a 1 to 10 sample taken from Pittsylvania (Personal) Property, 1800, 1810, and 1820.

27. Ibid.

28. Hart, *The Valley of Virginia*.

29. U.S. Manufacturing Census, 1810 and 1820. The early development of manufacturing in the Shenandoah Valley is chronicled in Mitchel, "The Upper Shenandoah Valley."

30. In 1820 the white populations of Pittsylvania and Augusta counties were 11,500 and 12,000, respectively.

31. For discussions of Augusta as a center of the Virginia yeomanry, see Hart, *The Valley of Virginia*.

CHAPTER 2

1. Dorfman, *The Economic Mind*, pp. 540–41.

2. *Calendar of Virginia State Papers*, 15 January 1818. For a discussion of the importance of expectations in the founding of towns, see Smolensky and Ratajczak, "Cities," pp. 90–131.

3. Clement, *History of Pittsylvania*, p. 231.

4. Pittsylvania Petition, October 1793.

5. Clement, *History of Pittsylvania*, pp. 231–32.

6. Among Peter Wilson's progeny were some of the leading citizens of Danville, as well as two governors of North Carolina and one of Georgia. Usery, "Overseers," pp. 31–32; Clement, *History of Pittsylvania*, pp. 44, 52, 58–61, 94–95, 116, 139–40.

7. The size of Wilson's tobacco crop is inferred from information provided in

Appendix D of Robert's *The Tobacco Kingdom*. Wilson was wealthy enough at the time of his death somewhere around the War of 1812 to bequeath to each of his eleven children a home, livestock, and furniture.

8. Information on the twelve trustees was compiled from scattered references in Clement, *History of Pittsylvania*, and Usery, "Overseers."

9. Clement, *History of Pittsylvania*, p. 232.

10. Pittsylvania (Personal and Real) Property, 1800.

11. Pittsylvania (Real) Property, 1800.

12. Pittsylvania Petition, 16 December 1801.

13. Hairston, *Danville*, p. 31; Clement, *History of Pittsylvania*, p. 233.

14. Robert, *The Tobacco Kingdom*, pt. II, and Herndon, "A History of Tobacco."

15. Clement, *History of Pittsylvania*, p. 236; Pollack, *Sketchbook*, p. 11.

16. Hagan, *Danville*, p. 56. Hagan notes that the Pittsylvania representative of the Roanoke Navigation Company was Nathaniel Wilson, son of John Wilson. In the 1820s Cabell and Colonel William F. Lewis built flour, corn, and linseed oil mills along the canal.

17. Quoted in Stokes, "Milton," p. 3.

18. Quoted in Clement, *History of Pittsylvania*, p. 236. The opening of the Dismal Swamp Canal began to attract trade from the northwest corner of Pittsylvania County, which was close to Lynchburg and had traditionally traded there. In 1818 planter-entrepreneurs Charles and Abner Anthony established a town they named Monroe. It was located on their land on the banks of the Staunton River at a ford where they operated a ferry. Their request to the legislature for a town charter stated that the petitioners acted "in the belief that this town in a short while will become a better market for their produce than the more distant towns on the James River, in as much as the Staunton River, with some additional improvements, will afford safe and easy navigation for batteaux into Roanoke and from there by way of the Dismal Swamp Canal to Norfolk, our most valuable town for foreign commerce" (Pittsylvania Petition, 12 December 1818).

While Monroe was being established in northern Pittsylvania along the Staunton, Chatham, the county seat since 1807, was growing in central Pittsylvania along the banks of the Banister River. Like the Dan and the Staunton, the Banister flowed into the Roanoke so that Chatham too was caught up in the expectations engendered by the Roanoke improvements. In 1807 Chatham had little more than a courthouse and a store; by 1820 it had 6 landowners, 12 lots, $4,600 in buildings, and property valued at $7,700.

19. Pittsylvania Petition, 17 December 1818.

20. *Calendar of Virginia State Papers*, vol. 2, p. 461.

21. For more on the Hairston family, see Chapters 7 and 8 below.

22. The profile of Cabell in this and succeeding paragraphs was pieced together from Dame, *Historical Sketch*; scattered references in Clement's *History of Pittsylvania*, Hagan's and Hairston's histories of Danville, and Pollack's *Sketchbook*; U.S. Census for 1840; and the surviving issues of the *Danville Reporter* (9 March 1833, 30 April and 27 August 1836, 6 September 1837)

published under Cabell's editorship. For Cabell's role in the opening of the Dismal Swamp Canal, see Chapter 8 below.

23. Dame, *Historical Sketch*, p. 37.

24. *Danville Reporter*, 9 March 1833.

25. Sam Pannill from his Green Hill estate and workshops, to Samuel Pannill, Jr., and Crispen Dickerson in Danville, 19 February 1830, Wilson Papers.

26. Ibid., 11 April 1828.

27. Ibid., 6 June 1828.

28. Ibid., 21 November 1828.

29. Ibid., 19 July 1829.

30. Ibid., 29 August, 1829.

31. Goldfield's *Urban Growth* provides striking discussions of planter capitalism in the late antebellum period. For a description of planter-entrepreneurs similar to those of the Danville area, see Wood, "Henry Edmundson," pp. 305–20.

CHAPTER 3

1. For a general description of the efforts to bring about political reform, see Pole, "Representation," pp. 17–50; Green, *Constitutional Developments*; and what is far and away the most valuable source, Sutton, "Constitutional Convention." The ideological dimensions of the reform movement are analyzed in Siegel, "The Paternalist Thesis."

2. Virginia Acts, 28 January 1828.

3. Pittsylvania Petition, 17 December 1822.

4. *Roanoke Sentinel*, 20 March 1824.

5. Stokes, "Milton."

6. Pittsylvania (Personal and Real) Property, 1820.

7. Thirty-one people signed this petition of 15 January 1828. Sixteen of the thirty-one owned property in Danville. Of the sixteen, ten were slaveholders with a mean holding of sixteen slaves. Two of the sixteen had small-scale tobacco manufacturing operations in Danville and three were skilled craftsmen. The legislature responded to the petition by authorizing a joint stock company with a capital stock not to exceed $50,000 to be raised in $50 shares. Virginia Acts, 10 February 1829. The company floundered and collapsed, and in 1835 the assembly passed legislation to revive the failed company.

8. *Roanoke Sentinel*, 20 March 1824.

9. Ibid.

10. See n. 1 above.

11. Sutton, "Constitutional Convention," p. 53; Pittsylvania Petitions, 10 December 1810.

12. Sutton, "Constitutional Convention," p. 57.

13. There were repeated efforts by the citizens of northwestern Pittsylvania to secede and form a new county. See, for instance, Pittsylvania Petition, 17 December 1836.

14. *The Telegraph* (a short-lived Danville weekly), 3 December 1827.

15. Virginia Acts, 27 January 1827. Sutton, in his conclusion to "Constitutional Convention," describes the pivotal position played by delegates from swing counties like Pittsylvania.

16. The governor and the upper house were relatively weak. For a discussion of the divisions animating state politics, see also Siegel, "The Paternalist Thesis" and "The Virginia Ideology."

17. George Townes, the son of a wealthy Episcopalian planter, was born near Danville in 1791. A wealthy man himself, in 1830 he owned nearly 2,500 acres of land, 30 slaves, and property in Danville. He represented Pittsylvania in the assembly as a young man in the 1818–19 sessions and later in 1848–49; in between, during the 1830s and 1840s, he served on the Danville town council. He played a crucial role in Danville's history at two points: first, as just described in the text, during the Constitutional Convention; and later when, during his service in the 1848–49 session of the assembly, Danville, through his and Whitmell Tunstall's efforts, was able to secure a charter for a Richmond to Danville railroad.

Townes typifies the planter businessmen who were so central to Danville's development. His Masonic eulogizer summarized some of his career: "I am not certain that he held any official position therein [with the Mason's lodge], but his high standing in our county and his great and deserved popularity make it proper that he should be noticed as one of our past Worthies [sic]. He was a Colonel of the artillery branch of the state service . . . one of the most ardent and active friends of the Richmond and Danville Railroad system, and was well known as a great advocate of anything which elevates the people and improves their condition." This brief profile was based on the eulogy to Townes printed in George Dame's *Historical Sketch of the Roman Eagle Lodge* (p. 23), as well as passing references to Townes in Hairston, *Danville*, and Clement, *History of Pittsylvania*.

18. Sutton, "Constitutional Convention," p. 90.

19. On these and a number of other points, Ambler's venerable *Sectionalism* was invaluable.

CHAPTER 4

1. Quoted in Hagan, *Danville*, chap. 2, pp. 25–49.

2. Hall, "Soil Erosion," p. 100.

3. Pittsylvania's enviable position as a swing county is explained in Sutton, "Constitutional Convention," chap. 2.

4. Hagan, *Danville*, chap. 2. The contours of Coleman's account are confirmed by the discussion of Pittsylvania in this period in *Martin's Gazeteer* and Pollack's *Sketchbook*.

5. Pittsylvania Petition, 15 December 1828. Among the other signatories were Sam Pannill and Sam Pannill, Jr.; William Linn, the pioneer tobacco manufacturer; and the Williams brothers, who are discussed in Chapter 10 below.

6. Pittsylvania Petition, 2 January 1833; Pollack, *Sketchbook*, p. 27.

7. Danville City Council Minutes, 1833. Scattered minutes remain for 1833 through 1847.

The composition of the first town council tells us something about the nature of the social order in Danville. The council included two of the town's master craftsmen, both of whom became heavily involved in the efforts to make the town a transportation and hence marketing center. One of the two, James Macallister, a tailor and small property owner, was also one of the ruling elders of the Presbyterian Church. The other, William O'Neil, was a relative newcomer, coming to Danville from Boston in 1823. In 1826, only three years after his arrival, O'Neil was elected to the exalted position of Master of Mason's Lodge. The active members of the lodge included the town's most prominent business leaders, such as B. W. S. Cabell and James Lanier. Norris, "First Presbyterian Church."

8. *Danville Reporter*, 9 February 1833.

9. Ibid.

10. This was to be the first of a number of abortive attempts to link Danville to Evansham by road or rail.

11. Virginia Acts, 2 April 1831.

12. *Danville Reporter*, 9 February 1833; Virginia Acts, 25 February 1833. For a description of the state government's involvement in internal improvements, see Goodrich, "The Virginia System."

13. Virginia Acts, 10 February 1833.

14. For a good description of the intense rivalry between Virginia's coastal port cities for the trade of the interior, see Stewart, "Railroads and Urban Rivalries," pp. 4–22. Stewart's article describes the ways in which Virginia's urban development was limited by fierce political and economic competition between Norfolk and Richmond, and between Norfolk and Petersburg.

15. The story of these complicated dealings was uncovered by piecing together scattered newspaper information with the relevant Virginia Acts (21 January, 31 March, and 24 February 1837) and the crucial long petition of 1838, which outlines the story.

16. For the Norfolk perspective, see Wertenbaker, *Norfolk*.

17. Clement, *History of Pittsylvania*, p. 231.

18. Whitmell P. Tunstall was the grandson of William Tunstall, a planter from the Tidewater's King and Queen County, who became Pittsylvania's first county clerk. William Tunstall became renowned for importing from England Koulihan, "a horse of the finest blood" (Clement, *History of Pittsylvania*, p. 211), considered one of the thirty-nine most noted horses imported into Virginia before the Revolution. Like many other Pittsylvania planters, including John Wilson, William Tunstall was an ardent patriot who served on the local Committee of Safety and in the militia.

William's son, William Tunstall, Jr., father of Whitmell, shared a similar mix of republican enthusiasm and aristocratic pretense. We can see this mixture in a letter he helped to write honoring the teacher of his children: "In a free and extensive country where learning is encouraged and usefull improvements and discoveries rewarded, it will naturally result that young and ingenious minds will forever be exerted to excell in the most plausible pursuits. A Young man sincere and moral in all his deportments will hardly fail to meet with the friendship and patronage of every good man, but when these virtues shine in a conspicuous manner with sentiments polished and refined by a classical education, we may and do expect such a one to meet not only with respect but encouragement in whatever business his qualifications may induce him to undertake" (Clement, *History of Pittsylvania*, p. 213). In short, the successful young man should be a classically educated entrepreneur. The sons and sons-in-law of William Tunstall, Jr., were examples, as were Whitmell's partner in the drive for a railroad, the planter/banker George Townes, and the planter/merchant Nathaniel Wilson, son of the famous John Wilson and himself a strong supporter of internal improvements (Clement, *History of Pittsylvania*, pp. 17, 104).

19. Pittsylvania Petition, 20 February 1837.

20. Ibid.

CHAPTER 5

1. Glasgow, *The Deliverance*, p. 6.

2. Ibid., p. 35.

3. Cocke, *Tobacco*, p. 28. For a general discussion of the widespread criticism of tobacco, see Robert, *The Tobacco Kingdom*, chap. 2.

4. Quoted in Robert, *The Tobacco Kingdom*, p. 26.

5. Ibid., p. 27.

6. Cocke, *Tobacco*, pp. 7–8.

7. Quoted in Robert, *The Tobacco Kingdom*, p. 25.

8. For a discussion of the early impact of tobacco culture, see Morgan, "The Labor Problem," pp. 595–611, and Diamond, "From Organization to Society," pp. 457–75.

9. Morgan, "The Labor Problem," p. 598.

10. Ibid. In Western Europe from the fourteenth century on, the typical response to a scarcity of labor had been to induce work through increased freedoms. The situation in Virginia, however, was more like that of Eastern Europe, where an increased demand for grains coupled with a high demand for labor led to the increasing subjugation of the peasant population. For an interesting conceptual discussion of this process, see Domar, "Slavery or Serfdom," pp. 18–32.

11. Edgar Thompson, "The Natural History of Agricultural Labor," pp. 110–74; Ballagh, *White Servitude*, p. 44; Dunn, *Sugar and Slaves*, p. 73; Palmer, "Servant into Slave," pp. 355–70. On the lack of mobility for freed indentures, see Morgan, "Headrights and Head Counts," p. 361.

12. On the cultural and commercial impact of London, see Hill, *Reformation to Industrial Revolution*, and Wrigley, "A Simple Model of London's Importance, 1650–1750," pp. 44–70. The significance of this commercial orientation is spelled out in Rubin, "Growth and Expansion of Urban Centers."

13. Rainbolt, "The Virginia Vision," chap. 3.

14. Myrdal, *Rich Lands, Poor Lands*, chap. 5. On the issue of linkages, spread effects, and balanced versus unbalanced growth, see Hirschman, *Strategy of Eco-*

nomic Development; and for a range of articles concerned with this problem, see Meier, *Leading Issues in Development Economics*, chap. 5, sec. 2. Rothstein, "Ante-Bellum Wheat and Cotton Exports," provides the basis for my description of wheat marketing.

15. Earle and Hoffman, "The Urban South," p. 50.

16. Craven, *Soil Exhaustion*, pp. 32, 57; Papenfeuse, "Planter Behavior and Economic Opportunity in a Staple Economy," pp. 297–313.

17. Bruce, *Virginia in the 17th Century*, p. 260.

18. Hall, "Soil Erosion," p. 15.

19. Philips, *Life and Labor*, p. 4.

20. Hall, "Soil Erosion," p. 3.

21. Ibid.

22. Ibid.

23. Gray, "The Market Surplus Problem of Colonial Tobacco," pp. 1–34; Craven, *Soil Exhaustion*.

24. Gross, "Dairy Cattle and Climate," p. 13.

25. Jones, "Environment, Agriculture and Industrialization," pp. 491–502; Hall, "Soil Erosion," p. 9; Gross, "Dairy Cattle and Climate," p. 8.

26. Rubin, "The Limits of Agricultural Progress," pp. 367–73; Gross, "Dairy Cattle and Climate," p. 7.

27. Rubin, "Comparative Economic Development," p. 5.

28. Hall, "Soil Erosion," p. 136.

29. Ibid.

30. Rubin, "The Limits of Agricultural Progress," p. 367.

31. Weld, *Travels*, pp. 204, 205. Elijah Fletcher, a native Vermonter who moved to the western Piedmont, noted in his diary that Albemarle, like the Shenandoah Valley, reminded him of his native state. Von Briesen, *Letters of Elijah Fletcher*.

32. Cason, *90 Degrees in the Shade*, p. 31.

33. William C. Bruce, *Below the James*, p. 11. George Washington, among others, saw his section of Virginia, the northern neck, as a part of the middle states.

CHAPTER 6

1. Weld, *Travels*, pp. 232–33.

2. Schlebecker, "Farmers," pp. 464–65.

3. Gates, *The Farmers Age*, p. 110. On Hairston and Pittsylvania see also Eaton, *Growth of Southern Civilization*, p. 316; Fields, "The Agricultural Population," p. 316. Hart (*The Valley of Virginia*), in discussing the beginning period covered in this volume, and Perry ("A History of Farm Tenancy"), in covering the later period, come to similar conclusions about the size of landholdings.

4. My statistical information was derived from one in ten samples of the U.S. Census, Population Schedule, 1850, 1860, and from one in ten samples of the Pittsylvania (Real and Personal) Property, 1820, 1840, and 1860.

5. Hart, *The Valley of Virginia*, p. 38.

6. U.S. Census, Agriculture Schedule, 1860.

7. Table 6-4 shows how the people who owned the highly valued plots of land fit into decile rankings based on the total number of acres an individual owned and the total value of the acreage owned. Thus in 1840 of the 40 people who owned plots valued at $6 or more an acre, 18 (45 percent) owned acreage so large as to place them in the top two deciles in terms of the total number of acres they possessed.

8. Mitchel, in "The Upper Shenandoah Valley," found that by 1800 about 30 percent of the adult male population of the valley was composed of landless day laborers.

9. Ibid., p. 255.

10. This percentage was derived as follows:

$$\frac{1,265 \text{ (approximate number of rural slaveholding families)}}{3,166 \text{ (approximate number of rural households)}} = 40\%$$

The number of rural households was determined by dividing the size of the average household (5.4 people) into the total rural population.

As shown in the table below, slaves had comprised a sizable percentage of Pittsylvania's population even before the first boom following the War of 1812, and the county was 43 percent slave by 1830. Between then and the Civil War, there was only a slight increase in the slave population.

Pittsylvania Slave Population, 1790–1860
(Rounded off to the Nearest Hundred)

Year	1790	1800	1810	1820	1830	1840	1850	1860
Number	3,100	4,200	6,400	8,700	11,300	12,100	13,500	15,000
Percent	27%	33%	37%	40%	43%	45%	46%	46%

11. This percentage was derived as follows:

$$\frac{1,140 \text{ (approximate number of rural slaveholders)}}{1,750 \text{ (approximate number of rural landowners)}} = 65\%$$

It is necessarily high because it does not take into account landless individuals who owned slaves.

12. The best discussion of the economic and geographic organization of the Shenandoah appears in Miller, "The Shenandoah Valley."

13. Ibid., chap. 2. For a general discussion of the way different American agricultural areas were either able or unable to benefit from English developments, see Jones, "Creative Disruptions."

14. Schlebecker, "Farmers," p. 476.

15. As Mitchel ("The Upper Shenandoah Valley") has made clear, Augusta, as well as the rest of the Valley, enjoyed a thriving town life almost from the onset of settlement in the mid-eighteenth century.

16. Numerous travelers commented on the importance of towns to the commercial life of the Valley. The observations of Johann David Schoepf, a German, were typical. In *Travels*, he noted that, "of the county of Augusta, Stanton is the capital, a place by no means inconsiderable, carrying on much trade with the farther mountain-country. The town lies in the remarkable long, fertile limestone

valley which between the north and south mountain runs through the greatest part of North America, and contains many other towns already mentioned, as Lebanon, Carlisle, and Shippensburgh in Pennsylvania, Winchester in Virginia, Hagerstown in Maryland" (p. 69). Robert Sutton, in "Virginia Consitutional Convention" (chap. 5), provides a detailed description of the diversity and fluidity of Augusta's social order in 1830.

17. Although the growing season was shorter in the Valley than in the Piedmont, crop failures from early frosts were rare. Only occasional summer droughts posed a major problem for Valley farmers. The certainty of the growing season minimized some of the traditional vicissitudes of farming.

18. Descriptions of these shifts during the Revolution are provided by Herndon in "Hemp in Colonial Virginia," p. 83, and "A War Inspired Industry," p. 301; see also Gray, *History of Agriculture*, vol. 2, chap. 26. For the late antebellum period, chapters 38 and 39 of Gray's *History of Agriculture*, vol. 2, are useful, along with Miller's "The Shenandoah Valley." For the postbellum period, Allen Moger's "Industrial and Urban Progress," p. 307, was useful, but particularly important were Catlett and Fishburne's "Economic and Social Survey of Augusta County," and Gee and Corson's "Statistical Study of Virginia."

CHAPTER 7

1. Ortiz, *Cuban Counterpoint*, p. 8.
2. Ibid. This chapter owes a great deal to Ortiz's extraordinarily nuanced discussion of the way the characteristics of an area's dominant crop affect the society dependent on that crop.
3. Philips, *Life and Labor*, p. 112.
4. Robert, *The Tobacco Kingdom*, p. 18.
5. Ibid.
6. Ibid., chap. 3.
7. Ibid., p. 39.
8. Ibid., p. 37.
9. Tilley, *The Bright Tobacco Industry*, p. 85.
10. Philips, *Life and Labor*, p. 114; Humphries, "The Impact of Tobacco."
11. Tilley, *The Bright Tobacco Industry*, p. 37.
12. Ortiz, *Cuban Counterpoint*, p. 39.
13. Cathey, *Agricultural Developments*, p. 123.
14. Robert, *The Tobacco Kingdom*, p. 18. See also McColley, *Slavery and Jeffersonian Virginia*, p. 17.
15. DeCoin, *History and Cultivation of Tobacco*.
16. Quoted in Robert, *The Tobacco Kingdom*, p. 42.
17. Ibid., p. 42.
18. Tilley, *The Bright Tobacco Industry*, pp. 188–91.
19. Olmsted, *The Cotton Kingdom*, pp. 69–70.
20. Robert, *The Tobacco Kingdom*, pp. 20–21; Herndon, *William Tatham and the Culture of Tobacco*, p. 104.
21. Virginia Writers' Project, *The Negro in Virginia*, p. 224.

22. Ibid., p. 322.

23. Ibid., p. 281.

24. Yetman, *Voices from Slavery*, p. 24. Some slaves developed special skills in stripping and topping (Gray, *History of Agriculture*, vol. 2, p. 407; Robert, *The Tobacco Kingdom*, p. 37), and Gray (*History of Agriculture*) has argued that there was a sharp increase in slave productivity in the decades before the Civil War.

25. Tilley, *The Bright Tobacco Industry*, p. 13.

26. Hall, "Soil Erosion," pp. 82, 96; Whitney, "Soils," p. 144; Wingo, *Virginia's Soils*, p. 205.

27. U.S. Department of Agriculture, *Soil Survey of Pittsylvania County*; Fuller et al., *Pittsylvania County Geographic Supplement*; Tilley, *The Bright Tobacco Industry*, pp. 27, 32.

28. Robert, *The Tobacco Kingdom*, p. 42; Herndon, "A History of Tobacco," p. 41.

29. Abisha Slade sold the extraordinary crop at premium prices in Danville to the Johns brothers, two of the town's pioneering tobacco manufacturers.

30. Tilley, *The Bright Tobacco Industry*, p. 21.

CHAPTER 8

1. These figures are based on data taken from the Population, Agricultural, and Manufacturing Schedules of the U.S. Census, 1850 and 1860, and on Pittsylvania (Real) Property, 1850 and 1860.

2. Elliot and Nye, *Virginia Directory*; Howe, *Historical Collection of Virginia*, p. 133; Clement, *History of Pittsylvania*, chap. 8.

3. Clark, "The First Quarter Century"; Goodrich, "The Virginia System"; Clement, *History of Pittsylvania*, pp. 241–42. The careers of Tunstall and Townes are described in Chapter 4 above.

4. Pittsylvania Petition, 13 February 1847.

5. *Danville Register*, 5 February 1848.

6. Ibid. The newspaper described Hairston as a "plain, practical and successful planter."

7. Pittsylvania Petition, 10 January 1851.

8. *Danville Register*, 5 February 1848.

9. At the same time interest was also revived in a lesser project, the improvement of the Banister River which moved west to east along Pittsylvania's midsection. Whitmell Tunstall and Nathaniel Wilson were among the leaders of a group of central Pittsylvania planters and businessmen who formed a company to improve the river for bateau navigation. It was hoped that the river could serve as a feeder route for the Richmond and Danville Railroad, which would cross the Banister in eastern Pittsylvania.

10. Virginia Acts, 29 April 1852, 14 March 1853; *Danville Republican*, 15 April 1854.

11. *Danville Republican*, 9 December 1853.

12. Information on sixteen of the twenty Pittsylvania representatives was

pieced together from scattered and generally fragmentary references in Clement's *History of Pittsylvania* and the Hagan and Hairston histories of Danville. Of the sixteen, nine made Danville their chief residence, three made Chatham their chief residence, and four lived primarily on their estates. In terms of occupation, seven were businessmen, three were tobacco manufacturers, two were planters, two were professional politicians, one was a judge, and one was an editor. Of the ten whose political affiliations could be identified, eight were Whigs, and two were Democrats.

13. Clement, *History of Pittsylvania*, pp. 260, 242; *Danville Register*, 7 July 1848; Scarborough, *Diary of Edmund Ruffin* (quotation, p. 10).

14. Witcher was an uncompromising proslavery advocate during the famous 1832 legislative debate that followed Nat Turner's Rebellion. On Witcher's role in that debate, see Robert, *Monticello*, chap. 2. For his position in the 1836 campaign, see Eaton, *Freedom of Thought Struggle*, p. 205.

15. The evidence from Pittsylvania strongly supports Seller's contention that "the towns dominated the countryside . . . the elements of leadership, impetus, financing and propaganda were furnished mainly by the commercial groups of the cities and towns." "Who Were the Southern Whigs?" p. 335.

16. Wooding, "Sketch of Danville."

17. *Danville Republican*, 27 January 1854.

18. U.S. Census, Population Schedule, 1850, 1860. Only seven of the thirty-nine new clerks can be identified as the younger sons of Danville merchants.

19. Pittsylvania (Real) Property, 1820, 1830, 1840, 1850.

20. The percentage for Danville proper is somewhat deceptive, particularly for 1850. The 43 percent figure does not include the planters who lived within close proximity to the town. And given the town's limited boundaries in 1850 (during the 1850s these boundaries would be expanded by the legislature), even a few of the businessmen lived beyond the town limits. Of the new investors, most were from the neighboring counties to the west of Pittsylvania, counties which, unlike those to the east, were also benefiting from the development of bright tobacco, and from Richmond and Lynchburg.

21. Pittsylvania (Real) Property, 1850, 1860. The residence of the owners was found by matching the Danville tax lists against the U.S. Census, Population Schedule, 1850, 1860.

22. U.S. Census, Population Schedules, 1850, 1860; Pittsylvania (Real) and (Personal) Property, 1850, 1860.

23. Robert, *The Tobacco Kingdom*, pp. 178–79.

24. Table 8-3 was developed by matching the county tax lists with the lists of occupations found in the census. For the years before 1850 a wide variety of sources, including letters and newspaper accounts that sometimes made reference to a man's occupation, was used.

25. According to *DeBow's Review* (vol. 18, January 1885, p. 53) and the *Alabama Beacon* (Greensboro, 2 June 1854), Samuel Hairston owned between 1,600 and 1,700 slaves and managed 1,000 more belonging to his grandmother, Ruth Stoval Hairston. In 1855, his plantations were valued at $600,000 and his total wealth at between $3 and $5 million. Samuel's lavish home at Oak Hill, northwest of Danville, was only one of his 21 Pittsylvania properties, which

included more than 1,200 acres of land valued at $65,000 and buildings worth $9,500. His main residence at Oak Hill was valued at $6,000 and a lesser house at Cascade near the Henry County border was valued at $2,000. In neighboring Henry County and across the North Carolina border, the operations of his brother Peter Hairston were described as a study in managerial efficiency by Scarborough, the historian of plantation procedure, in *The Overseer*.

The Wilsons and Hairstons had been intermarrying for three generations. Both families were bulwarks of the local Methodist church. Samuel Hairston's maternal grandmother, Ruth Stoval Hairston, had married her cousin Peter Wilson, son of John Wilson, one of the founders of Danville (see Chapter 2 above for an account of John Wilson). Peter Wilson was the brother of Robert and Nathaniel Wilson, both of whom played prominent roles in the development of Danville. Samuel's mother, Agnes (the daughter of Peter Wilson and Ruth Stoval Hairston), had also married a cousin, Samuel Hairston, Sr. Together they sired Peter, George, and the great Sam, Jr. Through the Wilsons, the Hairstons were connected to two of the other major families of the area. Robert Wilson married the daughter of Samuel Pannill, and Nathaniel Wilson married the daughter of William Tunstall.

Despite the wealth and prominence of these families, they largely eschewed politics (Eaton, *Freedom of Thought Struggle*, p. 316). There is no indication, for instance, that Samuel Hairston ever held political office or was even active behind the scenes. His brother George, however, did sit in the state senate from 1817 to 1821.

26. *Danville Republican*, 24 March 1854.

27. *Martin's Gazeteer*; Grasty Family Papers. The bulk of the Grasty collection deals with the mercantile records of different Grasty enterprises. The story of the Grastys described in the following three paragraphs is taken largely from a reading of these records.

28. Grasty Family Papers; *Danville Reporter*, 21 August 1840.

29. Ibid.

30. Grasty Family Papers; U.S. Census, Manufacturing Schedule, 1860.

CHAPTER 9

1. For a description of this development see Goldfield, *Urban Growth*, chaps. 1–3.

2. Dodd and Dodd, *Historical Statistics*. Success came more easily to the tobacco manufacturers than to their counterparts in textiles, for a number of reasons. First, tobacco manufacturing required a minimal initial investment compared to textiles. Indeed, one of the early problems was that entry was so easy that the growth of numerous part-time plantation manufactories hindered the development of larger, full-time urban operations. Nor was there a political problem: a protective tariff was not needed to foster the industry. Finally, because tobacco manufacturing was relatively simple, no Northern advantage in machinery and expertise had to be overcome.

3. *Danville Register*, 26 October, 1849.

4. Robert, *The Story of Tobacco*.

5. Axton, *Tobacco*, pp. 55, 59; the quotation is found on p. 59.

6. Heimann, *Tobacco*, p. 151.

7. Robert, *The Tobacco Kingdom*, pp. 176–77; the quotation is found on p. 175.

8. Heimann, *Tobacco*, p. 148. Tobacco consumption was always a matter of taste and style. At the same time that bright leaf wrappers were becoming popular for chewing, dark leaf wrapped cigars were becoming the rage in the North.

9. Heimann, *Tobacco*, p. 32; Robert, *The Tobacco Kingdom*, p. 213.

10. Tilley, *The Bright Tobacco Industry*, p. 198; Pollack, *Sketchbook*, p. 32.

11. Tilley, *The Bright Tobacco Industry*, p. 199.

12. This almost exclusive focus on manufacturing caused some problems, as noted by the *Danville Register* on 5 February 1848: "The market of course must be less stable so long as the present system is kept up than it would be if the tobacco were sold in hogsheads; and for this reason: that at every good harvest season a large quantity is brought in loose, and in bad order. Which is thus forced on the manufacturer who is unable to give it houseroom, because he must either hang it up to dry or permit it to rot in the bulk. And when sold in this condition all other buyers, the shippers for instance were excluded; whereas if it were in hogshead it would give the shipper an equal chance with the manufacturer and the planter would certainly be the gainer to the extent of this increased competition. Besides another advantage the planter would gain by this change would be found in the fact that he would thus force the purchaser here to pay the Richmond and Petersburg prices (freight off) or he would send it to one of those markets."

13. Robert, *Tobacco Kingdom*, p. 194.

14. Tilley, *The Bright Tobacco Industry*, p. 529.

15. Here is how the turnover was distributed by sections of the county:

Danville: —Of the seven manufacturers in 1850, two had died by 1860.

—Of the seventeen firms in 1860, twelve had opened since 1850. Of these twelve, ten firms were new, one had moved to Danville from northern Pittsylvania, and one was a partnership formed between two manufacturers already operating in Danville.

Whitmell: —Of the twenty-two firms in 1850 (producing more than $500 of manufactured tobacco), thirteen had disappeared by 1860 and six had closed because of death.

—Of the fourteen firms in 1860, five were new.

Central and Northern Pittsylvania: —Of the fourteen firms in 1850, ten had gone out of business by 1860; only one had closed because of death.

—Of the eight firms in 1860, five were new.

Based on the U.S. Census, Manufacturing Schedule, 1850, 1860, newspaper obituaries, and death notices.

Between 1850 and 1860 there was a great increase in the size of the individual tobacco manufacturing companies. In the northern district, for instance, the mean value of the capital investment tripled, the mean number of hands increased by two and one-half times, and the value of goods produced increased three and one-third times. Considering the Basin as a whole (including Danville and the tobacco factories that ringed it to the north, northwest, and west), the mean number of hands increased from 24 in 1850 to 30 in 1860; the mean capital invested, from $2,076 to $6,675; and the mean output, from $19,500 to $32,500, an increase of almost 70 percent. The largest firms were in Danville and their mean output was $43,800.

16. All but two of the twenty-one tobacco manufacturers in Danville in 1860 were born either in Pittsylvania or an adjacent county.

17. See the petitions to the legislature of 17 January 1852, 10 July 1852, and 6 December 1852.

18. Information on the earlier occupations of the Danville manufacturers was derived from the U.S. Census, Population and Manufacturing Schedules, and from the brief accounts of their lives scattered throughout Clement (*History of Pittsylvania*), Pollack (*Sketchbook*), Hairston (*Danville*), and Hagan (*Danville*).

19. As a young man, Mastin Williams had fought for American independence. After the war he acquired considerable property by his marriage to the daughter of James Walker, a local planter of standing and property. Walker, a man of some distinction, was renowned for the quality of his library. Among the investments Mastin bequeathed to his son James were the thirty acres of land near the canal. By 1830 this land was valued at $400 per acre. Clement, *History of Pittsylvania*, pp. 139, 162, 172–73.

20. *Danville Reporter*, 30 April 1836.

21. Pollack, *Sketchbook*, p. 38.

22. Ibid., p. 142.

23. The chief investors in the company were from Norfolk: Banister Anderson, known as the "Napoleon of tobacco manufacturers," and Thompson Coleman. Coleman's father, Stephen Coleman, was a leading planter who owned an extensive estate in the middle of the county along the Banister River. Thompson's brothers, Daniel and Stephen, Jr., became planters; Daniel also served several terms in the legislature. In 1829 Thompson left his family estates and went to Danville, where he would play a prominent role in the town's economic life. Clement, *History of Pittsylvania*, pp. 197–99, 287–89.

24. U.S. Census, Manufacturing Schedule, 1850, 1860.

25. Alexander Patten, "Scenes in the Old Dominion."

26. Many of the figures given in the census summaries are useful only as approximations. The figures used here are based not on the summaries per se, but on an evaluation of the summaries in conjunction with the manuscript census for population and manufacturing. Where possible the manuscript figures have been checked against the tax lists. In short, a variety of sources were used in tandem to eliminate the oversights or errors in any one source.

27. The bulk of Sutherlin's papers are at the University of North Carolina at

Chapel Hill, but the Duke University Library also has a substantial number of his papers. The information presented on slave hiring is derived almost entirely from the Chapel Hill collection.

28. In 1860, for instance, when Sutherlin had a $6,000 investment in his manufacturing plant, the cost of hired slave labor for that year was at least $3,000. If the prorated cost of his slaves were added, labor costs may have represented as much as 69 percent of his fixed investment.

29. On a number of occasions, Sutherlin hired labor late in the year. His choice was probably based on a rough calculation of what neoclassic economists call the marginal productivity of labor. The women and boys did the unskilled stemming and cooking work, while the men engaged in the semiskilled twisting and prizing operations.

30. Grasty Family Papers. Information on Grasty's interest in hiring was derived both from his account books and correspondence. For a summary of Grasty's career, see Chapter 8 above.

31. Robert, *The Tobacco Kingdom*, pp. 211–18. The famous lumpers of Danville were reportedly able to gauge the weight of a lump as accurately as a scale. Heimann, *Tobacco*, p. 165.

32. U.S. Census, Manufacturing Schedule, 1860; Robert, *The Tobacco Kingdom*, p. 171.

33. On the limited amount of machinery required in tobacco compared to other industries, see the sample inventory in Robert, *The Tobacco Kingdom*, pp. 252–54, and *The Story of Tobacco*, p. 85, and the U.S. Census, Manufacturing Schedule, 1860. It was only with the smoking tobacco era that machinery would be used in all phases of production.

34. Robert, *The Story of Tobacco*, p. 85.

35. *Danville Republican*, 24 July 1856, 19 November 1857; *Memorials of the Life, Public Services, and Character of William T. Sutherlin*, p. 37.

CHAPTER 10

1. U.S. Census, Population Schedule, 1850; Thompson Coleman's extended account of Danville in 1829 from Hagan, *Danville*.

2. U.S. Census, Population Schedules, 1850, 1860.

3. *Danville Republican*, 27 January 1854 (quotations); Grasty Family Papers. The city council first authorized such patrols in 1833, but the authorization was rarely acted upon.

4. Pittsylvania Petitions, January and March 1854; *Danville Republican*, 9 December 1853. For a general account of the way these restraints were developed and imposed in Southern cities, see Wade, *Slavery in the Cities*, pp. 155–60.

5. Hustings Court Records, 1855–60.

6. Thomas Grasty (merchant), E. J. Bell, J. W. Pace, S. H. Holland (tobacco manufacturers), and others to the Hustings Court, 1855. For a general account of the importance of temperance in movements for social control, see Joseph Gusfield, *The Symbolic Crusade* (New York, 1965).

7. The statistical information on timepieces in Pittsylvania and Augusta in the following paragraphs is taken entirely from Pittsylvania and Augusta (Personal)

Property 1815, 1850, 1860. For a general discussion of the development of clock manufacture and use in the United States, see Brown, *Modernization*.

8. Genovese, *Roll, Jordan, Roll*, p. 291. The pathbreaking discussion of this topic was Thompson's "Time, Work Discipline and Industrial Capitalism."

9. Brown, *Modernization*, p. 134.

10. In the *Danville Post*'s special edition of 1879, devoted to the town's history, the editor noted that "William T. Sutherlin [is] a man who has displayed more public spirit, perhaps in everything promoting the interests of the town of Danville than any other man connected with the history of the town."

11. Clement, *History of Pittsylvania*, pp. 232, 243; *Memorials of the Life, Public Services, and Character of William T. Sutherlin* (hereafter cited as *Memorials*), pp. 5, 27, 71. Thanks to Robert, *The Tobacco Kingdom*, pp. 171–73, it is possible to clearly gauge Sutherlin's standing among the rising class of Virginia tobacco manufacturers. In 1850, at age 28, Sutherlin was a middle-sized operator in an industry where much of the production was still done in small plantation factories. In that same year, he ranked in the top 40 percent of all of Virginia's tobacco manufacturers in the amount of capital he had invested in tobacco manufacturing, in the top third in the number of workers he employed, but in the top 10 percent in the value of the goods he produced. The high value of his output is probably attributable to the premium placed on bright tobacco. Between 1850 and 1860 there was a substantial shift away from small-scale rural production units and toward the growth of the larger urban factories. In the more developed situation of 1860, Sutherlin ranked in the top 2 percent in capital invested and in the top 3 percent in the number of hands employed and the value of the goods produced.

Capital Investments of William T. Sutherlin, 1850–1869

	1850	1854	1860 (alone)	In partnership w/Ferril
Capital Invested	$6,000		$17,000	$5,000
Raw Materials Bought				
lbs. of tobacco	370,000		590,000	340,000
lbs. of licorice			30,000	10,000
nails and boxes			5,540	4,000
Value of Materials Bought				
tobacco	$25,000	$37,984	$66,775	$40,000
licorice			$6,000	$2,200
Hands & Their Cost/Month				
male	30/$210		63/$945	40/$500
female	10/$30		12/$120	8/$100
Finished Product				
pounds			435,000	255,000
value	$55,000		$97,730	$70,000

12. Hagan, *Danville*, p. 41.

13. Dame, *Historical Sketch*.

14. During the Civil War, the Danville Milling and Manufacturing Company became heavily involved in the Confederate war effort. This involvement is discussed in a March 1862 letter from Sutherlin to William Grasty (Sutherlin Papers, University of North Carolina at Chapel Hill).

15. *Danville Register*, 5 February 1848; Sutherlin Papers, University of North Carolina at Chapel Hill.

16. Tilley, *The Bright Tobacco Industry*, p. 37; Sutherlin Papers, University of North Carolina at Chapel Hill.

17. The records on which the discussion in this and the next two paragraphs is based are scattered through Sutherlin's papers in both the Duke University and University of North Carolina at Chapel Hill collections. Most of the records referred to pertain to the period between 1855 and 1860.

18. Sutherlin to Levi Holbrook, 1855, Sutherlin Papers, Duke University.

19. *Memorials*, p. 81.

20. Ibid., p. 73.

21. Ibid., pp. 78, 80.

CHAPTER II

1. After the war, Holbrook wrote to Andrew Johnson asking for Sutherlin's immediate pardon. Even while living with Sutherlin, Holbrook brought food to the Yankee soldiers in the Danville prisons. Robertson, "Houses of Horror," pp. 329–46.

2. The crisis was set off by a combination of a bumper crop the year earlier and slackened Northern demand.

3. Robert, *The Tobacco Kingdom*, p. 229.

4. Ibid., pp. 233–34.

5. *Memorials*, p. 41.

6. Tilley, *The Bright Tobacco Industry*, pp. 199–201.

7. Witcher and Tredway made their sentiments public at an 1860 meeting held at the county courthouse in Chatham. The election statistics come from Pollack, *Sketchbook*, p. 34.

8. Pollack, *Sketchbook*, p. 110.

9. Henry Muse to William Sutherlin, 28 January 1861, Sutherlin Papers, University of North Carolina at Chapel Hill.

10. The leading voice for secession was the Danville Democratic newspaper, *The Appeal*, edited by Billy Coleman. After some harsh attacks on Sutherlin, Coleman's critics suggested that Coleman wanted disunion to keep his post office job. They said that he feared Abe Lincoln would give his job to a Whig. This information on Tredway is pieced together from passing references to him in Hagan (*Danville*), Hairston (*Danville*), and Pollack (*Sketchbook*). The scattered surviving election results indicate that Sutherlin and Tredway were sent to the convention by large majorities.

11. Sutherlin Papers, University of North Carolina at Chapel Hill, 9 February 1861.

12. Ibid., November 1860.

13. George Sutherlin to William Sutherlin, 2 March 1860, Sutherlin Papers, University of North Carolina at Chapel Hill.

14. James Sutherlin to William Sutherlin, 7 March 1860, ibid.

15. William Sutherlin's position on the war was described by Mrs. Sutherlin after the war in Avary, *Dixie after the War*.

16. J. B. Sharpe to William Sutherlin, 26 February 1861, Sutherlin Papers, University of North Carolina at Chapel Hill.

17. Pittsylvania Petition, 20 February 1837. The petition is quoted from at length in Chapter 4 above.

18. Quoted in Reese, *Proceedings*, vol. 2, pp. 705–29.

19. Grasty Family Papers, passim.

20. Emory Thomas, *The Confederacy as a Revolutionary Experience* (Englewood, 1971), p. 87; Brewer, *The Confederate Negro*, p. 41; Mary E. Massey, *Ersatz in the Confederacy* (Columbia, S.C., 1952).

21. A letter from James Sutherlin to William Sutherlin (28 February 1862, Sutherlin Papers, Duke University) discusses the broad range of William's activities. Initially William Sutherlin was also the commandant of one of the town's prisons, but he gave that task to Colonel Withers, later a figure of some significance during the Yankee occupation.

The expansion of business and industry was such that the legislature authorized the expansion of the town's boundaries on 7 March 1862.

On the skills of the slave population, see the letter of 30 January 1863 to Sutherlin from one of his employees (Sutherlin Papers, Duke University).

22. S. W. Davis to William Sutherlin, 25 January 1862, Sutherlin Papers, University of North Carolina at Chapel Hill; R. O. Davidson to William Sutherlin, March 1864, and James Sutherlin to William Sutherlin, January 1863, early February, 21, 28 February 1863, Sutherlin Papers, Duke University.

23. Tatum, *Disloyalty*, p. 160.

24. Withers, *Autobiography*, p. 211. In touring the North Carolina counties just south of Danville right after the war, John Dennett discovered that many of the "trifflin people of Caswell and Rockingham Counties had been unionists" (Dennett, *The South as It Is*, p. 103). Withers had claimed that there were numerous deserters in the mountains of Patrick, Henry, and Franklin counties.

25. Brewer, *The Confederate Negro*, pp. 43–51, 125; the quotation is found on p. 125. See Tilley, *The Bright Tobacco Industry*, p. 358, for evidence of the continued concentration on tobacco even during the war. The son of the editor of the *Milton Chronicle* summed up what was probably the view of many soldiers when he wrote to his father: "It would be glorious indeed for the Southern Confederacy if every Tobacco Factory in it were burned to the ground and their very ashes scattered to the four winds of heaven. *These money-making machines are mainly responsible for the exhorbitant prices now charged for the accessories of life.*" Quoted in Stokes, "Milton."

26. Heimann, *Tobacco*, p. 169.

27. Tilley, *The Bright Tobacco Industry*, p. 498. In fact, there was a postwar boom based on the mild and bright leaf. It was part of the concatenations that led to the emergence of the modern cigarette industry.

28. *Danville Appeal*, 14 January 1865.

29. Thomas Preisser, "The Virginia Decision to Use Negro Soldiers in the Civil War, 1864–1865," *Virginia Magazine of History and Biography*, 1975, p. 133; Maury Klein, *The Great Richmond Terminal* (Charlottesville, 1970).

Algernon S. Buford was born in Pittsylvania in 1826, the son of a middling planter from eastern Virginia who had settled in Pittsylvania before the Revolution. Buford was connected by marriage to George Townes, one of the central figures behind the creation of the Richmond and Danville Railroad. After the war, Buford became president of the Richmond and Danville.

30. The process of making Danville a rail center during the war had come in part through the dismantling of other commercially competitive, though less strategically important, lines than the Richmond and Danville. Johnston, *Virginia Railroads*.

31. Brewer, *The Confederate Negro*; Johnston, *Virginia*, pp. 56, 142. For an interesting discussion of the connection between slavery and racial control, see Roark, *Masters without Slaves*.

32. James Robertson, "Danville under Military Occupation," mistakenly saw Danville in just those terms. If Danville was the last capital of the Confederacy, he reasoned, it must have been the embodiment of the "lost cause."

33. Withers, *Autobiography*, p. 214; Pollack, *Sketchbook*, p. 65.

34. Withers, *Autobiography*, pp. 219, 227; Avary, *Dixie after the War*, p. 65; Wooding Papers; Robertson, "Danville under Military Occupation," passim. George Dame, in *Historical Sketch of the Roman Eagle Lodge*, describes how the lodge provided fraternal assistance to fellow Yankee Masons incarcerated in Danville's prisons.

35. *Memorials*, pp. 144–46.

36. Reid Papers.

37. Porter, *People, Places and Things*, p. 91.

CONCLUSION

1. Porter, *People, Places and Things*, p. 91.

2. Perry, "A History of Farm Tenancy," chap. 1; Tilley, *The Bright Tobacco Industry*, pp. 124–25.

3. "To this day tobacco is still harvested and cured largely by hand, *requiring more labor than the entire U.S. wheat and cotton crops combined.*" Quoted in Mann, *Tobacco*, the best and most recent discussion of the problem of modernizing tobacco production. The italics are mine.

4. Weld, *Travels*, pp. 204, 205.

5. Langhorne, *Southern Sketches*, p. 83.

6. William C. Bruce, *Below the James*, p. 41.

7. Thompson, *Urban Economics*, p. 11.

8. Berkeley, *Why Is Virginia Poor?*

9. North, "Location Theory"; Tiebout, "Exports" (see also the reply by North in the same issue).

❦ ❦ ❦

BIBLIOGRAPHY

PRIMARY SOURCES

MANUSCRIPT COLLECTIONS

Duke University, Durham, North Carolina
   Grasty Family Papers
   William T. Sutherlin Papers
University of North Carolina at Chapel Hill
   William T. Sutherlin Papers
   Robert Wilson Papers
University of Virginia, Charlottesville
   Lanier Family Papers
   Richard Reid Papers
   Wooding Family Papers

NEWSPAPERS

Danville Appeal
Danville Register
Danville Reporter and Roanoke Commercial Gazette
Danville Republican
Danville Telegraph
Roanoke Sentinel
Richmond Enquirer
Richmond Whig

STATISTICAL MATERIALS

Catlett and Fishburne. "An Economic and Social Survey of Augusta County." University of Virginia Record Extension Service, 1928.
Census Office. Second Decennial Census. Washington, 1801. National Archives.
Dodd, Donald, and Dodd, Wynelle. *Historical Statistics of the South, 1790–1970.* University of Alabama, 1973.
Gee and Corson. "A Statistical Study of Virginia." University of Virginia Research in the Social Sciences, 1927.
Heads of Families at the First Census of the United States, Taken in the Year 1790. Washington, 1907–8.
Pittsylvania County and Augusta County, Virginia (Personal) Property Book for

1782, 1800, 1810, 1815, 1820, 1830, 1840, 1850, 1860. Virginia State Library, Richmond.

Pittsylvania County and Augusta County, Virginia (Real) Property Book for 1800, 1810, 1820, 1825, 1830, 1840, 1850, 1860. Virginia State Library, Richmond.

U.S. Bureau of the Census. Third Census (1810), Report on Manufactures. Washington, 1814. National Archives.

U.S. Bureau of the Census. Fourth Census (1820), Report on Manufactures. Washington, 1823. National Archives.

U.S. Bureau of the Census. Fourth Census (1820), Report on Population. Washington, 1823. National Archives.

U.S. Bureau of the Census. Fifth Census (1830), Report on Population. Washington, 1833. National Archives.

U.S. Bureau of the Census. Sixth Census (1840), Report on Manufactures. Washington, 1841. National Archives.

U.S. Bureau of the Census. Sixth Census (1840), Report on Population. Washington, 1841. National Archives.

U.S. Bureau of the Census. Seventh Census (1850), Schedule 1, Free Inhabitants; Schedule 2, Slave Inhabitants; Schedule 4, Products of Agriculture; Schedule 5, Products of Industry. Washington, 1853, 1859. National Archives.

U.S. Bureau of the Census. Eighth Census (1860), Schedule 1, Free Inhabitants; Schedule 2, Slave Inhabitants; Schedule 4, Products of Agriculture; Schedule 5, Products of Industry. Washington, 1864, 1866. National Archives.

OFFICIAL RECORDS AND DOCUMENTS

Acts of the Virginia Legislature. Virginia State Library, Richmond.

Calendar of Virginia State Papers. Richmond, 1893. Virginia State Library, Richmond.

Danville City Council Minutes, 1833–47. Danville Town Hall.

Petitions to the Legislature, from Pittsylvania, Henry, Patrick, Franklin, Wythe, and Halifax Counties. Virginia State Library, Richmond.

Proceedings of the Virginia Constitutional Convention of 1851. Richmond, 1930. Virginia State Library, Richmond.

Records of the Danville Hustings Court, 1855–60. City Courthouse, Danville, Virginia.

Reese, George, ed. *Proceedings of the Virginia State Convention of 1861.* 3 vols. Richmond, 1965. Virginia State Library, Richmond.

U.S. Department of Agriculture. *Soil Survey of Pittsylvania County, Virginia.* Washington, D.C., 1922.

CONTEMPORARY OBSERVATIONS,
TRAVEL ACCOUNTS, AND GAZETEERS

Avary, Myra. *Dixie after the War.* New York, 1906.

Berkeley, C. N. *Why is Virginia Poor?* Richmond, 1884.

Cocke, John H. *Tobacco, the Bane of Virginia Husbandry.* Richmond, 1860.

Dame, George. *Historical Sketch of the Roman Eagle Lodge: Danville, Virginia, 1820–95.* Richmond, 1895.
DeCoin, Colonel Robert L. *History and Cultivation of Tobacco.* London, 1864.
Dennett, John. *The South as It Is, 1865–1866.* New York, 1965.
Elliot and Nye. *Virginia Directory and Business Review.* Richmond, 1852.
Glasgow, Ellen. *The Deliverance: A Romance of the Tobacco Fields.* New York, 1904.
Langhorne, Ora. *Southern Sketches from Virginia.* Charlottesville, 1964.
Martin's Gazeteer of Virginia. Richmond, 1835.
Memorials of the Life, Public Services, and Character of William T. Sutherlin. Danville Public Library, 1894.
Norris, George. "The History of the First Presbyterian Church." Danville Public Library, n.d.
Patten, Alexander. "Scenes in the Old Dominion—Number 2—A Tobacco Market." *New York Mercury* (4 November 1859).
Perdue, Charles, ed. *Weevils in the Wheat.* Charlottesville, 1976.
Pollack, Edward. *Sketchbook of Danville: Its Manufacturing and Commerce.* Richmond, 1885.
Porter, Duval. *People, Places and Things.* Lynchburg, 1895.
Scarborough, William, ed. *The Diary of Edmund Ruffin,* Vol. 1. Baton Rouge, 1972.
Schoepf, Johann David. *Travels in the Confederation, 1783–4.* Philadelphia, 1911.
Smyth, J. F. D. *A Tour of the United States.* London, 1784.
Virginia Writers' Project. *The Negro in Virginia.* New York, 1940.
Von Briesen, Martha, ed. *The Letters of Elijah Fletcher.* Charlottesville, 1965.
Weld, Isaac. *Travels through the States of North America.* London, 1807.
Withers, Robert E. *Autobiography of an Octogenarian.* Roanoke, 1907.
Wooding, Harry, Sr. "Sketch of Danville." University of Virginia, n.d.
Yetman, Norman, ed. *Voices from Slavery.* New York, 1970.

SECONDARY SOURCES

UNPUBLISHED PAPERS, THESES, AND DISSERTATIONS

Chinitz, Benjamin. "Patterns of Agglomeration: Pittsburgh and New York." Seminar paper, University of Pittsburgh, 1967.
Clark, Malcolm. "The First Quarter Century of the Richmond-Danville Railroad, 1847–71." Ph.D. dissertation, George Washington University, 1959.
Fields, Emmet. "The Agricultural Population of Virginia, 1850–60." Ph.D. dissertation, Vanderbilt University, 1953.
Fleetwood, George. "Southside Virginia in the Middle Period." M.A. thesis, Wake Forest University, 1940.
Gross, Leo. "Dairy Cattle and Climate in the Southern United States." Ph.D. dissertation, University of Maryland, 1963.

Hall, Arthur. "Soil Erosion and Agriculture in the Southern Piedmont." Ph.D. dissertation, Duke University, 1948.

Herndon, G. Melvin. "A History of Tobacco in Virginia." M.A. thesis, University of Virginia, 1956.

Miller, Leroy. "The Shenandoah Valley in Virginia: An Economic and Geographic Interpretation." Ph.D. dissertation, George Peabody University, 1937.

Mitchel, Robert. "The Upper Shenandoah Valley of Virginia during the 18th Century." Ph.D. dissertation, University of Wisconsin, 1969.

Mitchell, Dora. "A Political and Social History of Henry County Virginia as Disclosed in the County Court Records." M.A. thesis, University of Virginia, 1962.

Nichols, Mike. "Origins of the Virginia Southside, 1703–52: A Social and Economic Study." Ph.D. dissertation, College of William and Mary, 1972.

Perry, Kathleen. "A History of Farm Tenancy in the Tobacco Region of Virginia, 1865–1950." Ph.D. dissertation, Harvard University, 1956.

Rainbolt, John. "The Virginia Vision." Ph.D. dissertation, University of Wisconsin, 1966.

Sutton, Robert. "The Virginia Constitutional Convention of 1829–30." Ph.D. dissertation, University of Virginia, 1968.

Usery, Robert. "The Overseers of the Poor in Accomac, Pittsylvania and Rockingham Counties, 1768–1802." M.A. thesis, College of William and Mary, 1960.

BOOKS AND ARTICLES

Ambler, Charles. *Sectionalism in Virginia from 1776 to 1861*. New York, 1964.

Axton, W. F. *Tobacco and Kentucky*. Lexington, 1974.

Baldwin, Robert. "The Pattern of Development in Newly Settled Areas." *Manchester School of Economic and Social Studies* 24 (1956): 161–79.

———. "Export Technology and Development from a Subsistence Level." *Economic Journal* 73 (1963): 80–92.

Ballagh, James C. *White Servitude in the Colony of Virginia: A Study of Indentured Labor in the American Colonies*. Baltimore, 1895.

Berlin, Ira, and Gutman, Herbert. "Natives and Immigrants, Free Men and Slaves: Urban Working Class Men in the Antebellum South." *American Historical Review* 88 (1983): 1175–1200.

Breen, T. H. *Tobacco Culture: The Mentality of the Great Tidewater Planters on the Eve of the Revolution*. Princeton, 1985.

Brewer, James. *The Confederate Negro*. Durham, 1969.

Bridenbaugh, Carl, and Bridenbaugh, Roberta. *No Peace Beyond the Line: The English in the Caribbean, 1624–1690*. New York, 1972.

Brown, Richard. *Modernization, the Transformation of American Life 1600–1865*. New York, 1976.

Bruce, Kathleen. *Virginia Iron Manufactures in the Slave Era*. New York, 1931.

Bruce, Philip A. *Virginia in the 17th Century*. New York, 1896.

Bruce, William C. *Below the James: A Plantation Sketch*. Boston, 1927.

Cason, Clarence. *90 Degrees in the Shade*. Chapel Hill, 1935.

Cathey, Cornelius. *Agricultural Developments in North Carolina*. Chapel Hill, 1956.

Clement, Maude Carter. *The History of Pittsylvania County*. Lynchburg, Va., 1929.

Cowdrey, Albert. *This Land, This South: An Environmental History*. Lexington, Ky., 1983.

Craven, Avery. *Soil Exhaustion as a Factor in the Agricultural History of Virginia and Maryland: 1606–1860*. Gloucester, Mass., 1965.

David, Paul, and Temin, Peter. "Capitalist Masters, Bourgeois Slaves." In *Reckoning with Slavery*, edited by Paul David. New York, 1976.

Davis, David Brion. *The Problem of Slavery in the Age of Revolution*. Ithaca, N.Y., 1975.

Diamond, Sigmund. "From Organization to Society: Virginia in the 17th Century." *American Sociological Review* 43 (1957–58): 457–75.

Domar, Evsey. "The Causes of Slavery or Serfdom: A Hypothesis." *Journal of Economic History* 30 (1970): 18–32.

Dorfman, Joseph. *The Economic Mind in American Civilization*. New York, 1946.

Dunn, Richard. *Sugar and Slaves: The Rise of the Planter Class in the English West Indies, 1624–1713*. Chapel Hill, 1973.

Earle, Carville, and Hoffman, Ronald. "The Urban South: The First Two Centuries." In *The City in Southern History*, edited by Brownell and Goldfield. Port Washington, N.Y., 1977.

Eaton, Clement. *The Growth of Southern Civilization*. New York, 1963.

———. *The Freedom of Thought Struggle in the Old South*. New York, 1974.

Fields, Barbara. *On the Middle Ground: Slavery in Nineteenth Century Maryland*. New Haven, 1985.

Fogel, Robert, and Engerman, Stanley. *Time on the Cross*. 2 vols. Boston, 1974.

Forster, Robert. "Achievements of the *Annales* School." *Journal of Economic History* 38 (1978): 58–76.

Freehling, William. "The Founding Fathers and Slavery." *American Historical Review* 77 (1972): 81–93.

Fuller, Margaret, et al. *Pittsylvania County Geographic Supplement*. Danville, 1925.

Gates, Paul. *The Farmers Age, Agriculture 1815–60*. New York, 1960.

Genovese, Eugene. *The Political Economy of Slavery*. New York, 1967.

———. *Roll, Jordan, Roll*. New York, 1974.

———. "A Reply to Criticism." *Radical History Review* 3 (1977): 94–111.

———. *The Fruits of Merchant Capital: Slavery and Bourgeois Property in the Rise and Expansion of Capitalism*. New York, 1983.

Ginther, Herman. *Captain Staunton's River*. Richmond, 1968.

Goldfield, David. *Urban Growth in the Age of Sectionalism: Virginia, 1847–61*. Baton Rouge, 1977.

Goodrich, Carter. "The Virginia System of Mixed Enterprise: A Study of State Planning of Internal Improvements." *Political Science Quarterly* 64 (September 1949): 355–87.

Gray, Lewis. "The Market Surplus Problem of Colonial Tobacco." *Agricultural History* 2 (1928): 1–34.

———. *History of Agriculture in the Southern United States to 1860.* 2 vols. Washington, D.C., 1933.

Green, Fletcher. *Constitutional Developments in the South Atlantic States.* New York, 1966.

Greenberg, Michael. "William Byrd II and the World of the Market." *Southern Studies* 16 (1977): 429–56.

Griffin, P., Young, R., and Chatham, R. *Anglo-America: A Regional Geography of the United States and Canada.* Toronto, 1962.

Hagan, Jane. *The Story of Danville.* New York, 1947.

Hairston, Beatrice. *The Story of Danville.* Richmond, 1955.

Hart, Freeman. *The Valley of Virginia in the American Revolution.* Chapel Hill, 1942.

Heimann, Robert. *Tobacco and Americans.* New York, 1960.

Herndon, G. Melvin. "Hemp in Colonial Virginia." *Agricultural History* 37 (1963): 86–93.

———. "A War Inspired Industry: The Manufacture of Hemp in Virginia during the Revolution." *Virginia Magazine of History and Biography* 74 (1966): 301–11.

———, ed. *William Tatham and the Culture of Tobacco.* Coral Gables, Fla., 1969.

Hill, Christopher. *Reformation to Industrial Revolution.* London, 1967.

Hirschman, Albert. *The Strategy of Economic Development.* New Haven, 1958.

Howe, Henry. *Historical Collection of Virginia.* Charleston, S.C., 1845.

Humphries, William. "The Impact of Tobacco upon North Carolina Towns." Paper presented at the East Carolina University Tobacco History Symposium, 27 March 1974.

Johnson, Michael. *Toward a Patriarchal Republic.* Baton Rouge, 1977.

Johnston, Angus. *Virginia Railroads in the Civil War.* Chapel Hill, 1961.

Jones, E. L. "Creative Disruptions in America Agriculture, 1629–1820." *Agricultural History* 48 (October 1974): 510–28.

———. "Environment, Agriculture and Industrialization in Europe." *Agricultural History* 51 (July 1977): 491–502.

Kolko, Gabriel. "Max Weber and America: Theory and Evidence." *History and Theory* 1 (1960–61): 243–60.

Luraghi, Raimondo. *The Rise and Fall of the Plantation South.* New York, 1978.

McColley, Robert. *Slavery and Jeffersonian Virginia.* Urbana, Ill., 1973.

McWhiney, Grady. "The Revolution in 19th Century Alabama Agriculture." *Alabama Review* 31 (1978): 3–32.

Main, J. T. "The One Hundred." *William and Mary Quarterly*, 3rd ser. 11 (1951): 354–84.

Mann, Charles. *Tobacco: The Ants and the Elephants.* Salt Lake City, 1975.

Mannheim, Karl. "Conservative Thought." In *From Karl Mannheim*, edited by Kurt Wolff, pp. 177–222. New York, 1971.

Marx, Karl. *Capital.* Vol. 1. Chicago, 1909.

Meier, Gerald. *Leading Issues in Development Economics.* New York, 1964.

Moger, Allen. "Industrial and Urban Progress in Virginia from 1880 to 1900." *Virginia Magazine of History and Biography* 38 (1958): 307–36.

Morgan, Edmund. "The Labor Problem at Jamestown." *American Historical Review* 76 (June 1971): 595–611.

———. "Headrights and Head Counts: A Review Article." *Virginia Magazine of History and Biography* 80 (July 1972): 361–86.

Myrdal, Gunnar. *Rich Lands, Poor Lands.* New York, 1957.

Nichols, William. "An Agricultural Surplus as a Factor in Economic Development." *Journal of Political Economy* 71 (1963): 1–29.

North, Douglas. "Location Theory and Regional Economic Growth." *Journal of Political Economy* 63 (1955): 243–58.

Oakes, James. *The Ruling Race.* New York, 1982.

Olmsted, Frederick Law. *The Cotton Kingdom.* Edited by Arthur Schlesinger, Jr. New York, 1953.

Ortiz, Fernando. *Cuban Counterpoint: Tobacco and Sugar.* New York, 1970.

Palmer, Paul. "Servant into Slave." *South Atlantic Quarterly* (Summer 1966): 355–70.

Papenfuse, Edward. "Planter Behavior and Economic Opportunity in a Staple Economy." *Agricultural History* 46 (April 1972): 297–313.

Phillips, U. B. *Plantation and Frontier.* 2 vols. Cleveland, 1910.

———. *Life and Labor in the Old South.* Boston, 1929.

Plumb, J. H. *In the Light of History.* Boston, 1973.

Polanyi, Karl. *The Great Transformation.* New York, 1944.

Pole, J. R. "Representation and Authority in Virginia from the Revolution to Reform." *Journal of Southern History* (1958): 17–50.

Primack, Martin. "Land Clearing Under 19th Century Techniques." *Journal of Economic History* 22 (1962): 448–71.

Reich, Robert. *The Next American Frontier.* New York, 1983.

Risjord, Norman. "The Virginia Federalists." *Journal of Southern History* 33 (1917): 486–517.

Roark, James. *Masters without Slaves.* New York, 1977.

Robert, Joseph. *The Road from Monticello.* Durham, 1941.

———. *The Story of Tobacco.* New York, 1952.

———. *The Tobacco Kingdom.* Gloucester, Mass., 1965.

Robertson, James. "Houses of Horror, Danville's Civil War Prisons." *Virginia Magazine of History and Biography* 69 (1961): 329–46.

———. "Danville under Military Occupation." *Virginia Magazine of History and Biography* 75 (1967): 331–48.

Rothstein, Morton. "Ante-Bellum Wheat and Cotton Exports: A Contrast in Marketing Organization and Economic Development." Seminar paper presented at the University of Pittsburgh, 1971.

Rouse, Park. *Below the James Lies Dixie.* Richmond, 1955.

Rubin, Julius. "The Comparative Economic Development of American Regions." Seminar paper, University of Pittsburgh, 1965.

———. "The Limits of Agricultural Progress in the 19th Century South." *Agricultural History* 49 (1975): 362–75.

———. "The Growth and Expansion of Urban Centers." In *The Growth of*

Seaport Cities, edited by David Gilchrist. Charlottesville, 1976.

Rubin, Julius, and Fischbaum, Marvin. "Slavery and Economic Development in the American South." *Explorations in Entrepreneurial History* 6 (1968): 116–27.

Russel, Robert. "The General Effects of Slavery upon Southern Economic Progress." *Journal of Southern History* 4 (1938): 34–54.

Scarborough, William. *The Overseer: Plantation Management in the South.* Baton Rouge, 1966.

Schlebecker, John. "Farmers in the Lower Shenandoah Valley, 1850." *Virginia Magazine of History and Biography* 79 (October 1971): 462–76.

Schmidt, Frederika, and Wilhelm, Barbara. "Early Proslavery Petitions in Virginia." *William and Mary Quarterly,* 3rd ser. 30 (January 1973): 133–46.

Schultz, T. W. *The Economic Organization of Agriculture.* New York, 1953.

——. "Investment in Human Capital." *American Economic Review* 51 (1961): 13–31.

Sellers, Charles. "Who Were the Southern Whigs?" *American Historical Review* 59 (January 1954): 335–46.

Shalhope, Robert. "Race, Class and Slavery." *Journal of Southern History* 37 (1971): 73–94.

Shifflett, Crandall A. *Patronage and Poverty in the Tobacco South: Louisa County, Virginia, 1860–1900.* Knoxville, Tenn., 1982.

Siegel, Fred. "Time on the Cross: A First Appraisal." *Historical Methods Newsletter* 7 (1974): 299–303.

——. "Parameters for Paternalism?" *Radical History Review* 3 (1976): 60–67.

——. "The Paternalist Thesis: Virginia as a Test Case." *Civil War History* 25 (1979): 246–61.

——. "The Virginia Ideology." *Reviews in American History* 7 (1979): 344–50.

Smolensky, Eugene, and Ratajczak, Donald. "The Conception of Cities." *Explorations in Entrepreneurial History* 2 (1965): 90–131.

Stampp, Kenneth. *The Peculiar Institution.* New York, 1956.

Stewart, Peter. "Railroads and Urban Rivalries in Ante-Bellum Eastern Virginia." *Virginia Magazine of History and Biography* 81 (1974): 4–22.

Stokes, Durward. "Milton: The Growth and Decline of a Tobacco Town." Paper presented at the East Carolina University Tobacco History Symposium, 27 March 1974.

Tatum, George. *Disloyalty in the Confederacy.* Chapel Hill, 1934.

Thompson, Edgar. "The Natural History of Agricultural Labor in the South." In *Essays in Honor of William K. Boyd,* edited by D. Jackson, pp. 110–74. Durham, 1940.

Thompson, E. P. "Time, Work Discipline and Industrial Capitalism." *Past and Present* 38 (December 1967): 56–97.

Thompson, Wilbur. *A Preface to Urban Economics.* New York, 1965.

Thornton, J. Mills. *Politics and Power in a Slave Society: Alabama, 1800–1860.* Baton Rouge, 1977.

Tiebout, Charles. "Exports and Regional Economic Growth." *Journal of Political Economy* 65 (1956): 331–45.

Tilley, Nannie M. *The Bright Tobacco Industry*. Chapel Hill, 1948.

Wade, Richard. *Slavery in the Cities*. New York, 1964.

Weaver, F. Stirnton. "Positive Economics." *Science and Society* 35 (1971): 168–76.

Wertenbaker, Thomas. *Norfolk: Historical Southern Port*. Durham, 1962.

Whitney, Milton. "Soils in Relation to Their Crop Production." *The Agricultural Yearbook*. Washington, D.C., 1894.

Willis, Roy. "The Contribution of the *Annales* School to Agrarian History: A Review Essay." *Agricultural History* 52 (1978): 538–48.

Wingo, Alfred. *Virginia's Soils and Land Use*. Richmond, 1949.

Wood, Walter. "Henry Edmundson, The Allegheny Turnpike and 'Fotheringay Plantation,' 1805–1847: Planting and Trading in Montgomery County, Virginia." *Virginia Magazine of History and Biography* 83 (1975): 305–20.

Wrigley, E. A. "A Simple Model of London's Importance in the Changing English Society and Economy, 1650–1750." *Past and Present* 60 (1967): 44–70.

INDEX

Accomac County, 16–17
Adams, John Quincy, 43
Adamson, George, 28
Agriculture: soil and climate and diversification of, 68–74, 85–86, 87; reform of, 70, 71–74; production in Pittsylvania and Augusta counties compared, 86–87; alternatives to tobacco, 165
Albemarle County, 72–74
Anderson, Abner, 150
Anderson, Banister, 141
Animal parasites, 71, 72
Artisans, 115, 130
Atkinson, Thomas, 110
Auctions, 124–25, 128, 149
Augusta County, 23, 72–74, 75–92, 138; slavery in, 72; white landed population of, 76–78; size and value of property in, 78–80; landless white population of, 80–83; organization of landholding in, 84–86; organization of economic activity in, 86–88; timepieces in, 138
Ayres, William, 127

Backward linkages, 66
Banister River, 9, 12, 13, 14
Banister Valley, 42
Banks and banking: in Danville, 32–33, 40–41, 43, 47; during secession and Civil War, 147, 148
Barnett, John, 30
Beavers, Jonathan, 116–17
Bedford County, 12
Before Breakfast Secessionists, 155
Bell, John, 150
Berkeley, William, 65
Blacksmiths, 121

Boom-and-bust cycles, 45–58, 87; in Danville from 1829 to 1847, 45–58, 102; and tobacco factories, 48–49; and town government and internal improvements, 49–55; and Tunstall's campaign for railroad, 55–57; in Augusta County, 87
Botetourt County, 54, 55, 106
Breckinridge, John C., 150
Bright tobacco, 100–102, 123, 142; crop rotation and, 71–72; difficulty with, 100–101; rise of, 100–102; soil and, 101; Civil War and, 156
Brooke, John, 15
Brookneal, 15
Bruce, Alexander, 118
Bruce, William Cabell, 164
Brunswick County, 11
Buford, A. S., 157
Building values, 72
Byrd, William, 69

Cabell, B. W. S., 25–26, 31, 32–33, 34–35, 44, 51, 53, 54, 109, 114, 117, 158
Cameron, William, 134
Campbell County, 15
Capitalist school of Southern history, 1–3
Carrol County, 52
Caswell County, N.C., 102, 110
Cattle breeding, 119
Charlotte County, 15
Chatham: population of, 86
Chewing tobacco, 122–23
Christianity: and slavery, 20–21
Cities. See Towns and cities
Civil War, 2, 146–61; Danville as economic beneficiary of, 153; war ef-